# The Great Crashes

'Linda Yueh's analysis of what past financial crises have in common is an important contribution that can help society anticipate and tackle potential crashes in the future'
Christine Lagarde, President of the European Central Bank

'An accessible and insightful overview of modern financial crises, incorporating both historical detail and thoughtful analysis'
Kenneth Rogoff

'A masterclass in spotting the early signs of a crisis. Linda Yueh expertly shows how we can understand these crashes better when they occur and even prevent them from happening in the future. An accessible yet rich study of our most turbulent economic years'
Nouriel Roubini, author of *Megathreats*

'This well-written book draws out the many different ways in which markets can crash and she's willing to chance her arm predicting the next one'
Vince Cable, author of *How to be a Politician*

'A timely and instructive book on the big financial and economic crashes. It comes in the midst of a global polycrisis that threatens the economic and social well-being of all, especially the world's poorest citizens. Linda Yueh makes a heroic effort to tease out lessons fundamental to managing future crises. The question is: will we learn?'
Dr Ngozi Okonjo-Iweala, Director-General of the World Trade Organization and former Finance Minister of Nigeria

'Demonstrates how that old saying – "this time is different" – is both so true and so wrong!'
Lord Green

'Crashes are an integral part of the history of capitalism. The last century has seen plenty of them. All crashes begin with debt-fuelled euphoria and end in disappointment. Yet how bad that disappointment turns out to be also depends on where in the economy the crash falls, and how determined and credible are the responses. In this lively and blessedly brief book, Linda Yueh does a lovely job of explaining the history, and drawing the necessary lessons'
Martin Wolf, Chief Economics Commentator, *Financial Times*

# The Great Crashes

## LINDA YUEH

BUSINESS

PENGUIN BUSINESS

UK | USA | Canada | Ireland | Australia
India | New Zealand | South Africa

Penguin Business is part of the Penguin Random House group of companies
whose addresses can be found at global.penguinrandomhouse.com.

First published 2023
001

Set in 12/14.75pt Bembo Book MT Pro
Typeset by Jouve (UK), Milton Keynes
Printed and bound in Great Britain by Clays Ltd, Elcograf S.p.A.

The authorized representative in the EEA is Penguin Random House Ireland,
Morrison Chambers, 32 Nassau Street, Dublin D02 YH68

A CIP catalogue record for this book is available from the British Library

HARDBACK ISBN: 978-0-241-42275-5
TRADE PAPERBACK ISBN: 978-0-241-42276-2

www.greenpenguin.co.uk

MIX
Paper from
responsible sources
FSC® C018179

Penguin Random House is committed to a
sustainable future for our business, our readers
and our planet. This book is made from Forest
Stewardship Council® certified paper.

To the pack

# Contents

Introduction The Great Crash of 1929     I

1. Three Generations of Currency Crises     11

2. The US Savings and Loan Crisis of the 1980s     29

3. Japan's Real-Estate Crash of the Early 1990s     43

4. The Dot Com Crash, 2000–2001     67

5. The Global Financial Crisis of 2008     81

6. The Euro Crisis of 2010     107

7. The Covid-19 Crash of 2020     137

8. The Next Great Crash?     163

Epilogue     185

*Acknowledgements*     197

*Notes*     199

*Bibliography*     217

*Index*     233

# Introduction
## The Great Crash of 1929

'There can be few fields of human endeavor in which history counts for so little as in the world of finance. Past experience, to the extent that it is part of memory at all, is dismissed as the primitive refuge of those who do not have the insight to appreciate the incredible wonders of the present,' observed J. K. Galbraith, the eminent economist who advised US presidents, including John F. Kennedy.[1]

The near century since the Great Crash of 1929 has proven to be as financially tumultuous as the centuries that came before. It has witnessed multiple financial crises striking nations, regions and – in more recent years – the global economy. *The Great Crashes* tells the stories of ten of these events. They serve as a series of cautionary tales, each with its own set of lessons. As this book will show, there is very little that is certain in economics, but there will always be another financial crisis. The chapters that follow will aim to analyse the crashes of our past to determine how best to mitigate the damage of financial crashes in the future, when they inevitably come.

Each of the ten crashes that follow has a unique set of causes and consequences but, despite their differences, they all feature three distinct phases: euphoria, credibility and aftermath. Euphoria or exuberance, often used interchangeably, leads people to invest in markets they believe will rise and rise. To resolve a financial crisis, credible policies are essential. These two aspects can shape the aftermath: the difference between a quick recovery or a long, protracted recession. In each chapter the past responses (or lack thereof) of governments or institutions to these early phases will be analysed to determine which led to the best outcomes, and which to the worst, in the hope that these lessons will help us understand how best to act in the future.

The Great Crash of 1929, and the ensuing depression of the 1930s, is understood to be among the worst of all time. It holds a special place in the annals of financial crises throughout history. Some of the lessons hard-won in this period went on to inform policy in the crashes that followed. So, it's a good place to begin.

In the period after the First World War, the US economy recovered and boomed. It was growth fuelled by the belief of investors in the transformative impact of innovations such as the expansion of the telephone and highways networks, the electrification of millions of homes and the mass production of cars. Real-estate prices rose too, though not as exuberantly as stocks. The US blue-chip stock index, the Dow Jones Industrial Average, had increased six-fold between August 1921 and September 1929 during the economic expansion that occurred during the period known as the Roaring Twenties.[2] Euphoria drove the stock market to dizzying heights, almost tripling its value between the beginning of 1927 and September 1929.[3] But the boom couldn't last and, when the market collapsed a month later, it was the worst financial crash in American history.

The great economist Irving Fisher was caught up in this belief in an ever-rising market. After the Great Crash, he insisted: 'the ensuing rally will see the markets quickly return to previous highs'.[4] Unfortunately for him, it did not. He lost not only his $10-million fortune (about $170 million in today's money), but also his reputation. Like other investors who believed that prices would only go up, he borrowed from his sister-in-law to invest in shares, believing he could recoup his losses. He never did and ended up indebted to her until her death.

The stock market was booming despite a mild recession in 1927, which led to a rise in unemployment and a drop in production as well as falling prices known as deflation. The US central bank, the Federal Reserve, became concerned about the booming market and raised interest rates in 1928, which further dampened economic activity by increasing the cost of borrowing.[5]

On what was later called Black Monday, 28 October 1929, the Dow declined by nearly 13 per cent, falling into correction territory, which is a 10 per cent drop, caused by investors selling their shares as they lost confidence in the contracting economy. And on Black Tuesday, the Dow fell an additional 12 per cent and collapsed into a bear market (a term usually referring to share prices falling by 20 per cent). Within a couple of weeks, the index had declined by nearly 50 per cent. Investors saw the value of their shares, or their wealth held in stocks, cut in half. But it was to get worse. In the ensuing Great Depression, the stock market continued to fall for several years, hitting its lowest value in the summer of 1932. The Dow closed at 41.22 at its trough, which was a staggering 89 per cent below its peak, and did not recover to its pre-crash high for another two decades, until November 1954.[6]

The Great Depression saw widespread bank failures as property prices crashed. When the market is surging, an increase in household wealth leads to greater spending. As people begin to feel wealthier due to their stocks performing well, they tend to spend more, including on homes. For instance, the housing market in Manhattan is correlated with the bonuses on Wall Street, New York's financial centre.[7] Similarly, firms invest more, and in riskier projects, when their cost of borrowing falls. But when the market turns, and when asset prices fall, economic activity slows. Those riskier investments that households or firms might have made are not undertaken in case they don't pay off. As the number of borrowers defaulting on their repayments rises, banks and lenders get into trouble. And in 1929, this was exactly what happened: real-estate loan defaults were the largest factor in bank failures and an astounding one third of all US banks failed between 1930 and 1933.[8]

Around one in four Americans lost their life savings. The US economy contracted by a staggering 29 per cent. Prices fell by some 25 per cent. Millions of people lost their jobs. Around a quarter of the country's workforce were unemployed and many were in desperate circumstances, poignantly captured in John Steinbeck's Pulitzer Prize-winning novel, *The Grapes of Wrath*. Steinbeck said: 'I want to put a tag of shame on the greedy bastards who are responsible for this [Great Depression].'[9]

Yet it wasn't until February 1932 that the Fed injected cash to try to reflate the economy. Its actions helped industrial production and commodity prices start to recover. In the summer of that year, when deflation seemed to be under control, the Fed discontinued its supportive policies despite the ongoing depression.[10]

The slowness to act and then the premature withdrawal of support worsened the Great Depression. This was the conclusion of the seminal work of another great economist, Milton Friedman, and his co-author, Anna Jacobson Schwartz. In their 1963 book *A Monetary History of the United States, 1867–1960*, their crucial observation was that the money supply contracted by one-third between August 1929 and March 1933, which meant that there were fewer funds available to fuel economic activity. Despite the stock market and the economy both being in crisis, the Fed only belatedly offered monetary support and then withdrew it too soon.

The economy hit rock bottom in March 1933. The brake on its downward spiral was applied by the actions of the new US president. Franklin D. Roosevelt was inaugurated on Saturday 4 March 1933, and immediately had to contend with a month-long bank run. The next day, he declared a bank holiday and shut down the entire banking system and the stock market. On 9 March, within days of his becoming president, Congress passed the Emergency Banking Act of 1933. It included a provision that essentially provided 100 per cent deposit insurance. On Sunday 12 March, in FDR's first 'fireside chat' radio broadcast to millions of Americans, he reassured the country that only the sound banks will reopen: 'I can assure you that it is safer to keep your money in a reopened bank than under the mattress.'[11] They believed him. The next day, people were queuing to deposit rather than withdraw their money. On 15 March, the first day of reopening, the stock market also registered its largest ever one-day rise. This marked the turning point of the Great Depression. FDR had managed in a few days what his predecessor Herbert Hoover could not in three years. Why? Because the unprecedented bank holiday and 'fire-side chat' – backed up by legislation – were viewed as credible.

But the depression was far from over. Despite, or perhaps because of, his misfortunes during the 1929 Great Crash, Irving Fisher devised the influential debt-deflation theory. Deflation happens after a crash because firms and households are repaying debt, also known as deleveraging. After a financial crash, the prices of securities and commodities fall. This leads to a decline in the value of those securities and commodities that banks hold as collateral against money they have loaned. These lenders would then 'call in' the loans, that is, ask for them to be repaid, since the securities that secured the loans are worth less. This leads firms to sell those assets in a 'fire sale', since they need the money to repay their loans regardless of the price they can sell at. Households are also affected, since they may also need to sell securities to repay debt. This drives further price falls, and firms will begin to fail. Firms either can't borrow or postpone borrowing, since they are not investing, so prices fall further. Falling prices also lead people to put off purchases, since they expect the items to be cheaper in the future. Lower demand in turn contributes to falling prices. As prices collapse, there are more firm failures. Banks are also incurring losses and failing too. As banks fail, depositors will take their money out, which can precipitate bank runs. (This was especially so during the Great Depression, since deposit insurance didn't exist until after the 1930s debacle.) When people withdraw their deposits, banks have to call in more loans, which leads to more 'fire sales' by companies. Until deleveraging is complete, this dynamic drives the debt-deflation cycle, which is highly damaging and difficult to break out of.

Global deflation was also worsening the situation, exerting downward pressure on prices in the United States. There was growing stress on the gold standard, which was a system of fixed exchange rates whereby currencies were pegged to gold at a set rate. In May 1931, Austria stopped intervening to support its currency after speculators sold off the Schilling because they did not believe the parity with gold could be maintained. Contagion followed as speculators sold off other currencies, including sterling. After the UK's departure from the gold standard in September 1931, foreign investors feared that the United States would do the same and began converting their dollar assets to gold. Speculators also did not believe that the US would defend the $20.67 per troy ounce parity to gold and attacked the dollar. It wasn't until March 1933 that the US established a new parity of $35/oz, but also left the gold standard shortly thereafter. Speculators then turned their attention to the 'gold bloc' countries of France, Belgium, Italy, the Netherlands and Switzerland, who started buying gold to offset speculators selling their currencies, which added to global deflation. The 'gold bloc' suspended their currencies' convertibility into gold in 1936. Thus, the gold standard worsened deflation during the most protracted depression in American history.

In 1937–38 there was in the US a 'double dip' downturn, known as the 'recession within a depression', where GDP fell by 10 per cent and unemployment rose to 20 per cent.[12] It was also due to premature withdrawal of monetary support when policymakers thought the economy had recovered but it hadn't sufficiently. Throughout the 1930s, the economy was stuck in the debt-deflation cycle. It wasn't until 1941 that the Great Depression finally ended, in the midst of the Second World War.[13] The severity and length of the 1929 Great Crash have given it an unrivalled status in the history of financial crises.

Economists around the world learned a great deal from this catastrophic event. They extracted lessons that helped inform their responses to future crashes. We will try to do the same. First, by analysing the three phases, euphoria, credibility and aftermath, displayed clearly by the events of the Great Crash. Euphoria, whether in a stock or housing market or in an entire country or region, is the belief (always proved wrong) that markets will continue to rise, and so growing debt levels are not a source of concern. The 1929 crash was fuelled by a belief that technological marvels would lead to ever-rising stock markets, and so investing in the market was a sure-fire way to make money.

Next, we saw the importance of credibility. The slowness of the US central bank in loosening financial conditions to support the economy contributed to the depth of the Great Depression. FDR restoring confidence in the banks started the recovery. It also highlighted the importance of having effective banking regulations, specifically the need for deposit insurance so depositors can feel confident that their money is safe. Thus, credible economic policies matter. And go a long way to determining the aftermath.

The 1929 Great Crash led to the worst depression in US history because the market crash brought down the entire banking system. It takes a long time to recover from a systemic banking crisis; banks must be rescued and there's a 'credit crunch' since banks aren't lending, which affects firms and households, who can no longer readily borrow or invest. The mistakes of the Fed and the slowness of the US government in sorting out the banks meant that policymaking was found lacking. Thus, the combination of a banking crisis and a lack of credible policies meant the aftermath of the Great Crash was not a swift recovery but rather the Great Depression, in which millions of people suffered hardship for a decade.

Despite the lessons learned after the Great Crash, the late twentieth century and early twenty-first century have seen a bonanza of financial crises. A series of financial crises of all kinds, including banking, housing and stock market crashes, and currency and sovereign debt crises, have accompanied the opening up and globalization of financial markets. Since the 1970s, the expansion in offshore banking and currency trading has led to close linkages among markets, with the result that an economic downturn can spread rapidly from country to country. Although there have been crises of all shapes and sizes over the centuries, the past several decades have seen a series of financial disasters regularly encompassing economies around the world.

There have been three generations of currency crises since this globalization of financial markets. The first was the early 1980s Latin American currency crisis. It was followed by the 1992 collapse of the European Exchange Rate Mechanism, whereby European currencies had been pegged to the German Mark. The third-generation model was the 1997–98 Asian financial crisis, which ultimately spread across the world to Turkey, Russia, Brazil and Argentina. Simultaneously, a savings-and-loan crisis was raging in the United States and a spectacular real-estate crash was toppling the once-thriving economy in Japan.

At the start of the twenty-first century, there was no respite as the dot com bubble burst, triggering a recession in the US that spilled over into the international market. Then the world witnessed the worst systemic banking crisis since the 1929 Great Crash. The 2008 global financial crisis, with its origins in reckless sub-prime mortgage lending in the US, led to a near meltdown of the American financial industry that almost brought down the British banking system and deeply affected others.

In the slipstream of the US sub-prime crisis came the 2010 euro crisis, which saw the bailouts of Ireland, Portugal and Greece (the largest in history) as well as the rescue of the entire banking systems of Spain and Cyprus. Shortly thereafter the world was hit by the Covid-19 pandemic. The ensuing market crashes were the sharpest in history. Financial markets fell from record highs and unemployment claims jumped more sharply than at any time since the Great Depression. The financial markets rebounded, but the real economy struggled. The massive government actions to rescue the economies around the world revealed the extent to which the lessons from history have been heeded or ignored.

What will spark the next great crash? China's recent property-market woes could point to it being the next global meltdown. There will undoubtedly be financial crises in other countries and other sectors that could arrive first, but China stands out as its sheer economic size makes any crisis a potentially seismic one – not only for itself but also for the global economy. And China is overdue for one. Its economy has the rare distinction of having escaped a serious financial crisis during four decades of pretty much uninterrupted growth. It has, of course, had booms and busts, but not yet a crash. One reason is because of the state dominance of the financial system, which benefits from government support. But, with mounting debts and looming fragility, it would be entirely consistent with economic history throughout the ages for China to experience one. If so, then it would likely be a true 'great crash'. Even though the nature and impact of a crisis in China will be distinct, the traits of debt driven by euphoria and the challenge to the credibility of its institutions already point to similarities with other financial crises.

Often, crises will involve several elements. For example, the late-1990s Asian crisis was both a financial crisis and a currency crisis. The 2008 global financial crisis was both a housing market collapse and a banking crash. So, a single taxonomy will never quite cover the complexity and unique features of each crisis, but the broad contours help in assessing what the aftermath of the next crisis could look like.

As with all books like this one, choices have had to be made about which events to cover. There have been many more financial market crashes than are included here, but not all of them ended up inflicting widespread economic pain. All of the crises in the book led to recession, which also marks them out as 'great crashes', since not all financial crises lead to an economic slump, even though all recessions come with a stock market decline. For instance, Black Monday on 19 October 1987 was the worst one-day stock market fall in history until the 2020 pandemic crash. US and global markets fell dramatically into bear markets in a matter of days and yet no recession ensued.[14] By contrast, the dot com bubble bursting in 2000–2001 led to a US recession, though not a deep one, and so it is covered while others are not. There have also been numerous housing market crashes, but most did not trigger financial meltdowns like the US sub-prime crisis that precipitated the 2008 global financial crisis. That was certainly the case with the Japanese crash. The early 1990s real-estate crash wasn't limited to Japan; a number of countries experienced the bursting of a housing bubble after an exuberant 1980s, which led to a global recession. However, those economies did not end up in a long stagnation, unlike Japan, which, three decades on, is still struggling to recover its pre-crash growth rates. Thus, Japan warrants a chapter because focusing on that economy offers lessons to try to minimize the impact of a housing bust, and avoid it resulting in lost decades of growth.

All the crashes in this book qualify, in one way or another, as 'great'. Financial folly has existed for centuries and will surely continue. *The Great Crashes* aims to highlight what we can learn, if not to avoid the inevitable next crisis, then at least to avoid the worst when it arrives. And we can only hope that enough lessons have been learned from history to prevent another global meltdown.

# 1    Three Generations of Currency Crises

Since the 1970s, the scale of international investment has grown dramatically. The majority of this funding is known as 'hot money', short-term and highly liquid capital that can move quickly in and out of markets and from country to country, leading to episodes of high volatility in currency markets. Too much 'hot money' can trigger a currency crisis by putting a currency under huge selling pressure on international foreign exchange markets, forcing a very large and dramatic devaluation. Currency crises can be extremely damaging to developing and emerging economies.

This chapter will look at three generations of currency crises that have resulted from changes in the international market. The first is the Latin American crisis of 1981–82 and the second is the European Exchange Rate Mechanism crisis of 1992. The third, the Asian financial crisis of 1997–98, is somewhat different because it was a combined currency and a financial crisis, as opposed to currency only, stemming from domestic financial crises in a number of Asian countries that led to dramatic money outflows.

The past fifty years have seen a tremendous change in the nature and the scale of financial markets. For much of the twentieth century, most financial activity was purely domestic, with financial institutions acting as intermediaries between domestic savers and borrowers. Most countries imposed exchange controls, which restricted both the access of households and firms to foreign currency and international capital mobility. Consequently, opportunities for international trades were scarce.

Since the 1970s, though, there has been a dramatic reduction in exchange controls globally, leading to much greater movement of capital across borders. This has helped to promote international trade, and particularly so in financial assets. As a result, the world's financial markets have become increasingly interlinked.

There are three main factors that have promoted the development of this international financial market: the historical change in exchange rate regimes, the growth in offshore banking and currency trading, and a change in ideology.

From the end of the Second World War until the 1970s, most countries operated a fixed exchange rate policy as laid down in the Bretton Woods Agreement. The agreement was the result of a meeting in Bretton Woods, New Hampshire, in July 1944 that led to the establishment of the International Monetary Fund (IMF) and the World Bank. Led by Harry Dexter White of the United States and John Maynard Keynes of the United Kingdom, forty-four countries signed up to a new system designed to prevent competitive devaluations and to promote greater cooperation in the aftermath of the war. Countries pegged their currencies to the US dollar, which would convert to gold at a fixed exchange rate of $35 per ounce.[1]

By 1971 the amount of foreign-held US currency had exceeded America's gold stock, causing President Richard Nixon to end the dollar's convertibility to gold. The dollar's central role as the world's reserve currency meant that this was the collapse of the Bretton Woods system. Many countries that had pegged to the dollar were affected (although this elicited little sympathy from US Treasury Secretary John Connally, who remarked: 'the dollar is our currency, but your problem').[2]

An important factor in the end of Bretton Woods was the growth of the Eurodollar market, an offshore short-term repository for US dollars. Here, the value of the dollar was determined in currency trading outside the boundaries of the United States. Consequently, any attempt made by the US Federal Reserve to assert exchange rate control could be circumvented by trading in the Eurodollar market, as this lay outside the jurisdiction of the US.

This was a large part of the second factor in the growth of international financial markets. There was a rapid expansion in the Eurodollar market when large banks and corporations started to operate offshore during the 1960s to gain greater control over their finances.[3] (For instance, an increase in the US interest rate couldn't be passed on by banks because there was an interest-rate ceiling imposed on deposit accounts by the federal government under a measure known as Regulation Q.) The consequence was a move of US dollar-denominated deposits from US domestic banks to offshore banks, including foreign branches of US banks that were not subject to these ceilings.[4]

At the same time, commodity-exporting countries in the Middle East also increased their demand for US dollar securities due to growing exports of oil, which is priced in dollars. In the autumn of 1973 oil prices increased by a factor of five after the Arab–Israeli conflict known as the Yom Kippur War. Oil prices jumped again by a factor of three at the end of that decade, following the Iran–Iraq War. Oil exporters accumulated dollars at a rapid pace and invested them in US government debt so they could earn a return on their foreign exchange reserves. This added to the foreign holdings of US dollars, so contributing to the demise of the Bretton Woods system.

The third factor was a notable change in ideology towards opening up domestic financial markets. The abolition of the Bretton Woods era of exchange controls and the increasing freedom to undertake international financial transactions mirrored the deregulation in domestic financial markets. This change in ideology culminated in the 'Big Bang' in 1986 in the UK that deregulated the City of London and permitted foreign competition, amidst similar moves to open up financial markets around the world. By the 1980s, an international financial market was born.

International financial markets enable investors to invest anywhere. They can move their funds in order to achieve the highest return wherever that is in the world. But money invested in a country can just as easily be withdrawn when investors lose confidence.

What makes investors decide to sell up and get out? Why would anyone attack a currency? How do speculators make money from devaluations?

This is how. If a speculator thinks that a currency will devalue, then they can submit an order to the markets to sell the currency now and buy it back at a later date. If, in the meantime, the exchange rate depreciates, it means that the speculator is selling the currency for far more than it will be bought back for, representing in many cases a sizeable trading profit.

To maintain a fixed exchange rate, the government must use its gold and foreign exchange reserves to intervene in the currency markets. If a speculator tries to sell the currency, then the government will use some of its reserves to buy it, increasing demand and aiming to reduce downward pressure on the exchange rate. If the government isn't wholly successful and a devaluation occurs, the currency loses value. In this case, the speculators' profit is the loss that the government suffers through its intervention.

When the government runs out of reserves and is no longer able to defend the fixed exchange rate against heavy selling by speculators, a currency crisis will usually emerge. The actions of speculators are a vital part of the anatomy of a currency crisis. Speculators know that when the government is low on reserves, they may be able to force a devaluation and make a profit. Whether or not a speculative attack occurs depends on it having a good chance of succeeding, and this is most likely to occur when the government has few resources with which to defend against it.

What makes a currency vulnerable to attack? There are at least three possibilities. First, a balance of payments crisis, which occurs when a government runs down its reserves in the official financing of a trade deficit. Because reserves are limited, official financing cannot sustain deficits for ever. Eventually, the balance of payments deficit will require an exchange rate devaluation.

Second, runaway inflation, which will erode competitiveness since there will be no offsetting exchange rate depreciation. Because the currency value is fixed, it cannot fall even as everything costs more in the country and inflation reduces the buying power of the currency. This will lead to the exchange rate being overvalued, which means it's more expensive to sell exports, so reducing competitiveness and worsening the trade position. This again will require an exchange rate devaluation.

Third, a government running a substantial level of debt may be encouraged to produce some inflation (known as seigniorage revenues) in order to reduce the real value of its debt. Therefore, large deficits may be seen as inflationary, with similar consequences for competitiveness and the balance of payments as outlined above.

Speculators will strike as soon as they believe that an attack will be successful, usually when the government's reserves fall to some critical level. Heavy selling will then exhaust those that remain. The fixed exchange rate is ultimately unsustainable because of the above fundamental factors. The actions of speculators just accelerated its demise.

The first generation of currency crisis, the Latin American crisis of 1981–82 exemplified these conditions. Chile, Brazil, Mexico and Argentina were operating a fixed exchange rate, collectively called the Tablita, in the form of a pre-announced schedule of depreciations against the US dollar known as a 'crawling peg'.

Just as abruptly as the 'hot money' flowed into these emerging economies, the flows reversed when the US, under new Fed Chairman Paul Volcker, raised interest rates in late 1979 to curb inflation in the aftermath of the second oil price shock of that decade. Higher interest rates made it tougher for these Latin American countries to finance their external indebtedness since the cost of borrowing had increased. Moreover, monies started to flow back into the United States due to better returns from the higher interest rates on US securities. Pegged against the dollar, the Tablita exchange rate came under pressure, particularly as there was also a substantial inflation differential between these countries and the US. Inflation in these Latin American economies rose in excess of the currency depreciations, which eroded their competitiveness and put pressure on their balance of payments.

The crisis erupted when these commodity-exporting countries said that they could not pay the interest on their external loans, which had jumped from $125 billion in the late 1970s to a staggering $800 billion. The combination of high interest rates and commodity prices falling due to the global recession meant that they were at risk of defaulting on their debt. For the next seven years, Latin American countries negotiated with their creditors.

It wasn't until March 1989 that the Brady Plan, named after then US Treasury Secretary Nicholas F. Brady, saw the crisis finally resolved. The Brady Plan was premised on how US domestic corporations were treated when they could not service their debts. First, bank creditors would grant debt relief in exchange for 'Brady bonds' that were backed by US Treasury bonds, which offer greater assurance of repayment. Second, the debt relief would be linked to economic reforms, and third, the debt would be made more tradable so that creditors could diversify their own risk.

Over $160 billion of Brady bonds were issued not only by Latin American emerging economies but by others as well, including Argentina, Brazil, Bulgaria, Costa Rica, Côte d'Ivoire, Dominican Republic, Ecuador, Jordan, Nigeria, Panama, Peru, the Philippines, Poland, Russia, Uruguay, Venezuela and Vietnam. About a decade and a half later, most Brady bonds had been exchanged or bought back by the debtor nations. Brady bond trading had accounted for 61 per cent of emerging market debt in 1994; it had dropped to just 2 per cent by 2005.[5]

The set of countries to suffer what would become known as the second-generation currency crisis would encompass not only those in the emerging economies of Latin America but also in the advanced economies of Europe.

After the end of the Bretton Woods system, European countries looked to fix their currencies against each other. As intra-European trade grew, these countries saw the benefits of having stable rates of exchange. The 1970s also saw the drive to deepen European integration, so the European Exchange Rate Mechanism (ERM) was created in 1979.

At its inception, the ERM members were Belgium, Denmark,

France, Germany, Greece, Ireland, Italy, Luxembourg and the Netherlands, all of whom pegged to the anchor currency, the German Mark. Other countries subsequently joined, including Spain (1989), the UK (1990) and Portugal (1992). Finland, Norway and Sweden were not officially in the ERM, but effectively pegged their currencies to it by fixing their values against either the ECU (a predecessor to the euro) or the German Mark.

These countries believed that Germany's low inflation would serve as an external anchor to keep their inflation under control after the bouts of high price increases that occurred during the 1970s. The problem was that this policy was at odds with the financial liberalization of the 1980s, which saw capital flowing more freely across borders, moved by investors and speculators.

But this all changed in the early 1990s, when German monetary policy loosened to fund the reunification of West and East Germany. German inflation rose, which didn't suit the other European countries, and the Mark lost its place as the anchor. This economic divergence severely disrupted the pegged exchange rate system, which eventually led to the collapse of the ERM in 1992.

All these countries fit the second-generation model well, but the UK example is particularly illuminating.

The UK's decision to join the ERM in 1990 was the cornerstone of its policy against inflation. By fixing the pound against the Mark, Germany's low-inflation discipline could be imported, and this worked for a time as inflation came under control from its peak in 1990. But that all changed when German interest rates began to climb.

German reunification was largely paid for by borrowing, and in order to control inflation, the German central bank, the Bundesbank, substantially increased German interest rates. If the UK wished to keep its fixed parity, then it would need to follow.

Operating high interest rates did not suit the British economy at the time. The UK was in a severe recession and suffering high unemployment. Britain needed lower interest rates in order to invigorate the economy and bring down unemployment. This was impossible as long as the UK was in the ERM, where German interest rates were actually rising, so there was a clear argument for the UK to abandon the fixed exchange rate.

Speculative pressure on the pound rose because of this conflict of policy objectives. If the pound came under heavy selling pressure, it would seem a very reasonable policy for the UK to simply let it devalue and sacrifice ERM membership. To defend the pound by raising interest rates would be intolerable for domestic reasons.

In the summer of 1992, hedge fund manager George Soros was one of those exerting pressure. He questioned the credibility of the currency peg and accumulated a short position of more than $10 billion by placing a 'sell' order on the pound in foreign exchange markets and agreeing to buy it back at a later date. He bet that the pound would fall in value by then. Soros's Quantum Fund led other speculators to sell off sterling. On what became known as Black Wednesday, 16 September 1992, the selling was so frenzied that the Bank of England was buying £2 billion of sterling an hour.[6]

At 11 a.m., Prime Minister John Major convened a meeting of key ministers, including his Chancellor, Norman Lamont. They agreed to raise interest rates from 10 per cent to 12 per cent. By the end of the day, interest rates were raised to an eye-watering 15 per cent. This did not avert the attack, but the UK could have imposed higher interest rates if it had wanted to. (For example, Swedish overnight interest rates jumped to 500 per cent at one point.) However, when 15 per cent did not work, the UK government announced it was leaving the ERM at 7.40 p.m. that day, prompting a collapse in the pound against the German currency.

In many ways, the UK's exit from the ERM wasn't such bad news. It enabled interest rates to come down sharply and the depreciation in the exchange rate that resulted boosted UK competitiveness. The economy began to grow, and unemployment declined. Some people refer to Black Wednesday as White Wednesday for this reason.

The day after Black Wednesday, much of the British press attacked George Soros, who personally made more than £1 billion from the pound's devaluation. He became known as the person who 'broke the

Bank of England'. However, given the UK's strong economic performance subsequently, there have even been calls to put a statue of him up in Trafalgar Square![7]

The anatomy of the ERM crisis illustrates the conflict at the centre of the second-generation currency crisis. The UK government had an incentive to raise interest rates to preserve membership of the ERM, but also an incentive to leave in order to loosen monetary policy and lower unemployment.

This choice is why second-generation crises are described as self-fulfilling. If speculators decide to attack and can coordinate their actions, then the attack will likely be successful in forcing a devaluation. A feature of the crisis is that the costs of defending the fixed exchange rate will increase as it becomes increasingly expected that the parity will be abandoned. As the belief rises that the government will drop the currency peg in order to reduce unemployment, the expectation of a currency depreciation becomes greater. This adds extra risk to holding sterling-denominated assets, so interest rates must rise further to compensate the holders and maintain the fixed exchange rate.

Thus, attacks are self-fulfilling in the sense that, once they start, they are likely to succeed, owing to the rising cost to the economy of maintaining the currency peg; but there is a degree of arbitrariness about them because (a) the government can choose to defend the exchange rate by raising interest rates despite it being detrimental to the economy and (b) a country that does not come under attack can continue to maintain parity. This is unlike the Latin American countries in the 1980s. Those economies suffered from poor economic fundamentals, so their exchange rates were doomed to collapse.

But when speculators like George Soros believe that a government won't choose the fixed exchange rate over employment, that can trigger a currency sell-off and a crisis. This was different from the first-generation crises.

The third-generation currency crisis was again different, and, rather surprisingly, took place among the fast-growing economies of Asia. At the end of 1997 and the beginning of 1998, the Asian

Five – Thailand, Malaysia, South Korea, Indonesia and the Philippines – suffered a collapse in their currencies brought on by large outflows of financial capital. Up until this time, these currencies had been held relatively fixed against the US dollar. It is clear that, as in the crises already described, a rapid drop in the exchange rate was involved, but that is where the comparisons finish.

Although there were those who questioned the extent of Asia's economic miracle, few expected the region to suffer the crisis that it did. It certainly didn't follow the conventional pattern set by the first- and second-generation models. On the eve of the crisis, inflation was low and there were none of the large budget deficits that had been a problem in the Latin American crisis. Indeed, the Asian countries were considered to be the model for emerging economies. Leading up to the crisis, the so-called 'Asian miracle' countries had seen impressive growth and low unemployment. There was apparently no reason to abandon their fixed exchange rates. Most risk assessments of the area in mid-1996 showed no signal of what was to come in the following months.

Unlike the first- and second-generation models, the Asian experience was part of a larger financial crisis as currency collapses were accompanied by falling asset prices and bank failures. The crisis also spread infectiously across the entire region, affecting not only the four Southeast Asian economies that were strongly linked by trade, but also South Korea in East Asia, which was not.

Several factors triggered the rapid withdrawal of investor funds in the region that led to the crisis, reversing the strong capital inflows it had previously enjoyed. In 1996, private net flows into these economies totalled $93 billion, mostly from private creditors and portfolio investment. Direct investment in physical items such as factories made up a very small part of the inflow. Rather, the vast majority (some 92 per cent) of the private capital flowing into the region was lent on a short-term basis. Developing countries would prefer to have more long-term investment that built infrastructure than loans that could quickly be pulled by creditors, so this ratio was far from ideal.

These large-scale inflows were encouraged by several factors. First, continuing high rates of economic growth gave confidence to foreign investors. Second, wide-ranging deregulation enabled banks and domestic corporations to tap into foreign finance for domestic investments. Third, the Asian Five's exchange rates were pegged to the US dollar, hence there was no exchange rate uncertainty, which helped to encourage inward investment. All this was bolstered by government policies that incentivized foreign borrowing, for example the absence of reserve requirements for foreign exchange loans.

These countries were among those classed as emerging markets, or EMs. Since 1988, there has been an Emerging Markets benchmark share index that comprises listed companies from EMs. The designation led many institutional funds that followed the EM index to invest in those countries. The Asian economies were especially popular since faster growth meant higher returns for investors. Moreover, with manufacturing moving out of a more expensive Japan, these countries were experiencing inflows of investment to fuel their places in the global supply chain. The 1990s were later dubbed a period of hyper-globalization as investment surged into emerging markets, and nowhere did it surge more rapidly than in Asia.[8]

Stock prices soared. In the first half of the 1990s, Thailand, Malaysia and Indonesia saw share prices rise by 300 to 500 per cent. In the East Asian region, stocks doubled in value in 1993 alone. Real estate boomed along with the economy. In many of these countries, the listed companies were substantial property owners, so the real-estate boom contributed to the stock market rise.

The crisis was brought on by the sudden reversal of a long and sustained period of inflows. In 1997, the net inflows into the Asian Five dropped from $93 billion and reversed to an outflow of $12 billion, a swing of $105 billion, which was about 11 per cent of their collective GDP. Foreign direct investment remained constant at about $7 billion, so most of the decline came from private short-term money flows: 'hot money'.

Why did this sudden reversal take place? Beneath the euphoric rise in markets, a number of fragilities in the corporate and banking systems were exposed when the inevitable bust followed. In Thailand, for example, finance companies borrowed short-term money, often in US dollars, and then lent to long-term speculative investors, particularly in real estate. When the short-term loans were recalled, they struggled to repay them since the money was tied up in long-term investments. The banking system in many Asian countries was somewhat murky. Although there were no explicit government guarantees, most banks had strong political connections and there was a belief that, if there was a default, the government would bail them out to prevent a banking collapse. Such a system of 'crony capitalism' is likely to lead to risky investments, which offer the opportunity to make large returns.

Risky bank lending contributed to the asset-price boom, particularly in real estate and stocks. High asset prices and equity values meant that property companies and other businesses could use these assets as collateral for more loans. The banking system was prepared to borrow from overseas to do so. The extent of bank lending meant that the real-estate and corporate sectors became increasingly indebted to banks, who were themselves increasingly indebted to foreign creditors. However, the fragility was masked by high asset prices, which gave a sense that the loans were collateralized, and an implicit trust that, even if anything did go wrong, there would be a government rescue package.

The fragility of the banking sector became apparent with the bursting of the asset bubble. Banks had advanced loans on what they perceived to be good collateral, but falling prices reduced that collateral's value, and banks ended up holding loans with little security. The banks had also borrowed substantially from overseas, so were vulnerable to foreign creditors recalling their loans.

Everything was set up for a potential crisis. If foreign investors suffered a loss of confidence, they would call in their loans, forcing the banking sector to call in some of its own loans. But because the collateral supporting these loans was no longer of sufficient value to repay them, any attempt by the banks to liquidate firm assets would lead to a succession of corporate bankruptcies and defaults. Worried foreign creditors would panic and attempt to salvage as much as possible by withdrawing as quickly as possible, which would lead to a downward spiral of bankruptcies, default and further panic.

There were several triggering factors that led to foreign investors losing confidence. When combined with the fragile economic conditions, this led to panic and large outflows, and therefore crisis.

In late 1996, Thailand's consumer finance companies started to report large losses. Many of these had been set up by Thai banks to circumvent the regulations that limited their offerings of consumer loans. Notably, Somprasong Land missed payments on its foreign debts, signalling the demise of the property market and the beginning of the end for the finance companies that had lent heavily to property investors. In June 1997, the Thai government removed support from a major finance company, Finance One, and announced that creditors – domestic and foreign – would incur losses. Foreign lenders became concerned and the flow of funds to Thailand fell. With less demand for the Thai baht, the Bank of Thailand struggled to maintain the fixed exchange rate. In July 1997, the attempt was abandoned and the baht fell in value.

In South Korea, there was also a growing number of corporate failures. In early 1997, Hanbo Steel collapsed owing almost $6 billion. This was the first Korean bankruptcy of a *chaebol*, a conglomerate, in a decade. Sammi Steel and Kia Motors suffered a similar fate. This put banks under pressure.

Following the collapse of the Thai baht, creditors became wary of the region as a whole, and the Asian financial crisis ensued. The currencies of Malaysia, the Philippines and Singapore fell in value by 30 per cent or more within six months. The Indonesian rupiah declined by more than two-thirds. Hong Kong was affected too. All these economies witnessed dramatic stock market collapses; share prices fell by 30 to 60 per cent. Real-estate prices dropped sharply. More foreign money left. With the exception of those in Singapore and Hong Kong, which had better financial regulation, most banks failed. In Indonesia, for example, the government closed sixteen banks but still couldn't stymie the crisis; it ended up guaranteeing the liabilities of all the banks and setting up a fund to restructure the banking system.[9]

The extent of the fallout from the Asian crisis came as a surprise to many. The contagion led to investors moving monies out of other emerging markets. In 1998, Russia suffered a crisis, followed shortly by Turkey in 1999 and then Brazil and Argentina. The US was also affected. Long-Term Capital Management (LTCM), which was the largest hedge fund in the US, needed to be rescued.

The hedge fund had a stellar pedigree of investors, it seemed. It was founded and managed by John Meriwether, a well-known bond trader from Salomon Brothers. It also counted among its ranks not one but two Nobel Prize-winning economists: Myron Scholes and Robert Merton. They had won the top prize in economics together with the late Fischer Black for devising the Black–Scholes–Merton model, a pioneering formula to value stock options. LTCM had also brought on board a former vice-chairman of the US Federal Reserve Bank, David Mullins, who had quit his job to become a partner at the firm.

In the early summer of 1998, LTCM's bet on emerging markets didn't seem to be such a great one. During the boom, it was highly profitable and also highly leveraged, as hedge funds are wont to be. But in August, when the Asian financial crisis spread to become a wider emerging markets crisis, the Russian rouble fell by more than 50 per cent and the country subsequently defaulted. LTCM had to sell securities in a falling market to repay short-term loans. Each sale was driving down the prices of the other assets that it owned. In a 'fire sale' of securities there are few eager buyers since they suspect that the prices of these securities will continue to fall. Since the same class of assets is identically priced across all firms, other financial institutions could also end up with losses on their balance sheets. In other words, LTCM could drag down others with it. The government believed the troubled hedge fund posed a potential risk to the entire financial system, and the New York Fed essentially forced the fourteen banks that were lenders to LTCM to convert their loans worth $3.5 billion into equity. These banks ended up owning 90 per cent of LTCM and wound down the firm by 2000.

The Asian crisis ended with Thailand, Indonesia and South Korea being rescued by the IMF. The Philippines drew more funds from an existing IMF package. The bailouts were sizeable and depleted the IMF's funds. Like other supranational organizations, the IMF has a pot of money that is funded by creditor countries such as the US and the EU. At the end of 1998, the IMF needed to increase its capital and its stakeholders agreed to do so to contend with the ongoing crisis.

Malaysia did not seek loans from the IMF as it wanted to avoid the conditionality of those loans, which usually include imposing fiscal austerity and opening up markets in exchange for rescue funds. Instead, rather controversially at the time, Malaysia imposed capital controls to prevent monies from leaving the country. It refused to allow foreign investors to withdraw their funds. The prime minister, Dr Mahathir Mohamad, blamed speculators like George Soros for causing the crisis.

An indicator that often rings alarm bells is when countries start to construct the biggest buildings in the world. That could cause speculators to take notice of a bubble and attack that country's currency, expecting it to fall in value alongside the economy during a bust. Before the crash, Malaysia had claimed the world's highest building and had plans to build the world's longest one. Soros, in reply to Dr Mahathir, declared that he had not shorted the ringgit despite these signs, and insisted that speculators provided a kind of shock treatment for governments that had ignored warning signals to get their economic houses in order. After the crisis, Malaysia put those record-breaking building plans on hold.[10]

Despite the scale of the crisis, the recession was V-shaped in Asia. From 1999, economic growth recovered quickly in the region after a sharp downturn, just as had happened after the second-generation crisis in Europe and for similar reasons. The large currency depreciations greatly increased the export competitiveness of the Asian nations, resulting in large current-account inflows which supported the recovery. Unlike in Europe, however, some of these emerging economies needed to be rescued, which made this a more devastating financial crisis than the European one.

Throughout history, the impact of a currency crisis is rarely limited to just one country. As seen in Latin America, Europe and Asia, its neighbours often suffer a similar fate. The regional nature of a currency crisis might be accounted for by the fact that countries that are close to each other geographically are often integrated with each other through trade. A crisis in one country leading to a large and rapid devaluation in the exchange rate might severely affect the competitiveness of neighbouring countries. Also, nations that are close geographically tend to export similar goods and services, so are competitors in global markets and/or part of the same global supply chains. A large devaluation in one might lead to speculation that similar devaluations will be required in the others in order to maintain the competitiveness of their exports.

The fact that neighbouring countries may share similar cultures and languages might point to their having not only similar economic structures, institutions and policies but also similar weaknesses. The financial crisis in Asia may have spread due to a general lack of confidence in the banking sector in the entire region.

An important lesson of the third-generation crisis is its contagion, which is when a shock or a crisis that originates in one country spreads to others. The crisis in Asia led to large-scale capital outflows from South America, for example, even though the economies were very different structurally, geographically far apart and exhibited few trade or financial links, which are typically a more gradual conduit in any case.

One explanation for contagion is that investors' appetites for risk may diminish in times of market stress and increased uncertainty. Emerging market economies can grow strongly, but this growth can also be fragile since a lack of well-established formal institutions at their stage of development could make those economies more prone to shocks. Assets in emerging markets may offer higher returns, but at the price of more risk. Advanced economies offer a slightly different type of portfolio. As these are large, wealthy and mature economies, assets are less risky, but the relative return will also be lower.

Although emerging markets may exhibit different fundamentals, they might all be affected by a general increase in risk aversion. It is evident from the third-generation model that emerging market crises become more likely as investors become more risk averse. If a crisis were to emerge, no investor would wish to be at the back of the stampede to exit the country since default might occur before they could liquidate their positions. Such nervousness can be infectious, generating the 'herding' behaviour among investors required to precipitate a currency crisis.

There have been a large number of currency crises around the globe since the early 1980s. Each generation exhibited exuberant behaviour in the run-up to the crisis, where 'hot money' flowed into countries that had promised to keep their exchange rates fixed and stable. The currency crises were triggered by speculators finding a lack of credibility on the part of governments in Latin America in the first generation and in Europe in the second generation to defend their currency pegs. The same can be said for Asia in the third generation, even though the crisis there stemmed from overextended financial markets. All three generations shared these traits.

But there were also differences, the biggest being the aftermath. Whereas the emerging markets required bailouts, the British economy grew well after crashing out of the ERM. The UK government, despite the about-face on the exchange rate, enjoyed the confidence of financial markets. Indeed, the 1990s and early 2000s became known as the 'Great Moderation', describing a period of low inflation and strong economic growth in Europe and elsewhere. Depending on the second shared trait of credibility, the post-crisis fate of countries can differ greatly even if the crises shared similar aspects leading up to the crash.

For policymakers, the three generations of currency crises offer different lessons. For the first-generation model, they should be wary of running excessive trade and budget deficits. When economic fundamentals are weak, as in Latin America in the 1980s, speculators could sell off a country's currency in anticipation of a collapse. In the second-generation model, because there's a conflict between maintaining the fixed exchange rate or preserving employment, as in the ERM crisis of 1992, speculators could decide to test the resolve of policymakers and cause a currency crisis. Maintaining credible policies is thus important because those economies did not have weak economic fundamentals, so a crisis was not inevitable. A final lesson derives from the third-generation model, which is contagion. Investors can quickly pull out 'hot money' across emerging markets, as seen in the late 1990s Asian financial crisis that spread far and wide. Since investors might treat emerging economies as a class, policymakers should aim to differentiate their country to prevent being included in indiscriminate selling that can trigger a crisis.

The legacy from these multiple generations of crises is a recognition that alongside the internationalization of financial markets is the internationalization of financial crises, which are no longer contained to regions but can spread rapidly around the world.

Given the global contagion from the Asian financial crisis, there is now greater international coordination of financial regulations, as seen in the establishment of the Financial Stability Forum in 1999. This later became the Financial Stability Board (FSB), after the 2008 global financial crisis. The FSB promulgates standards around capital and liquidity requirements that apply to large financial institutions. These international efforts actually began even earlier, with the Basel standards that were developed after the early 1980s Latin American crisis, which have since become influential standards governing major banks around the world. Crisis management has become global.

# 2  The US Savings and Loan Crisis of the 1980s

The savings and loan crisis of the 1980s was the worst US financial crisis since the Great Depression. It was the first, though not the last, systemic breakdown of the regulatory and deposit insurance system since the 1929 Great Crash. It ended with half of all savings and loans (also known as S&Ls) shutting down. It was a dramatic denouement for S&Ls, which were supposedly simple mortgage lenders, as captured in Frank Capra's classic 1946 movie, *It's a Wonderful Life*. Jimmy Stewart played a character named George Bailey who ended up using some of his honeymoon funds to prevent the local S&L from being acquired by the antagonist, a robber baron named Henry F. Potter.

Fast forward to the 1980s and the image of S&Ls was dramatically different, with Charles Keating becoming a real-life version of Henry Potter. Keating was a banker who bribed no fewer than five US senators, to buy their support for his failing S&L, Lincoln Savings and Loan. Keating had been charged by the Securities and Exchange Commission (SEC) for defrauding shareholders of his insurance company in 1979, and fined for approving $14 million in loans to himself and other officers of the company. In 1984, he moved into the growing S&L industry, acquiring the California-based Lincoln S&L. In just four years the bank's assets swelled from $1 billion to more than $5 billion, but he had cooked the books using shady accounting practices. For instance, he and his partners at Lincoln traded empty lots with other companies but listed those transactions as profitable in their books. He also invested a staggering two-thirds of Lincoln's federally insured deposits in risky assets such as junk bonds.

When the regulators started to ask questions, Keating called in favours from five senators to whom he had given over a million dollars in campaign contributions. He even boasted to reporters about his 'bribes'. The 'Keating Five' were Republican John McCain (Arizona) and Democrats Dennis DeConcini (Arizona), former astronaut John Glenn (Ohio), Alan Cranston (California) and Donald Riegle (Michigan). They were later investigated by the Senate Ethics Committee for their improper conduct in pressuring the regulator to overlook Keating's activities on the basis that Lincoln S&L was a major employer and provided jobs in their states. McCain, who was the Republican nominee for president in 2008, said later that it had been 'the worst mistake of my life'.[1]

Despite the lobbying, Lincoln S&L collapsed in 1989. Its failure led to the deposit insurer covering more than $3 billion in losses, which was the largest of the more than a thousand S&Ls that closed during the crisis. Keating was arrested and charged with seventy-three counts of fraud. He was sent to prison in 1991 and the government auctioned off his home and fined him $156 million. In 1996 his prison sentence was set aside for technical reasons, but in 1999 he again pleaded guilty to wire and bankruptcy fraud, and was sentenced to time already served.[2]

Although Keating became the face of the S&L crisis, it was a much broader phenomenon. The entire debacle cost the government an eye-watering $124 billion. The start of the S&L industry was a much more modest affair. In Pennsylvania in the 1830s, social collectives pooled people's savings and lent the funds to people who lacked the savings to buy a home outright. The repaid funds would then be lent to others in the community. At that time, commercial banks were not lending residential mortgages, so S&Ls, also known as thrifts, played an important role in the American dream of home ownership.

The idea worked well and, a century later, the Federal Home Loan Bank Act of 1932 formally established the S&L industry. In an effort to avoid a repeat of the bank and thrift failures of the 1929 crash, the government introduced a deposit insurance scheme to protect savers. In 1933, the Federal Deposit Insurance Corporation was established to insure deposits in banks. A year later, the Federal Savings and Loan Insurance Corporation was created to do the same for S&Ls.

S&Ls simply took in deposits and lent out mortgages. In both cases, they offered lower interest rates than banks. The model was described as a '3–6–3' business:[3] paying 3 per cent interest on deposits, charging 6 per cent on mortgages and arriving on the golf course by 3 p.m. In the 1970s and 1980s, the federal government greatly expanded the secondary markets for mortgages by introducing securitization. A bundle of mortgages could be sold to federal agencies and taken off the books of lenders, which increased the funding available for mortgages. Also, the federal income tax code allowed mortgage interest payments and local property taxes to be deducted from income, which essentially was a subsidy for homeowners. As part of the 'golden age' of economic growth in the 1950s and 1960s, the thrift industry saw its assets roughly double every five years between 1945 and 1965.[4] Growth then slowed but picked up again with the above changes, and by 1980 there were around 4,000 thrifts across the United States, with assets of more than $600 billion. Of those assets, the vast majority ($480 billion) were mortgages. Indeed, around 80 per cent of their balance sheets were mortgages. Thrifts were responsible for about half of all mortgages and more than a quarter of all deposits in the United States.

Like other financial institutions, S&Ls were highly regulated but also protected from competition by regulation. For instance, they could not lend mortgages to applicants living more than fifty miles from the S&L's home office. This insulated S&Ls from outside competition in their catchments.

In the 1970s, there were two oil price shocks. The first was due to the Yom Kippur War. After the Nixon administration offered aid to Israel in October 1973, the Arab states within the Organization of Petroleum Exporting Countries (OPEC) placed an embargo on sales of oil to the United States and also cut production. The price of oil quadrupled from $2.90 per barrel to $11.65 in early 1974.[5] The embargo was lifted in March of that year amidst disagreement among OPEC members, but oil prices remained high. This was followed by a second shock, also stemming from the Middle East. The 1978–79 Iranian Revolution and the Iran–Iraq War the following year saw damage to the country's oil production infrastructure, which drove up global prices since Iran was a major supplier. In 1981, oil stabilized at $32 per barrel.[6]

These two shocks heralded a period of high interest rates to tame inflation. Interest rates had begun to rise in the mid-1960s, but they remained below 10 per cent until 1973. They jumped with the first oil price shock, fell back and then rapidly shot up again after the second shock in 1979 and stayed in double digits for much of the next three years. Rapidly rising interest rates were bad for S&Ls. The long-term loans they offered, typically thirty-year mortgages, were financed by short-term deposits which could be withdrawn with little notice.

Bank deposit interest rates had been capped since 1933, and in 1966 Congress had placed a similar ceiling on the interest rates that thrifts could pay on deposits. Known as Regulation Q, the measure enabled them to earn a margin on their low-interest, fixed-rate mortgages. With rates elsewhere rising rapidly, both thrifts and banks started to compete to attract depositors by offering incentives such as electrical goods to new depositors when they signed up.

To help S&Ls, in 1970 Congress raised the minimum denomination of government bonds, known as Treasurys, from $1,000 to $10,000, to deter depositors from leaving thrifts and putting their money into government debt, which helped since the average deposit in a thrift was around $3,000.[7]

Thrifts wanted to offer variable-rate mortgages, as British building societies had been doing since the nineteenth century, which would have improved their business model, but Congress, concerned that thrifts would raise interest rates on mortgages when borrowers had few options, shot down any such proposal in order to protect consumers.

With rising rates and poor returns in thrifts and banks, money market mutual funds became an attractive alternative for savers. Mutual funds pooled the money of individuals and invested the funds in a variety of assets such as government debt and CDs (time deposits that pay higher interest if the money is left in the bank for six months to five years), all of which earned higher returns than an instant-withdrawal current account. Mutual funds were usually liquid, and even offered some limited chequing privileges. So, even though mutual funds were not insured, they generally invested in higher-quality assets and were considered relatively safe. They grew rapidly during the late 1970s.

As the S&L crisis was emerging, Regulation Q was relaxed slightly so that thrifts and banks could pay market rates to savers who deposited over $10,000 and left their money in for at least six months. But since the average deposit was only $4,750, few mutual-fund depositors were lured away to S&Ls.[8]

By the early 1980s, more than one-third of S&Ls were making losses and the entire industry was estimated to be around $100 billion in the red.[9] The federal insurer did not have enough funds to cover the deficit as it held just $6 billion in reserves.[10] The government reacted by passing the Depository Institutions Deregulation and Monetary Control Act and the Garn–St. Germain Depository Institutions Act, in 1980 and 1982 respectively, in an attempt to buy the S&Ls more time to weather the interest rate squeeze and avoid using taxpayer money to rescue them. These laws lowered the minimum level of capital that S&Ls needed to hold, which enabled them to report better financial positions. They also gave the regulators the ability to recognize new forms of regulatory capital as well as lowering the enforcement standards for S&Ls that were close to insolvency. This enabled previously insolvent S&Ls to report otherwise, so delaying the day of reckoning.[11]

Thrifts were also finally allowed to offer adjustable-rate mortgages and to lend nationally. Federally chartered S&Ls could now also provide consumer loans and credit cards, while state-chartered thrifts could invest a larger portion of their assets in commercial real estate and make commercial loans. They were at times granted even more latitude than their federal counterparts. In other words, thrifts were allowed to become more like commercial banks. The authorities weren't concerned about thrifts abandoning mortgages, trusting that

the tax advantages to thrifts of mortgage lending would be a sufficient incentive for them to carry on doing so.

Although these measures were intended to help the thrifts become
more viable, they also created new risks. The intention was that
allowing business and geographic diversification would enable S&Ls
to adopt a strategy for risk and return that was superior to their previous narrow remit of taking in short-term deposits and lending
long-term mortgages to local borrowers. But borrowers are far more
likely to default on other types of loans and investments than on their
mortgages. Even more troubling, unlike mortgages which are secured
by the property, the newly permitted types of loans included those that
were unsecured.

As S&Ls entered banking territory, competition heated up in the
commercial real-estate market loan business, which fuelled the
emerging property bubble. To make matters worse, S&Ls were inex-
perienced in such lending, which undermined their ability to deliver
a growth strategy that was also prudent.

For those S&Ls that were in reality insolvent but still operating
owing to the new government measures, it was worth taking excessive
risks. They were shielded by limited liability laws, so were liable only
to the extent of the equity they held in the business. Also, if it all went
wrong, the deposit insurance fund would cover their losses. And if it
worked, then they would reap the rewards. In the absence of regulation to monitor increased risk, the stage was set for catastrophe.

By 1983, nearly one in ten S&Ls was bankrupt. The Federal Savings
and Loan Insurance Corporation needed $25 billion to pay out on
insured deposits due to S&L failures, but it had less than a quarter of
that amount. Even worse, the lack of an effective regulatory system
meant that struggling S&Ls continued to operate like zombie companies. Their balance sheets eventually deteriorated even further,
adding more cost to the inevitable looming rescue.

Commercial banks were not immune from the challenging environment either. In 1984, the largest bank failure prior to the 2008
sub-prime crisis occurred. The seventh-largest bank in the US,

Continental Illinois, had bet on the oil price going up. When it went the other way, the bank suffered its second run in two years. It was rescued by the deposit insurer but shareholders, including the bank's directors, lost their money and the executives in charge lost their reputations as well. Like the zombie S&Ls, Continental Illinois remained in business on account of the various relaxed measures instituted by the government.

With growing losses, not only were the owners of thrifts inclined to take ever bigger risks, but also the community culture that had contributed to prudence in thrifts was quickly eroding. New entrants bought up failing thrifts or started their own and were able to grow fairly rapidly by investing in risky assets such as junk bonds, a financial 'innovation' famously peddled by Michael Milken at the investment bank Drexel Burnham Lambert in the 1980s. Milken was one inspiration for the fictional character Gordon Gekko in the 1987 film *Wall Street*, in which the character famously proclaimed, 'Greed is good,' which seemed to capture the ethos of that decade.

A junk bond, or high-yield bond, was a non-investment-grade bond issued by companies, many of which were 'fallen angels' – that is, they had previously been issued with a credit rating by one of the major credit rating agencies. There was a higher risk of default and risk that the company would stumble further. To compensate for the risk, junk bonds paid higher interest, some three to four percentage points more than investment-grade corporate bonds. The regulators prohibited many financial institutions from holding bonds below investment grade, so banks and insurance companies would be required to sell those bonds when they became 'junk', which pushed up the interest rates even further.

Higher returns for higher risk was how junk bonds were presented to potential buyers. There was the suggestion of a 'free lunch', because if the buyer bought a diversified portfolio of junk bonds, then the higher interest income would more than cover any losses in the event of default by any single company.[12]

The issuers weren't only 'fallen angels'. During the 1980s, leveraged buyouts – acquisitions financed by debt – were growing in number and size, one of the most notorious being Kohlberg Kravis Roberts & Company's leveraged buyout of RJR Nabisco, the conglomerate food and tobacco company, which became the subject of the book, and later film, *Barbarians at the Gate*. Such firms would raise as much as 90 per cent debt to buy a company and often dismantled or sold off parts of it (RJR and Nabisco subsequently became two firms). The buyouts would be financed by junk bonds, many of which were purchased by S&Ls. Some S&Ls even worked with Drexel Burnham Lambert as the underwriter to raise funds so that they could acquire firms themselves, since equity ownership by the thrifts was permitted.

Michael Milken was known as the 'junk bond king'.[13] At Drexel Burnham Lambert, he dominated the junk bond market that helped finance a wave of leveraged buyouts that changed the face of corporate America. Milken took full advantage of the economic environment of the 1980s, which saw a decline in interest rates and a growing economy, arranging junk bond financing for his friends and associates so they could gain control of firms such as thrifts and insurers.[14] Milken even provided 'letters of comfort' to entrepreneurs, assuring them that Drexel could raise the monies required. Once his friends and associates gained ownership of a company, his firm would issue junk bonds that were bought by thrifts and insurers that were also controlled by Milken's network. Drexel even established mutual funds, which pooled investors' money, to buy the junk bonds that it had underwritten, and earned fees from underwriting whenever its clients issued junk bonds. It also earned money from selling the junk bonds to its own mutual funds, levied fees for selling shares in the mutual funds to the public and charged management fees for running the mutual funds.

Unsurprisingly, many of the firms acquired by Milken's friends didn't earn enough to pay the interest on the junk bonds that they had issued. Milken then arranged for them to issue new securities that helped them pay the interest on their outstanding bonds, and Milken's network of thrifts bought those too.[15] His scheme ticked along until federal regulators clamped down and stopped S&Ls buying junk bonds. At the end of the 1980s, the junk bond market collapsed.

About half of the firms that had issued junk bonds through Drexel Burnham Lambert went into default. Drexel itself went bankrupt in 1992. The owners of junk bonds on average lost one-third of their money. It turned out that the additional interest income earned on these bonds did not cover the losses on the defaulted bonds.[16] There was no 'free lunch'!

The thrifts that had incurred such huge losses had done nothing illegal, but not so Michael Milken, who was jailed and paid a fine of $550 million. After his release from prison in 1993, he was still extremely wealthy.[17] He started the Milken Institute, a think-tank whose annual conference is held in Beverly Hills and attracts a number of his former Wall Street colleagues. Milken was pardoned by President Donald Trump in 2020, and could now apply to the SEC to lift the ban on him working in the securities industry, if he wished.

By the end of 1985 the S&L industry was over 50 per cent larger than it had been just three years earlier.[18] As it grew rapidly, the level of risk-taking rose with it. Instead of just lending mortgages, S&Ls increasingly lent to commercial real-estate buyers. The value of residential mortgages on their books grew by $120 billion, but as a percentage of total assets they declined from around two-thirds to just over 50 per cent between 1982 and 1985.[19] The rapid growth of S&Ls was propelled by investing in riskier assets.

As the Keating scandal illustrated, criminal activity was also fuelling growth. For instance, Empire Savings and Loan of Texas was involved in illegal land flips and other activities. Dubbed 'cash-for-trash', the practice involved flipping a property until its price was double or triple its market value, whereby an S&L would refinance each flip and end up with a more valuable asset. These loans were known as 'drag-away loans' since the intention was to default, which meant that the proceeds were dragged away by the S&L. That's what Empire S&L did to condominiums along the Interstate 30 highway near Dallas, despite a glut of properties in a state that was at the centre of the oil boom and thus a magnet for real-estate investors.[20] These phony profits from flipping properties caught up with Empire S&L, which eventually collapsed, costing taxpayers a staggering $300 million.

This mid-1980s peak in the real-estate bubble was also due to a change in tax laws and a rise in oil prices. The tax change was a shortening of the depreciation periods for real estate, which reduced taxable income, since this produces a larger annual loss on the property on paper, and thus increased profitability. But it was the expectation of oil prices rising ever higher that drove investor expectations during the 1980s. Even though oil prices peaked at $34 per barrel in 1981 and then gradually declined, investors believed that prices would triple within the decade.[21] Consequently, they piled into commercial real estate, with thrifts acting as a major investor, particularly in the American Southwest and Texas. No wonder Texas, booming from oil, was at the centre of the commercial real-estate boom.

But the tax treatment changed yet again just a few years later. In an effort to raise money after the recession, the US government passed the Tax Reform Act of 1986. This law reversed the previous tax code change by lengthening the depreciation periods for real estate. It also restricted the ability of real-estate investors to shelter income with their 'passive' or depreciation-related losses.[22] This led to a fall in real-estate values.

The timing coincided with a decline in oil prices. In 1985, instead of heading towards $100 per barrel, oil fell below its price in the early 1980s to around $24. Oil prices dropped even more in 1986, to below $10 during the summer. Even though oil prices settled at around $15 per barrel, this was less than half the price at the peak just a few years earlier. Commercial property prices dropped accordingly.[23] Although most of the US experienced modest declines, property prices in the South fared worse: while the value of offices fell by 10 per cent nationally, those in the South collapsed by more than one-third from their peak in 1983. For all commercial properties in the Southwest, including Arkansas, Louisiana, Oklahoma and Texas, prices eventually fell by nearly one-third during the following three years.

Unsurprisingly, since oil-rich Texas was the state with the most exuberant rises in real-estate prices, it was also the hardest hit by the S&L crisis. Half of all of the bankrupt thrifts were in the Lone Star State. As the real-estate bubble burst, land was auctioned at fire-sale prices. When this was coupled with falling oil prices, Texas entered recession.

Although it is true that the 'implosion of a bubble always leads to the discovery of frauds and swindles that developed in the froth of the mania',[24] the S&L failures were, in the main, due not to illegality but to risky behaviour, the institutional fragility of their lending model, inadequate regulation and, of course, euphoric belief in ever-rising real-estate prices. It was a disaster for investors. And it was disastrous for their lenders. Unfortunately, thrifts were both.

From 1985, the tighter regulations limited the rapid growth of S&Ls. With a larger headcount of regulators, the sector appeared to be stabilizing. But, despite this effort, the legacy of years of risk-taking remained. As the real-estate bubble burst in the South, the losses of S&Ls started to mount.

With the deposit insurer in trouble, the regulator raised the deposit insurance premiums paid by S&Ls by 150 per cent. That same year, the regulator attempted to inject more funds into the deposit insurer as the scale of the problem began to become apparent. But Congress did not act, reflecting a lack of urgency about the state of the S&Ls.

In the spring of 1987 the General Accounting Office, the government auditor, declared the Federal Savings and Loan Insurance Corporation was insolvent because of 'contingent liabilities'.[25] The liabilities of the insolvent thrifts were larger than the assets of the S&L deposit insurer. That prompted Congressional action. In the summer, Congress authorized $15 billion in additional borrowing authority for the corporation. But it was barely enough to dispose of the insolvent S&Ls 'along the highway from the airport to downtown Dallas'.[26]

By 1987, Texas was home to fourteen of the twenty thrifts with the biggest losses.[27] There were some profitable thrifts. But the two-thirds of S&Ls that made a profit of $5.6 billion in 1988 were dwarfed by the losses (some $6.8 billion) of the troubled remainder.

As the property market continued its decline in Texas and the Southwest, more government action was needed. It took until the end of the decade, but newly elected President George H. W. Bush revamped and rescued the sector. In 1989, Bush abolished the federal regulator and the insolvent deposit insurer. The newly instituted Resolution Trust Corporation resolved the insolvent S&Ls by selling their assets and using the proceeds to pay depositors. Bush's plan created a new borrowing authority of $50 billion to close down insolvent S&Ls. It also financed the prosecution of crimes by the Justice Department. It was the most dramatic change for the thrift industry since the 1930s.

The S&L crisis was over, but, with more than 1,000 S&L failures, it had cost a whopping $124 billion, of which the bulk was paid by tax-payers both through higher taxes and as levies charged on accounts held in S&Ls. The debacle was made more prominent by the political fallout associated with the Keating Five, which ensnarled a future presidential candidate and a former astronaut. Despite its headline-grabbing nature and motion-picture success, the S&L debacle shares the traits of financial crises throughout history. Notably, the exuberance of expecting property prices as well as oil prices to rise and rise fuelled the risky behaviour of S&Ls in the 1980s. But S&Ls were already in trouble before then. Their strict operating model of taking in deposits to lend out as mortgages and making money on the difference in deposit rates and lending rates came apart at the seams when interest rates shot up in the late 1970s.

By trying to loosen their model and liberalize their activities, regulators ended up introducing a perverse set of incentives. When the failing S&Ls were offered the chance to make commercial property loans with only limited downside for their executives, they seized the lifeline. Failing S&Ls went for broke; many just went broke instead.

The importance of the credibility of the regulatory system is the second trait that the S&L debacle shares with other financial crashes. The bankruptcy of even the deposit insurer underscored how far the supervisory system had lagged behind. As with other financial crises, its resolution required the restoring of credibility – and a lot more bailout funds. The 1989 measures replaced the ineffective supervisory bodies with a new structure that stabilized the S&L industry by resolving the failing ones. But it took another six years before the crisis came to an end, and the Resolution Trust Corporation was finally closed on 31 December 1995, its remit to resolve the insolvent S&Ls satisfied.

The aftermath was painful for taxpayers, but there was no lasting economic damage. Since then, thrifts have even attracted consumers disillusioned with big banks. In the twenty-first century they have again 'achieved great success by marketing themselves as community-oriented home lending specialists'.[28] There are more than 1,000 thrift institutions, making them the second-largest holder of deposits. The re-emergence of the sector and the rehabilitation of figures like Michael Milken contradict F. Scott Fitzgerald's famous observation: 'There are no second acts in American lives.'

# 3 Japan's Real-Estate Crash of the Early 1990s

In the second half of the 1980s, Japan was gripped with one of the biggest financial manias of the twentieth century. It was a crisis that would see the economy fall from that of a rising superpower vying with the United States to a bust that would lead to its 'lost decades' of economic growth.

In the years preceding the crisis, cheap and readily available credit flowed into soaring stock markets and inflated real-estate prices. At the time, these were viewed as the embodiment of Japan's post-war miracle economy. But the reality was a party that had been allowed to get recklessly out of control. The subsequent crash uncovered the cosy relationships between politicians, bureaucrats, businessmen, financiers and even organized crime that had allowed financial mismanagement not only to run rampant but also to be covered up.

After the Second World War, Japan's economy boomed. No other country, advanced or emerging, grew as quickly. In only four decades, Japan completed a transition from a lower-middle-income to a rich, advanced economy that became the second largest in the world, making it a model example of economic development.

Yet Japan's success story in many ways contradicted conventional thinking at the time. The World Bank's 1991 *World Development Report* was subtitled *The Challenge of Development*.[1] The report encapsulated the debate that had raged through the 1980s on the 'state versus market' approach to achieving rapid economic development. At its heart was the importance of productivity growth in sustaining fast output growth over the long term. It advocated a 'market friendly' approach – an open, competitive market with a limited role for government, any intervention by whom should be sparing, transparent and subject to checks and balances. Rather, the government's role would be to provide the social, legal and economic infrastructure that would enable the private sector to thrive.

The high-performing economies of East Asia, not just Japan but also South Korea and Taiwan, were cited by the bank as the best-in-class examples of this approach. Each had experienced a long run of growth after technologically upgrading their output and rapidly improving productivity. But this was only part of the picture in Japan. In reality, competition and openness were suppressed there. The state did not intervene reluctantly, but aggressively through a comprehensive industrial policy led by the Ministry of International Trade and Investment (MITI). Japan's success, in fact, was largely due to a 'market unfriendly' approach, with the state questioning not whether to intervene, but how.[2]

The war had left Japan with a labour-surplus economy. Abundant workers facilitated a productive textiles and basic, light manufactured goods market. In the short term, this was where Japan's comparative advantage lay, but it would not support the improvement of the standard of living to European or American levels or beyond in the longer term. This was explained by Vice-Minister Yoshihisa Ojimi of MITI at a seminar held in Seoul in April 1990:

> The MITI decided to establish in Japan industries which require intensive employment of capital and technology, industries that in consideration of comparative cost of production, should be the most inappropriate for Japan, industries such as steel, oil-refining, petrochemicals, automobiles, aircraft, industrial machinery of all sorts, and electronics, including electronic computers. From a short-run, static viewpoint, encouragement of such industries would seem to conflict with economic rationalism. But, from a long-range viewpoint, these are precisely the industries where income elasticity of demand is high, technological progress is rapid, and labour productivity rises fast.[3]

This quote suggests Japan's strategic identification of the key industries required to move from 'static' or short-run growth to long-term success. However, achieving this aim, particularly at the outset, required suppressing the open and competitive market conditions that the World Bank strongly recommended.

Between 1950 and 1970, the Japanese domestic capital markets were highly regulated and shut off from world capital markets. Only the government and its agencies were able to borrow from or lend abroad. Foreign direct investment was strictly controlled. Foreign firms were prohibited by either legal or administrative means from acquiring a majority ownership in Japanese corporations. MITI encouraged a variety of cartel arrangements in a wide range of industries to discourage excessive competition. These protections played an important role in promoting technical change, productivity growth and exports in these industries.

Japan's financial system had largely been set up to support these goals. The key factor was the direction of cheap finance to support long-term industrial upgrading. Close and long-term relationships between banks and corporations were strongly encouraged, so the banks themselves were vested in the economic goals of the Japanese government, which in turn gave them implicit state guarantees on their lending activities. The conglomerates that developed from these relationships were known as *keiretsu* (business networks), and included Japan's biggest bank, MUFG Bank, previously known as Bank of Tokyo-Mitsubishi, a company that was both a bank and a motor manufacturer.

During the high-growth miracle economy years of the 1960s, 1970s and 1980s, Japan's relationship system of banking was viewed positively when compared with the more hands-off approach of Western financial systems, particularly the Anglo-American banks. But the high-growth years also helped to conceal the deficiencies in the Japanese banking system, especially in terms of regulation, that were to leave Japanese banks fatally exposed to changing economic and international conditions.

Government involvement in the economy has been credited for Japan's rapid arrival as a rich country with high standards of living. At the centre of economic policy was the Ministry of Finance (MoF).

It emerged unscathed from the war when Allied officials accepted that a strong banking system was necessary for economic reconstruction. So, although many top officials were purged, the MoF remained largely intact.

In fact, the MoF held enormous sway over policy and regulatory jurisdiction. To put it into perspective, when compared with the US, the MoF authority was similar to the combined powers of the Federal Reserve Board, Treasury, Federal Deposit Insurance Corporation, Options Clearing Corporation, Bureau of Federal Credit Unions, Office of Thrift Supervision, Securities Exchange Commission, Inland Revenue Service, US Customs, National Association of Insurance Commissioners and the Commodity Futures Trading Commission. Unlike the US system, in which the economic levers of government were spread among ministries, the MoF was an all-powerful super-ministry controlling almost every aspect of the Japanese economy, and often described as a 'bureaucracy within a bureaucracy'.

Since the war, the Liberal Democratic Party (LDP) had governed exclusively in Japan, and would do so until 1993. With effectively one-party rule and a superministry, it was perhaps inevitable that close personal relationships would develop between the two. MoF appointments were seen as the most prestigious for career civil servants, with those in the budget and tax bureaus considered the most eminent as they were focused on by politicians. The top bureaucrats in the ministry tended to pass through those offices. Although Japanese bureaucrats must remain politically neutral, many top-ranking bureaucrats followed up public service careers by moving into the Japanese parliament, the Diet, having become LDP politicians. Marriage ties further cemented organizational relationships, with many daughters of prominent politicians wed to MoF officials. These close connections afforded the MoF political cover.

The reach of the MoF extended far beyond its own bureaucracy. *Shukko* describes the dispatch of civil servants from one agency to a temporary position in another. Large numbers of MoF officials were seconded to other government departments to the extent that MoF members often ended up colonizing new agencies. For example, when the Financial Supervisory Agency was eventually established in 1998 to be an independent regulator of financial services, twenty-four of its thirty-five employees were seconded from the MoF and very few of them actually had any prior regulatory experience.

The MoF also held strong control over the Bank of Japan (BoJ), which up until the late 1990s was considered one of the least independent central banks in advanced countries. Most aspects of its activities were legally controlled by the government via MoF directives. Although monetary policy was set at the central bank, the decision-making revolved around the finance minister, who convened the meetings of the BoJ policy board, where the only BoJ representative was the governor.

When it came to the commercial banks, networks played a large role in financial policymaking and regulation in Japan. Instead of the arm's-length regulatory processes found in the banking systems of advanced Western countries, relationships found in informal networks played a prominent role.

The *mofu-tan* were specific MoF liaisons in banks and securities firms. Their job was essentially to both build a rapport and negotiate with regulators, often seeking tacit and informal clearance of new activities. It was not uncommon for *mofu-tan* to visit the MoF daily, and they were expected to wine and dine the officials they followed, further cementing the relationship between banks and the ministry. *Mofu-tan* were predominantly graduates from Tokyo University in their late thirties who had been earmarked for senior management roles. For MoF officials, being entertained by the *mofu-tan* was seen as a perk of the job, but they would argue they used their contacts as a source of information about current issues in the sector.

The process of *amakudari* (literally, 'descend from heaven') refers to the dispatch of retired individuals from the MoF to the financial sector. *Amakudari* became an important incentive mechanism within the ministry and was largely viewed as an extension of the employment system. With public service salaries lower than those in the private sector, a plum job on retirement from the MoF was essentially considered a form of deferred compensation. *Amakudari* postings were highly prized, not just for their level of compensation and retirement allowance but also their status. For the banks, having a MoF 'old boys' network' was seen as a method of facilitating lines of communication and smoothing policy implementation.

In terms of the effectiveness of overseeing and regulating banks, however, the *mofu-tan* and *amakudari* systems had dysfunctional aspects. When post-retirement options depended on the goodwill of a predecessor, incumbent officials faced strong incentives to remain amiable with MoF alumni who had already descended. This might mean sharing information, overlooking past failures or allowing problems to perpetuate for not wanting to expose predecessors' failings. Such relationships hampered the regulation of banks, something laid bare during the crisis to come.

Until the mid-1990s, Japanese banks were regulated by two mechanisms. The first was price controls. Deposit ceilings were designed to prevent banks from competing with each other to raise deposits, the aim of this measure being to make funds available to be loaned to industry at favourable rates. The second part was the convoy approach to regulation (*goso sendan hoshiki*). As in a truck convoy, no bank was to be left behind and none was permitted to move so fast that it would endanger the viability of others. In essence this provided an assurance that no bank would fail. Entry and exit restrictions allowed the MoF to limit the number of banks and even control the expansion of their branches. In fact, MoF approval was required to open, close or relocate branches and headquarters. The MoF even issued guidance on physical aspects of bank branches, including their size and the facilities they could offer. It had a hand in every aspect of the banking industry.

For a time, the convoy-based regulation functioned well. The MoF would simply arrange for ailing banks to be taken over by stronger banks, which were selected based on existing relationships. For the stronger bank, it provided an opportunity to escape the regulatory limits on size and expand branches and depositors, so MoF-backed rescue mergers generally worked out well for both parties.

The regulatory structure with guaranteed margins and limited competition gave banks incentives to adopt a long-term view of lending and build deeper financial relationships with corporations. The 'main bank system' defined the special relationship with one bank used by a corporation for all its financial services. In return, the main bank would provide long-term fixed-rate lending and commit to extending extraordinary assistance in times of financial difficulties. These relationships were often cemented by the main bank being a shareholder in their own corporate borrower and having a presence on its board of directors.

The stability in long-term financing provided by the main bank system was lauded for high investment rates and lifetime employment in Japanese corporations, especially compared with Anglo-American banks. But under the Japanese main bank system, banks were effectively responsible for supervising their own borrowers, and employed weak processes for bad-debt resolution.

Formal supervision of the banks themselves was also weak, with monitoring of bank solvency largely absent. Banks tended not to be very transparent, and few demands were placed on them to be so, because the implicit government guarantees that banks would not fail lowered depositors' demands for information. All this made it difficult to discern the soundness of financial institutions.

On top of this, MoF bureaucrats typically had little technical knowledge and relied heavily on their informal networks within the financial sector for information about the state of affairs in the industry. Organizational resources allocated within the MoF to financial regulation bureaus were sparse, and elite-track officials were unlikely to go through them. The legacy of convoy regulation and rescues via mergers meant protocols for risk management were comparatively weak compared with those in other developed countries.

Despite these systemic flaws, from the 1950s to the 1970s the Japanese financial system was both stable and highly profitable. But with the real economy growing at about 10 per cent per year, high rates of business investment, low rates of corporate bankruptcy, markets protected from international competition, credit rationing meaning demand for loans always outstripping supply, and low-fixed deposit rates, it would have been difficult for Japanese banks not to make money. With an unblemished track record until the 1990s, there was little pressure from the Diet for the finance ministry to change its approach, but it had already become dangerously out of touch as the trends of globalization and deregulation began to increase the complexity of financial markets dramatically.

During the 1980s, Japan found itself in possession of a first-class manufacturing economy. However, its financial systems were, comparatively, in steerage. The political networks that had successfully helped direct and coordinate the economy between 1950 and 1980 now exposed the economy to financial meltdown.

On 22 September 1985, the finance ministers and central bankers of the G5 group of major economies (the US, Japan, the UK, West Germany and France) met at the Plaza Hotel in New York City. The US president Ronald Reagan was in his second term. With James Baker now Treasury Secretary, the administration moved from the laissez-faire stance that had characterized the first term to a more interventionist strategy. Reagan had always viewed a strong dollar as a vote of confidence in the US economy and preferred free markets, but Baker had a more pragmatic approach.[4]

The aim of the meeting was to strike an international agreement to drive down the value of the US dollar, which had appreciated during the early 1980s and was contributing to a burgeoning US trade deficit, particularly with Japan and Germany. The result was the Plaza Accord, under which the G5 agreed to depreciate the dollar's value via currency market intervention. But it soon became clear that the accord was too effective. The Japanese yen appreciated by nearly 50 per cent against the US dollar by the end of 1986.

On 22 February 1987, the finance ministers of the G7 group of major economies (the G5 plus Canada and Italy) convened at the Louvre in Paris to revise the Plaza Accord. At the signing of what became known as the Louvre Accord by six of the seven (Italy declined), they agreed to help to stabilize the dollar, which would require cutting interest rates in Japan and Germany to reduce their currencies' attractiveness. The Bank of Japan acted far more readily than the independently minded Bundesbank, reducing the rate from 5 per cent to a record low 2.5 per cent. The impact on lowering the cost and increasing the availability of credit in Japan further inflated the bubbles in stock markets and real estate already underway.

In August 1987, there was widespread anticipation of tightening by the Bank of Japan, but this action was deferred by the global panic and stock market crashes of Black Monday, 19 October, in the autumn of that year. By late 1988 and early 1989, MoF officials had become increasingly concerned over developments in the financial sector, but felt constrained by commitments made at the Louvre Accord to prevent the yen from strengthening. Monetary policy began tightening only in March 1989. With hindsight, the delayed action is regarded as one of the main contributing policy errors to Japan's subsequent crash and 'lost decades'. The tardiness in raising interest rates enabled the boom. GDP growth averaged 5.5 per cent between 1987 and 1990, unemployment fell to 2 per cent and the Nikkei stock index doubled from less than 20,000 to just under 39,000 at its peak on 29 December 1989.

Japanese banks invested heavily in the booming economy of the 1980s in an attempt to offset the negative impact of two trends undermining their traditional business revenues. First, the deregulation of interest rates from 1985 resulted in all deposits over ¥500,000 earning a higher rate determined by the market instead of one set by the government. This led to an increase in bank funding costs and squeezed profits. Previously, regulated deposit rates were below market rates, which allowed banks access to cheap funding and provided them with guaranteed profit margins. Banks restored their margins by not passing on rate increases to borrowers, instead investing in the Tokyo stock market. Vast capital gains from the red-hot market filled the growing holes in core operating profits from bank lending activities.

In the financial year ended March 1989, 42 per cent of profits from banks were earned from capital gains on securities. From 1984 to 1990, Japanese banks reported average annual profit increases of 13 per cent a year. However, if profits from sales of long-term securities and short-term stock market deals were excluded, profit growth was only 1 per cent per year – a measly rate of return from core banking activities, given the growth in the economy.

Reported bank profits, however, often equated to little more than paper shuffling. The *keiretsu* system of cross-shareholdings meant that banks typically owned a large number of shares in their clients, and vice versa, which cemented long-term relationships between borrowers and lenders. It also meant that any shares of those clients sold for profit by banks were bought back at higher prices, since the banks were committed to being shareholders in these companies. They also had to pay capital gains taxes on the profits, so, taken together, a bank's cash-in-hand was frequently much lower than might be expected from its reported profits.

The Bank for International Settlements (BIS) is known as the central banks' central bank due to its supranational standing in global banking markets. Japan's banks were aided and abetted by BIS rules that allowed them to count 45 per cent of unrealized share gains as capital, a highly controversial principle that was firmly opposed by the Bank of England. It meant that a rise in the stock market increased bank capital ratios, which then allowed banks to increase lending. The greater amount of lending in turn flowed into equities and property, which pushed up prices. When asset prices rise, the banks' holding of collateral based on those assets also rises, which leads to further cycles of higher bank capital and lending. All of this meant the capital position of Japanese banks became very dependent on the performance of the Tokyo stock market, in which they were also dominant players.

Another factor impacting the viability of the banks was a decline in loans made to their traditional clients. Blue-chip companies were raising increasing amounts through securities rather than bank loans, often in international markets after deregulation. In response, banks lent more to consumers and mortgage holders as corporate markets declined. Much of bank lending in real estate was indirectly via financial companies such as the *jusen* (housing loan companies), but the involvement of banks in real-estate lending was substantial by the end of the 1980s.

A historically feudal society, Japan equated the possession of land with status. Since the Second World War, land prices had grown faster on average than government bond rates, and a myth that land prices could only go upward had achieved widespread acceptance. This fuelled exuberance, and was especially the case in Tokyo, where tight zoning and building regulations created a 'permanent' land shortage. It helped to give banks the perception that any loan secured by real estate was unlikely to end up as a bad debt, and credit was readily available if real estate was posted as collateral. Land values were also underpinned by the tax system, which encouraged the acquisition of debt-financed real estate.

As the stock market hit its peak at the end of 1989, Japan's property markets were wildly exuberant. Sober estimates by the government's Management Coordination Survey valued Japanese real estate to be worth over ¥2,000 trillion, or five times Japanese GDP. That was four times the estimated value of all US property at the time, despite the US being twenty-five times Japan's physical area. In principle, at these valuations the Japanese could buy all of America by selling off Metropolitan Tokyo, or all of Canada simply by building on the grounds of the Imperial Palace. Tongue-in-cheek, Japan's land boom could be described as one of history's greatest accumulations of wealth in one country.

Between 1985 and 1991, taking together the real-estate markets of the six major cities of Tokyo, Yokohama, Nagoya, Kyoto, Osaka and Kobe, commercial prices were up 300 per cent, residential prices by 180 per cent and industrial prices by 160 per cent. Between 1989 and 1991, more than 160 golf courses were built in Japan, with a further 1,200 under construction or with planning permission. By then, there were 1,700 golf courses in the country, and 1.8 million people had membership of a golf club. The Nikkei even had a Golf Club membership index.

It wasn't just at home that Japanese bank lending fuelled the demand for real estate. After the MoF liberalized restrictions on foreign investment in 1983, Japan was becoming a powerhouse in the supply of credit worldwide. Following the Plaza Accord of 1985, the yen–dollar exchange rate went from 250 to 120, meaning that the dollar value of Japanese banks' assets doubled and overseas lending expanded. In the early 1980s, Japanese banks accounted for 4 per cent of international lending markets. By 1989 it was 40 per cent, with the US the favoured destination.

Unsurprisingly, American golf courses became a prime target. In September 1990, California's Pebble Beach resort was purchased by a Japanese real-estate developer for $831 million. Hawaii was a popular location. Japanese developers constructed resorts financed by Japanese banks, with little consideration of returns. The Grand Hyatt Wailea Resort and Spa in Maui, which opened in September 1991, claimed to be the most luxurious hotel ever built. Japanese banks had lent big in US property, especially in California, where the Japanese had financed virtually every new major building in Los Angeles. The Japanese foreign lending frenzy occurred at the same time as American property prices were booming, meaning most of the real-estate investments were acquired near the top of the market.

By late 1988, the same MoF officials who had held back the BoJ from increasing interest rates following the Louvre Accord had become increasingly concerned over developments in the financial sector. Excessive bank lending to real-estate and construction companies and the growing bubbles in stocks and property markets were now too rampant to ignore. In the spring of 1989, the MoF and BoJ finally acted, and interest rates began a steep climb, first from 2.5 per cent to 3.25 per cent and then five months later to 4.25 per cent as the Nikkei peaked at the end of the year.

Although there were further rate hikes to 6 per cent in 1990, the big move to quell the property market was made in April of that year. The BoJ and MoF committed to an orderly decline in land prices. There had been a political concern that rising land values had created 'easy wealth' that could undermine Japan's much-vaunted work culture; thus, Yasushi Mieno, governor of the Bank of Japan, was reportedly happy to see a 20 per cent fall in prices.[5] The MoF banking bureau gave out administrative guidance, which imposed restrictions that real-estate lending couldn't rise faster than total lending until the end of 1991.

Then, the unthinkable happened, the real-estate market collapsed. The Nikkei was in free fall. The stock market, which had increased four-fold in the previous six years to almost 40,000 at the start of 1990, had nearly halved in value by year end. It was a classic example of a mind-boggling boom followed by a spectacular bust.

Banks that had lent heavily against these assets saw rapid increases in bad loans as the value of collateral plummeted. The bursting of the twin stock-market and real-estate bubbles created balance-sheet problems for banks and corporations. The flow of credit that had fuelled the boom suddenly hit a full stop and went into reverse as the financial sector struggled under the weight of bad debts.

It was already pretty well understood that without the use of unrealized capital gains from latent shareholdings, many Japanese banks would be unable to achieve the 8 per cent capital adequacy level that was a requirement of the BIS. The 'Japan rate', a premium to lend to Japanese banks, became a well-known phenomenon in global markets. Now, with collapsing stock prices, capital ratios of Japanese banks were ravaged, leading to slower lending growth to the economy. By the end of 1990, land prices were falling in most parts of Japan. California's property market slumped, in part because Japanese investors were pulling back sharply on foreign assets to raise cash and strengthen balance sheets.

In late December 1990, the Bank of Japan, in an attempt to curtail the sharp fall in the stock market and offset the recessionary forces building in the economy, began reversing its rate increases. By April 1992, rates were back down to 3.5 per cent, but it was insufficient to prevent the Nikkei sliding further, and by late summer it was below 15,000.

The end of the property bubble was a disaster for Japanese banks. Collapsing land prices resulted in a deteriorating downward spiral of disappearing collateral, bank failures and fire sales of assets at home and overseas. Japan's property market turned from one where nobody wanted to sell to one where nobody wanted to buy. Bad debts in the financial system increased at an alarming rate as a result. In 1991, Salomon Brothers research into bad debts suggested they could reach ¥20 trillion as virtually every loan in the Japanese banking system had been collateralized by land. This would be as disastrous as the US savings and loan crisis discussed in the previous chapter. In fact, these predictions turned out to be conservative estimates of the sum of bad debts that actually accrued.

With the flow of credit interrupted, the Japanese economy become stagnant. From the final quarter of 1991 to the end of 1999, GDP growth averaged less than 1 per cent per annum and the country dropped from being the best-performing in the G7 to the worst, growing at a speed of less than half the G7 average. It would slow so much that the 'miracle economy' would lose its place as the world's second largest to a surging China.

As the stock market imploded and land values collapsed, waves of scandals and frauds in the financial sector came to light. One that caused huge public outcry was the use of *eigyo tokkin* accounts, whereby fund managers offered certain favoured investors guaranteed returns and even compensation for their losses. During the 1980s, these had become an endemic feature of fund management in Japan and viewed as a necessary tool for winning business. The process of loss compensation essentially worked through sales and purchases of bonds around the world, where the fund manager bought back the same bonds at a higher price than they had sold them to their clients at an earlier date, in a process that was easily hidden from the tax authorities.

In a fast-rising market, loss compensation was largely academic, but losses were now no longer theoretical. As markets crashed, the public were outraged at the sight of big fish being bailed out while small fry suffered losses. Although it was widely accepted in the financial district that favoured investors were protected in this way, it was a huge shock to the general population. The scandal ran on and on as more and more compensation payments came to light. The manipulation was judged to have helped push the stock market up to higher and higher levels as the risk of loss was essentially underwritten. James Walsh, president of America's Prudential Securities in Japan, likened the practice of reimbursing certain investors for their losses in securities as equivalent to an athlete on steroids.[6]

The MoF came out of the scandal badly. It had issued directives to ban loss compensation before the Nikkei reached its all-time high on the last trading day of 1989, but is alleged to have allowed securities firms to honour the existing guarantees they had made, and then turned a blind eye to the ongoing loss compensation made as the stock market collapsed. The tax authorities, however, were not so pragmatic and blew the whistle on the affair. Loss compensation was made a criminal offence, but the MoF was generally viewed as too slow to act.

A further wave of scandals uncovered the infiltration of organized crime into Japanese finance. The high returns from stock and real-estate markets were so great that they attracted gangsters away from the usual rackets of extortion, prostitution and drugs. Some became *sōkaiya* – professional extortionists. A common ruse was either to threaten to disrupt a company's annual general meeting unless they were paid off, or to demand 'protection money' to ensure that no awkward questions were asked. Because saving face is so important in Japan, executives were vulnerable to this type of extortion.

It was through such a relationship that Susumu Ishii, the head of Inagawa-kai, the Tokyo-based second-largest crime syndicate in Japan, persuaded the securities firms Nomura and Nikko to help finance Tokyu Corporation, a major railway company. In a six-month period in 1989, Ishii bought 2 per cent of the company with ¥36 billion borrowed from affiliates of Nomura and Nikko. After Ishii began buying, Tokyu's stock increased 164 per cent in the subsequent two months. The shares were heavily promoted through Nomura's branch network. In October 1989, Tokyu shares even came to represent 90 per cent of all share dealings in several Nomura branches. The MoF publicly announced their suspicions, but Ishii died of a stroke before any charges could be made.[7]

Another link between organized crime and finance was through the Yakuza. These gangsters had an informal and somewhat accepted role in Japanese society in reducing street crime to the 'organized' type and in resolving disputes without reverting to lawyers. Banks had often sold bad debts at a discount to Yakuza, and a gangster even joined the board of directors of a bank in Osaka.

The chairman of Sumitomo, one of Japan's most prominent banks, effectively allowed a gangster on the board of Itoman, a trading company that Sumitomo had absorbed in the early 1970s. Suemitsu Ito had been offered as a fixer to the board of directors after complications with a land deal, but he was really a front man for the Korean businessman Ho Yong Chung, who had underworld connections. Ito's appointment to the board precipitated a number of dubious investments. Sub-plots of land in Hawaii were bought from Ho's brother-in-law for much more than they were worth. The company extended loans to two paper companies owned by Ho's brother. The companies then passed on loans to two property developers. The bank started 'investing' in art, buying many paintings at inflated prices from companies owned by Ho. To finance these splurges, Itoman borrowed extensively from smaller banks, which were happy to lend, assuming Sumitomo was standing behind the firm. The loans were subsequently used to fund speculation in property, art and golf courses. In September 1990, after a five-month investigation, Sumitomo was obliged to rescue Itoman with estimated total debts of ¥1.4 trillion. Ito and other Ho associates were subsequently arrested in August 1991 and charged with using money borrowed from Itoman for personal use.[8]

Japan's banks were being looted not only by the violent underworld. On 25 July 1991, Taizo Hashida, the chairman and president of the world's third-largest bank, Fuji Bank, was forced to resign when it was discovered that three of the bank's Tokyo branches had been implicated in issuing forged certificates of deposits worth ¥260 billion, which were then used as collateral to raise loans from fourteen non-banks and invested in property companies, some with Yakuza connections. Within days of the Fuji scandal, Tokai Bank and Kyowa Saitama Bank admitted similar transgressions with forged certificates of deposit, again used to borrow from non-banks, for speculation in property and golf courses.[9]

For a few weeks, the Fuji scandal was Japan's largest ever bank fraud, but then came the involvement of Industrial Bank of Japan (IBJ) with Nui Onoue, the sixty-one-year-old owner of two Osaka restaurants. IBJ provided her with ¥240 billion in loans. Onoue became the largest individual speculator in the Tokyo stock market in the 1980s with 3.1 million shares in IBJ, making her the bank's largest individual shareholder. Her stock portfolio consisted of millions of shares in Japan's blue-chip companies, her strategy being simply to buy and hold large volumes of blue chips, especially bank shares. She was famous in brokering circles and generated large commissions. In August 1991, she was arrested for obtaining loans with false documents, including fake certificates of deposit. She had single-handedly engineered Japan's largest banking fraud.[10]

The series of scandals rocking the Japanese banking sector were heavily reported in the media. Each one undermined confidence in the banks and their management, but the MoF, already facing criticism as asset prices collapsed, was particularly keen to play down failures, believing public attention would turn to its incompetence in supervising banks. Blame was also attached to the Liberal Democratic Party (LDP). And in 1993, after almost forty years of single-party rule, it was toppled by an anti-LDP coalition.

The scandals made it politically very difficult for the government to use taxpayers' money to bail out and clean up the financial sector. Although individual institutions are typically a private concern, the financial system as a whole is very much a public one and vital to the functioning of the economy. Ultimately, it was the government's failure to be more aggressive in addressing the numerous scandals and tackling the huge extent of non-performing loans in Japanese banks that made the aftermath of the crisis so damaging.

A study by the International Monetary Fund found that the ten months following a crash are crucial in determining the long-term repercussions for the affected economy.[11] The report concluded that when governments acted slowly (over a period of four years or longer), their countries suffered more. Japan's response took eight years.

The government and the MoF's failure to act quickly could have been the result of the informal and relationship-based regulation that masked the true severity of the situation. In some cases, the books were window dressed by moving non-performing loans to paper companies and affiliates. Even when bad debts were written off by banks, they were not forced to appraise collateral at market prices but permitted to assume that it was recovered at purchase price. Perhaps the MoF was complicit in these actions not only to avoid acknowledging the size of non-performing loans hanging over the banks, but also in a desperate attempt to buy time in the vain hope that a rebounding economy would solve all the problems.

Even during the good times in the 1980s, low profitability from core operations had been an endemic feature of Japanese banks. The phasing out of fixed deposit rates in the late 1980s and early 1990s had ended a source of profits derived from regulation, while competition from taxpayer-funded, government-sponsored financial institutions offering subsidized loan rates made it hard to increase commercial loan rates. The banks themselves were reluctant to restore margins by increasing borrowing rates for their long-term corporate borrowers. As Hiroshi Kurosawa, the former president of the Industrial Bank of Japan, said in *Euromoney* in February 1998:

> Profit is very important. Our profit is too small. But profit is not the 100 per cent purpose of IBJ – it is not a purely commercial bank. Our philosophy is to serve our clients and Japanese industry. There must be profit, but profit must be reasonable. If we make too much profit, we are eating our clients' profits. We do not like to maximize our profits.[12]

With meagre profits no longer being propped up by cashing in past legacies, and with the faltering economy reducing opportunities for new business, as well as higher funding costs as a result of the 'Japan premium', there was little chance for Japan's financial institutions to resolve their own problems despite the remarkable forbearance shown to them by the MoF. With the compression of interest margins and large increases in credit costs from non-performing loans, it had become impossible for Japanese banks to cover losses and gradually write off bad loans out of current earnings alone.

By November 1997, the banks could mask the scale of the problem no longer. Sanyo Securities became the first brokerage firm to fail since the Second World War. On the 17th, Hokkaido Takushoku Bank, the tenth-largest commercial bank, also failed under the weight of its non-performing loans. On the 24th, Yamaichi Securities, the fourth-largest brokerage, effectively collapsed. And on the 26th of that month, the Tokuyo City Bank closed its doors.

These failures deeply shook the public perception that the MoF was in control. The bad loans discovered at failed financial institutions were subsequently found to be much larger than expected. Hokkaido Takushoku Bank had declared bankruptcy even though it paid dividends and posted profits for the financial year to March 1997. At the time of its bankruptcy, it reported capital of ¥300 billion, but inspections subsequently found negative equity of ¥1.2 *trillion*, which amounts to a total of ¥1.5 trillion of window dressing in its accounts. Likewise, Yamaichi Securities was found to have hidden ¥260 billion of losses on securities investments, more than 50 per cent of its equity capital.

The spurt of failures increased suspicions at home and abroad regarding financial statements and the supervision of Japanese financial institutions. All banks saw share prices fall and their cost of capital increase. Now there was a serious risk of 'credit-crunch' conditions spilling over into the economy and curtailing corporate investment, consumption and housing investments and setting off a vicious cycle of recession and further credit constraints.

On 29 November 1997, the go-ahead for the use of taxpayers' money to stabilize the banks was finally given, despite Prime Minister Ryutaro Hashimoto insisting it was 'not a policy shift'.[13] The Financial Reconstruction Law, enacted in February 1998, allocated ¥30 trillion to protect depositors at failed institutions and inject new capital into banks. Despite initial optimism, the injection failed to alleviate the crisis. The government claimed the funds were 'investments' rather than 'bailouts' and banks were not forced to take the funds, but the common view was that the recapitalization package was nothing more than another ad hoc stop-gap measure, described by the *Economist* magazine as the 'most expensive bandage in history'.[14]

The failure to restore confidence and trust in the banking system was now having a serious impact on business. By the summer of 1998, corporate restructuring and bankruptcy were rising, leading unemployment to hit its highest rate on record of 4.3 per cent. In September 1998, US Treasury Secretary Robert Rubin and US Deputy Treasury Secretary Larry Summers were applying pressure on the Japanese government to recapitalize viable banks in the wake of the wider Asian financial crisis and global stock market volatility following the near collapse of US hedge fund LTCM, discussed in Chapter 1.

At the October 1998 G7 finance ministers' meeting, Japan was being urged to take measures and use public funds to recapitalize weak banks. In late October, the Japanese government reacted by doubling the public money committed to the clean-up of the financial system from ¥30 trillion to ¥60 trillion, which was a sizeable 12 per cent of GDP. The Bank Recapitalization Act increased the funding available to ¥25 trillion. This time, the take-up was more active, characterized by Industrial Bank of Japan's President Masao Nishimura's famous comments about banks having social responsibilities:

> This is not about the interests of one bank, but the interests of the entire Japanese economy. If we do not do this, we will be forced to accept recapitalization, so we must do it. The government has prepared 25 trillion yen and we have a social responsibility to receive that.[15]

The Financial Revitalization Act accounted for the remaining ¥35 trillion. This was aimed at the orderly resolution of failing banks

by providing deposit insurance and meeting the costs of nationaliz-
ing them, merging them or shutting them down. It was under this
Act that Long Term Credit Bank and Nippon Credit Bank were
nationalized in October and December 1998, respectively. Both laws
helped stabilize the financial system and lay the ground for a muted
recovery of the Japanese economy. Facilitation of merger, and con-
solidation in the banking system, meant that the 'Japan premium' was
reduced, which all helped to abate the acute financial crisis that had
enveloped the economy the previous year.

But the ongoing problems were still severe. Between March 1992
and September 2001, Japanese banks wrote off an estimated ¥75 trillion from bad loans, which was around 15 per cent of the level of
Japan's GDP. Despite this, banks still had ¥36 trillion of disclosed bad
loans at the end of September 2001 and, according to the newly formed
Financial Services Agency, undisclosed bad loans of ¥68 trillion. The
persistent low profitability of the banking sector meant that loan
losses exceeded the gross profits of the banking sector in every year
from 1994 to 1999. In 2001, President Yoshifumi Nishikawa of Sumitomo Mitsui Bank summed up the situation when he said: 'We have
lost almost everything we have accumulated since the war. We are
down to the bare bones.'[16]

In the late 1980s, rising stock markets and low interest rates effectively allowed cheap money to wash across the economy. Between late
1986 and early 1991, investment and capital expenditure accounted
for an astounding two-thirds of Japan's economic growth. To give a
sense of the scale, each year, the expansion in the Japanese economy
equalled the entire size of South Korea's GDP. In five years, Japan
added the economy of France. And by the end of this run, Japan's
economy was nearly twice the size of Germany's, Europe's largest.

The bursting of the stock and land-price bubbles ushered in the
first of the 'lost decades' in the 1990s. Millions of homeowners found
themselves in negative equity. Having been pushed out into the sub-
urbs by sky-high prices in Tokyo, many found themselves stuck with
a two-hour commute from a property that they could not sell. With

the dramatic slowdown in economic growth from around 4 per cent to 1 per cent, they also had to adjust to their incomes doubling not every eighteen years but every seventy. Such is the dramatic impact of slowing national economic growth on average incomes experienced by Japanese people for not one but three 'lost decades' and counting.

Japanese banks were vulnerable to asset-price volatility and their ability to absorb non-performing loans was low. Capital injections to restore capital adequacy, which might have led to a speedier resolution and restored market confidence, were held back because using public funds was politically unpopular, and the LDP was electorally weak. This gave way to regulatory forbearance, a postponed realization of the true extent of the bad loans in the hope that the problem would go away as markets and the economy rebounded. Instead, non-performing loans increased, which crippled the balance sheets of Japanese banks and dragged down the economy.

The aftermath of the financial crisis has been unusually painful as Japan continues to struggle to grow and defeat deflation, a phenomenon that can become entrenched since consumers expect prices to fall and thus postpone their purchases. This has depressed demand in the economy and has been a drag on recovery. Shinzo Abe, proposed a series of reforms during his second term as prime minister, from 2012 to 2020, dubbed 'Abenomics', to try to revive the economy. Although there has been progress, Japan's economy serves as a warning about the lasting impact of a systemic financial crisis.

The crisis was triggered by the bursting of a stock-market and real-estate bubble driven by exuberance, a trait shared by other financial crises throughout history. Japanese policymakers repeated many of the mistakes from the Great Depression. By reacting too slowly and timidly, they allowed deflation or price falls to become entrenched, and a crash to become a depression. Notably, Japan's prolonged recovery has been characterized by slow economic growth and persistent deflation for three decades.

But it is the aftermath of the Japanese crash that exemplifies the importance of credibility. The Japanese government has been described as responding with 'extraordinary delay' to the bad-debt problems in the financial system, especially in 'the use of public funds to recapitalize banks, augment the depositor safety net, and establish a temporary agency to take control of failed banks and dispose of their assets'.[17] The MoF's slowness to act allowed the crisis to worsen and damaged its credibility. The Japanese public lost confidence in the MoF and did not countenance the use of taxpayers' money to bail out the banks, yet the government had no other choice as it faced a systemic banking crisis that had the potential to shut down the entire economy, since the country was too big to be rescued by the International Monetary Fund. The government's loss of credibility hampered its efforts to resolve the financial crisis, which contributed to its dire aftermath.

Japan's crisis shared the traits of exuberance and credibility that are the hallmarks of financial crashes throughout history. But it is alone among the crises in this book in its longevity, for the aftermath of the 1990–92 crash is still playing out three decades later.

# 4    The Dot Com Crash, 2000–2001

The dot com crash exemplifies euphoria in its most extreme form. During the 1990s, e-commerce emerged as an exciting new industry. With internet access becoming widely available, there was an opportunity to sell online. For those who remember having no choice but to go to physical stores to buy anything, it was revolutionary to be able to do so through websites. Dot com companies sprouted up to sell directly to consumers. Amazon famously sold books while others sold pet supplies, clothing and much more. There was even a dot com – CyberRebate – that sold electronics, jewellery and other items at highly inflated prices but offered a rebate of 50 to 100 per cent. It made money because only about half of its customers took the time to mail in and claim the rebate.[1] It seemed that a new internet economy was emerging and investors were keen to not miss the boat.

The dot com crash exemplifies the traits of financial crises throughout history. Investors poured their money into internet stocks and banked on e-commerce taking off. Until the bubble burst in the spring of 2000, dot com companies like Pets.com and eToys.com raised millions of dollars despite never having turned a profit. Now that may sound familiar, as tech start-ups today often seem pretty far removed from any black ink on their profit and loss statements, but, at the start of the millennium, investors were euphoric about the internet even though it was far from clear how dot coms could make money from 'eyeballs', since the monetization of website visits was in its nascent stages, and most households were still using glacially slow dial-up connections. But that did not stop the tech-heavy NASDAQ stock index from soaring by a staggering 440 per cent between 1995, when the web-browser company Netscape had its initial public offering (IPO) of shares on the New York Stock Exchange, or the bubble bursting in 2000, when the market fell by an astounding 78 per cent between March and October. This was when the term 'irrational exuberance' was coined.[2] It warrants a chapter in this book because it is a crash that led to a recession.

A company that is often regarded as epitomizing the dot com era is Pets.com.[3] It had the most valuable domain name in the pet supplies industry and was 50 per cent owned by Amazon. Pets.com ran a famous, and expensive, marketing campaign featuring a sock puppet that even made an appearance in the Macy's Thanksgiving Day Parade in 1999, the first dot com company to appear in the annual televised extravaganza, and launched its IPO just a few months later. By the following November, Pets.com had lost $147 million and shut its doors. Its opening IPO price of $11 a share jumped by around 30 per cent after its public listing to $14. But it quickly collapsed to $1 and remained there until the company's demise. It was sold to PetSmart.com in December 2000, though the sale did not include the sock puppet, which retained its fame and found a new home after auto loan company Bar None bought it in 2002. The sock puppet was soon back on TV, this time hawking loans instead of pet supplies.

Pets.com was started by entrepreneurs Greg McLemore and Eva Woodsmall, who spotted an opportunity and registered the noun-based web address in 1994, a common move at the time. (Others such as Garden.com, eToys.com and Webvan.com also found fortune for a short while.) They launched an online community for pet owners that attracted the attention of investors who added e-commerce to the website. In 1998, a seasoned CEO, Julie Wainwright, joined the company. Wainwright had successfully led Reel.com, which was sold to Hollywood Video for $100 million. She has since founded TheRealReal.com in 2011, which sells second-hand luxury items and has been valued at $300 million, which is still going strong in the 2020s.

Once in charge of Pets.com, Wainwright sold a 50 per cent stake to Amazon,[4] whose founder, Jeff Bezos, was looking for ways to diversify from books, videos and CDs, and sell consumers 'anything they might want to find online'.[5] He viewed pet supplies as part of that diversification. He wasn't the only one to see an opportunity.

Pets.com raised nearly $110 million from venture capitalists by the end of 1999, a year after the business was reconstituted and launched as an online shop. Pets are indeed a big market. Worldwide, the market for pet supplies was estimated at over $50 billion at the time, with the US accounting for just under half of that sizeable figure.[6] Almost two-thirds of US households have at least one pet, and time-strapped pet owners were Pets.com's target. Its marketing campaign included the slogan, 'because pets can't drive'.[7]

It was a highly competitive market. Pets.com tried to stand out with its expensive advertising as well as by offering more products than any online competitor. It even, uniquely, targeted the ferret. Most other pet stores focused on dogs and cats, but Pets.com needed to differentiate itself so it focused on serving America's then third most popular pet. It also started a newsletter that increased its potential customer base to over a quarter of a million people in which it offered advice from pet experts, breeders, vets and even legal experts specializing in animal matters.

It prompted a reaction from bricks-and-mortar pet stores. An established national retailer, PetSmart, launched a website to compete against emerging online challengers like Pets.com. With physical stores jumping into e-commerce, the already competitive market got even more competitive. It is ironic that PetSmart acquired what remained of Pets.com after its collapse.

Pets.com was far from alone in its experience. A seasoned market analyst observed of the dot coms that it was: '[a]lmost unprecedented to see an entire sector go from an idea to heavily funded to defunct in just a year and a half'.[8]

Pets.com was perhaps the best-known dot com failure at the time, but there were many others, such as Webvan.com, an online grocery delivery service.[9] At its peak, it was a unicorn (a private company worth more than $1 billion) at a time when that was a rarity. That status was confirmed at its November 1999 IPO, which raised $375 million, valuing the company at $1.2 billion. Webvan.com announced that summer that it would invest $1 billion in warehouses and expand to over thirty cities within a year. Its shares were buoyant at $30, but fell to just 6 cents in July 2001, when it shut down and laid off 2,000 employees.

Another online retailer, Garden.com, also saw its shares fall to a measly 9 cents a year after its IPO in September 1999, when its shares had jumped to over $20. It likewise closed its virtual doors. TheGlobe.com, one of the first social media websites that allowed users to create their own web pages, had a spectacular IPO in November 1998. Its offer price was $9, which jumped by a record 600 per cent on the first day of trading. The picture looked very different less than two years later when the company was delisted by the NASDAQ stock exchange for falling below $1 per share.

Other high-profile failures included online clothing retailer Boo.com, which failed before it went public. In June 2000, its assets were sold at a fraction of their value. Its back-end technology, distribution and fulfilment systems and physical assets, an infrastructure that had cost the company a staggering $200 million to develop, were sold for just $400,000.

Then, there was eToys.com. Founded in 1997, it quickly became a much-visited website for holiday shopping. It saw its share price soar to a high of $86 in February 2000 after a heady IPO in May 1999. It then fell to 9 cents a share and the company shut down in March 2001. At its peak, it was valued at $7.7 billion, which was 35 per cent more than the dominant 'traditional' toy store, Toys 'R' Us. This was extraordinary, since eToys.com's annual revenues in 1999 were $30 million when Toys 'R' Us made that much in a single day. After it failed, eToys.com sold most of its inventory for $5.4 million to KB Toys; the retail value of that inventory was eight times that amount. KB Toys also spent another $3.35 million on the website, name and logo of eToys.com.

eToys.com visibly embodied the ethos of the time: Get big fast. Build it, and they will come, costs will drop and profits will follow.[10] Its CEO, Toby Lenk, proclaimed: 'We're losing money fast on purpose, to build our brand.'[11] Lenk believed that gaining customers was key and revelled in claiming a 40 per cent monthly growth in revenue. Such sentiments are still frequently heard in the start-up world as companies try to take the market.[12] They reflect the competitive pressures on start-ups due to the low entry cost for web-based companies as compared with physical stores. Even Toys 'R' Us's early venture into online shopping failed so spectacularly that it was fined by the US Federal Trade Commission for failing to meet shipping guarantees,[13] although its link-up in 2000 with Amazon, whereby its website would be run by the e-commerce giant, meant that eToys.com struggled to compete against its newly partnered competitor.

The biggest winner of the dot com era was Amazon, now the most successful e-retailer in the world. The company weathered the 2000–2001 dot com crash, despite not posting its first profit until 2002. Jeff Bezos focused on cornering the online retail market even if it meant losses in the short term. This strategy worked for him because he kept a close eye on costs – unlike the numerous other dot coms that had failed spectacularly.[14] As the eminent economist John Kay pointed out: 'Unhappy businesses resemble one another; each successful company is successful in its own way.'[15]

So, how did the dot com bubble inflate so spectacularly?

Stock market bubbles are probably the archetypal examples of the trait of euphoria. And this one was so exuberant that it birthed a new phrase, 'irrational exuberance', to describe a rise in asset prices caused by a bubble rather than because their fundamental value has risen. The stock market is, after all, supposed to value companies based on what their future earnings are worth today. In other words, share prices are supposed to rise when assets are increasing in value. A bubble is formed when prices become based on something other than expected returns. Many have tried to explain this phenomenon throughout history. John Maynard Keynes described it as 'animal spirits' while, about a century earlier, Charles Mackay had called it the 'madness of crowds'.[16] Today we might call it a 'bandwagon effect'. What these phrases all describe is a reckless behavioural process whereby exuberance leads investors to observe what others are doing and simply join in.

Of course, it makes sense that a bull market (one that is rising) will attract investors, especially those with less experience, while a bear market (one that is falling) will discourage new entrants and cause existing investors to desert. But if, for whatever reason, investors share a collective belief that they are buying into an area from which could emerge the next Apple, their euphoria will pump money into that favoured sector, inflating the prices of every company in it. And that's what happened with the dot coms. Their prices became detached from the fundamentals of their businesses.

The euphoric mood accelerated through the 1990s, resulting in a highly inflated stock market. US equity prices had increased nearly five-fold between 1990 and the market peak in March 2000. In the second half of the 1990s, share prices rose by over 21 per cent on average each year, doubling the annual rate of growth of the first five years.[17] Market capitalization (the total of company valuations) tripled between 1995 and 2000, after doubling in the first half of the decade. This explosion wasn't limited to the United States. Major equity markets around the world also saw increases of about 8 per cent each year during the late 1990s.[18]

Given the potentially devastating impact on the economy of its collapse, concern about the stock market had been growing at the US central bank. The Fed had raised interest rates in 1994, and in 1996 its chairman, Alan Greenspan, delivered his famous 'irrational exuberance' speech, asking on 5 December, 'How do we know when irrational exuberance has unduly escalated asset values?'[19] Greenspan had heard arguments put forward both by economists from banks and from academics such as Yale's Bob Shiller about whether the exuberance was irrational.[20] His speech hit a nerve, and global equity markets fell by up to 4 per cent the next day. The Dow Jones stock index promptly fell by nearly 5 per cent, a level that's halfway to a correction. It led Greenspan to remark: 'We had a desirable effect.'[21] But it didn't last.

The acceleration in share prices not only caught the attention of the Fed but also is why the dot com bubble is popularly dated from 1995. Many view the IPO of Netscape Communications on 9 August 1995 as the start of the dot com boom. The fact that it had never made a profit from its Navigator browser did not prevent its shares from more than doubling at IPO. Netscape was worth $2.7 billion by the end of the day.

Not everyone is in agreement regarding the 1995 date. Economists Brad DeLong and Konstantin Magin argue that there was no significant bubble until around 1998.[22] They believe that the NASDAQ became bubbly around 1999, when it more than doubled in value without any 'plausible candidate for fundamental news to support such a large revaluation of equity values'.[23] They also point out that the collapse of the market was similarly devoid of fundamental news. It is indeed difficult to analyse a bubble: when it started, why it started, why it burst. There are no hard and fast definitions of a bubble, for one thing, and there are often a number of reasons for the bust, which does make analysis challenging for policymakers. Even Greenspan eventually abandoned his 'irrational exuberance' argument when he concluded that the market reflected the 'judgments of millions of investors, many of whom are highly knowledgeable about the prospects for the specific companies that make up our broad stock price indices'.[24]

Aside from Netscape, there were other dot coms that caught investors' attention as the bubble grew. During the holiday season of 1998, dot com companies such as Amazon were making millions in revenues. This reflected the rapid expansion of the internet economy, which grew 174.5 per cent between 1995 and 1998, and a pacey 68 per cent from 1998 to 1999.[25] These growth rates strengthened the exuberance that many were feeling about the untapped potential of online shopping. An estimated 50,000 entrepreneurs founded dot coms between 1998 and 2002.[26] The emergence of 'dot com millionaires' may have prompted more investors to want to be part of this new economy. It certainly felt that way at the dot com IPOs. During the period 1975–2001, the ten biggest first-day jumps in stock prices were all technology stocks whose IPOs were in 1998 and 1999.[27]

But soon thereafter, in April 2000, the tech-heavy NASDAQ dropped by more than 10 per cent, a dip widely regarded as a correction. After years of an extraordinary boom, the market was deflating and was set for one of the worst crashes in history.

There were numerous triggers for the bust. Part of the change in mood was due to rising inflation, which can be expected to squeeze consumer incomes and lead to reduced sales. Importantly, in November 1999, a US court investigating Microsoft deemed the company to be an unlawful monopolist.[28] The judge initially ordered it to be disbanded, dampening sentiment around investment in tech companies and leading investors to begin to question the business models and management of dot coms, which further threw cold water on the market even though the ruling was appealed.

Many people imagine that dot com companies are run by 'twenty-somethings',[29] as Bill Gates and Mark Zuckerberg were when they founded Microsoft and Facebook. In reality, management is more commonly by experienced executives. The average age of a successful start-up founder is closer to forty-five than twenty.[30] The difference in the dot com era was that management teams often lacked experience in the specific industry relating to their company. For Pets.com, although some managers had come from Petco, a bricks-and-mortar pet store, others had come from other dot coms. Without previous experience in the industry, a traditional business is more likely to fail.[31] In the case of dot coms, even though many had experienced managers, the lack of specific industry knowledge may have contributed to their failures. For instance, the management team of Garden.com extensively researched the industry, but they had no direct experience and also were not horticultural enthusiasts.[32]

Additionally, there was some questionable spending in a number of dot coms. Many had raised substantial funding both before and after their IPOs. With a 'wall of money' giving them a sense of security, perhaps they felt that they had the cash to spend in pursuit of market share. Clothing retailer Boo.com spent $42 million on a launch campaign for its website, which, it turned out, wasn't yet live. Since Boo.com was never a publicly traded company, it's not possible to know how much was spent on sales and marketing. Boo.com reportedly raised around $100 million as a private company. But that $42 million campaign for the website launch included $25 million of advertising in magazines and newspapers and on billboards.[33] That's a hefty chunk spent on one campaign. (By contrast, Amazon's marketing costs as a ratio to net sales were 10.7 per cent in 1999 and fell to 4.4 per cent by 2001.)

The poor management decisions didn't stop there. For example, a problem facing Pets.com was its distribution system. It offered a fixed shipping fee of $4.95 plus just $2 for anything over eleven pounds in weight. But it had only one distribution centre, in California, so shipped to other parts of the US at a loss. Pets.com was losing money on every sale of low-margin goods, including popular items like dog food. It also had poor returns from its expensive advertising. The famous sock puppet advert played at the January 2000 Super Bowl and was loved by the public; it was voted the fifth most popular ad at the time but it cost $2.2 million.[34] Customers may have gone to its website to buy the puppet, but unfortunately not its other products.[35] It failed to produce the sales to justify the hugely expensive ad.

Another mistake of management was a failure to ensure timely delivery, especially for Christmas. eToys.com described its use of a third-party delivery company as a 'disaster'.[36] After seeing a disappointed child's face on Christmas morning, parents would not be returning to the website.

These mistakes were worsened by managers who were struggling with the speed of growth. Pets.com grew to 320 employees in just over two years; Boo.com went from 5 employees in 1998 to having 420 people a year later; eToys.com grew from 13 to 235 employees in its first two years and then to 940 after its IPO.

On top of all this, things might just have been advancing too quickly for the dot coms as investors' expectations for e-commerce were running ahead of consumers and the available technology. For instance, Boo.com offered 3-D graphics on its website, but only a very small percentage of households had internet access with sufficient bandwidth to handle them, which meant that the vast majority could not properly view its website. By contrast, Pets at Home, the physical store, was founded in 1991 but didn't launch its website until 2008, when broadband availability had become widespread. Perhaps some of the dot coms might have endured had they started a decade later. Maybe they were just ahead of their time.

Then there were the new investors who were able to trade electronically via online platforms such as E\*Trade, an online brokerage that catered to retail investors who also shared the exuberance felt by the professionals in the new internet economy. And the internet allowed them to invest without having to use a broker. But that was part of the problem. Retail investors were seemingly more bullish on dot coms and took bigger risks, including investing on margin, which meant they were borrowing to invest in stocks. Investors trading on E\*Trade were seven times more likely to trade on margin than investors who used Merrill Lynch, a full-service brokerage that also held their assets as well as offering trading services.[37] A month before the market peaked in 2000, the internet sector accounted for 6 per cent of the market capitalization of all US public companies but 20 per cent of trading volumes.[38]

It wasn't just investors in public companies who fuelled the bubble. Venture capitalists (VCs) who provided the initial funding to dot coms when they were private firms were also less experienced in 2000. In the early 1990s, the share of investments made by VCs who had been in that role for less than five years was 10 per cent. By 2000, it had increased to 40 per cent. The newer VCs, perhaps more familiar with the internet but with less experience of investing, were making a significant share of the investments in dot coms compared with their more seasoned colleagues.[39]

All of these factors were probably why venture capitalists invested a great deal initially but then notably less in the second quarter of 2000.[40] The shift in funding and sentiment that often drives retail investors led to hundreds of dot com companies shutting down. Between January 2000 and June 2001, 564 dot coms closed.[41]

Viewed over a decade, the 1,000 per cent NASDAQ rally ended in March 2000. The NASDAQ fell by 78 per cent and did not recover its pre-crash level of 5,000 until March 2015.[42] More than half the companies that had floated their shares in the boom perished in the bust.[43] Indeed, only Microsoft of the so-called 'Four Horsemen' of tech stocks that drove a great deal of the dot com rally (the others being Cisco, Intel and Dell) had recovered from the bust a decade later.[44] Cisco and Intel remained below their highs in 2000 while Dell was relisted after being taken private. In terms of valuations, Microsoft at around thirty times price-to-earnings was still trading at less than half of what it reached during the dot com boom.[45]

The other major US stock markets also crashed. The Dow Jones Industrial Average of blue-chip stocks fell by 54 per cent, while the S&P 500, representing the broader market, lost 48 per cent of its value. Though not as much as the NASDAQ, these declines were far in excess of the 20 per cent drop that defines a bear market. The declines across the indices were concentrated in the dot coms. An index of 400 dot com stocks had increased ten-fold in value from 1997 to March 2000, and then fell by 80 per cent in the next nine months.[46] But because the dot com bubble was concentrated in tech stocks and related sectors, it limited the impact of the crash on the economy.

The dot com crash led to a short, mild recession. At the time, the IT sector was relatively remote from other sectors of the economy, so the dot com crash left little mark on GDP (which fell by only 0.3 per cent) and did no lasting economic damage. But, it did end a record, decade-long expansion of the US economy that began in March 1991 and finished exactly ten years later. According to the National Bureau of Economic Research (NBER), which is the official arbiter of US business cycles, the average recession since the Second World War lasts nine months once the outliers are discounted.[47] The recession that followed the dot com crash concluded after just eight months, in November 2001.

Whereas deep recessions tend to be followed by a strong rebound, and thus the commonly touted V-shape recovery, mild recessions tend to be followed by an equally mild recovery. This was the case with the dot com crash, the 2001 recession being similar to the mild recessions of 1969–70 and 1990–91, both of which had followed long expansions of the US economy. The NBER estimates peak-to-trough declines in real GDP during recessions that follow long expansions at about 1 per cent versus 2.6 per cent for other reces-sions.[48] Despite the historical similarities, the mild 2001 recession was still jarring since the period included the tragic events of 9/11. As a result, forecasters expected that the US economy would contract in the final three months of 2001.[49] That it did not was perhaps due to, or was certainly helped by, stimulative measures such as car compan-ies offering special financing incentives to buoy demand, causing light vehicle sales to reach a near-record high in October of that year.[50]

Rather unusually, personal incomes continued to grow owing to an increase in wealth accumulated by US households during the 1990s, which saw stronger than normal productivity growth translate into more disposable income. Consequently, unlike in most reces-sions, retail sales and the housing market both held steady throughout 2001.[51] Demand was also helped by the fact that interest rates were low before the recession hit. Despite the growth in incomes and wealth, inflation too was low during what has been called the 'Great Moderation' of the late 1990s and early 2000s. This had enabled the Fed to keep interest rates down, which helped support consumption through cheap loans.[52]

Although unemployment did not rise sharply, still the recession caused by the dot com crash saw more than 1.3 million people lose their jobs. The unemployment rate rose to 5.6 per cent in the fourth quarter of 2001, increasing from a thirty-year low of around 4 per cent at the end of 2000 and creating misery for the many people who lost their livelihoods.

Stocks are probably what most people think of when the term 'bubble' is mentioned, and the dot com boom seems to be an exem-plar of a rapid build-up in the market in which the companies driving the rise did not appear to have the business fundamentals to warrant the share price boom. It was a spectacular rise followed by a dramatic bust, remarkable for its speed and scale, which wiped out an entire sector in about a year and a half. The NASDAQ then took a decade and a half to recover, until the latest run-up in tech stocks that started in the late 2010s. So, despite the many differences between the stock market and other assets such as housing or exchange rates, stocks certainly share the trait of euphoria that has characterized financial crises throughout history.

The mild recession that followed the dot com bust, unlike the aftermath of the Great Crash of 1929, is also testament to the role of credibility. This second shared trait of financial crises emphasizes the importance of having credible institutions and policies that can ensure a better aftermath. The US had learned the lessons of the 1929 crash and the 1930s depression. The Federal Reserve had been monitoring the dot coms, as evidenced by Alan Greenspan's 'irrational exuberance' observation. All of this also led to rapid interest rate cuts to support the economy after the dot com crash to prevent the subsequent recession becoming deep or prolonged.

Those very interest rate cuts contributed to the next asset bubble, this time in US housing, but that is perhaps another lesson of financial crises. The remedies for the last crisis often contribute to the next. Cheap loans to bolster demand in 2001 were funnelled not into stocks, which were down, but into housing, which was looking up.

Is history repeating itself? As I write this in late 2022, the NASDAQ has recovered only some of the trillions of dollars wiped off tech companies' market value in the latest tech reversal. The 'Four Horsemen' have been replaced by the FAANGs (Facebook, Amazon, Apple, Netflix and Google). Microsoft, Apple, Amazon, Alphabet (Google's parent) and Meta (Facebook's parent) make up nearly one-fifth of the S&P 500.[53] At the height of the dot com boom, technology stocks accounted for over 35 per cent of the US benchmark index. It's a similar picture for the current market, which is why there are concerns that these sizeable tech companies could again drag the economy down if there is a crash.

There are certainly echoes of the dot com boom as investors fret over the high valuations placed on tech start-ups that have never turned a profit. Particularly for software or online-only companies that rely on building a large network of customers in order to gain market share, there is again a focus on gaining users over profitability. But, as the market began to fall, digital start-ups offering 'buy now, pay later' services such as Klarna started focusing less on growth and more on short-term profitability, since that was what investors were asking for.[54]

It's also worth bearing in mind that Amazon and Google not only survived but also became dominant after the dot com bust. Similarly, after the market collapse that followed the 2009 great recession discussed in the next chapter, start-ups like Airbnb, WhatsApp and payments company Stripe emerged. There are signs today of the great economist Joseph Schumpeter's 'creative destruction', in which there's a shake-out from a recession and the best companies thrive.[55] And it has been a big shake-out. Six months after the November 2021 peak, fintech companies (start-ups in the financial services sector) had lost more than 80 per cent of their value, consumer internet companies were down 70 per cent and firms offering business software had fallen by 65 per cent.[56]

Whether or not the latest run-up in the NASDAQ stock index was a bubble like two decades previously, the deflating of the market has meant that valuations have come down from what seemed to be euphoric levels. With less funding on offer, we may find out which firms have learned the vital lesson from the dot com era – the importance of controlling costs. As Mark Twain reportedly said, 'History doesn't repeat itself, but it does rhyme.'

# 5   The Global Financial Crisis of 2008

'We wondered if we broke the system this time,' a former bank CEO observed as the global financial crisis hit in 2008. Indeed, it was the first such episode since the Great Crash in 1929 that had the potential to bring down the entire global economic system.

In the United States, equities fell by a staggering 78 per cent, only a little less than in 1929 when the market fell by about 90 per cent from peak to trough. Unsurprisingly, given the historic parallel, the global financial crisis that occurred eighty years later led to the 2009 great recession. However, by learning some of the lessons from 1929, policymakers were able to prevent the recession from becoming a depression.

The technical definition of a recession is two consecutive quarters of economic contraction. A depression is significantly more severe than that. More than one economist has said: 'A recession is when your neighbour loses his job. A depression is when you lose your job.'

On Monday 15 September 2008, the 'most momentous day on Wall Street since the 1930s', the investment bank Lehman Brothers failed.[1] I remember it clearly. I was due to join a live BBC Radio 4 panel that evening to reflect on the first anniversary of the collapse of the British bank Northern Rock, which triggered the first bank run in the UK in over a century. The producer rang to inform me of Lehman's demise and that the agenda had changed to discuss what would happen next. That was going to be a tough question to answer, to say the least.

The events that followed the collapse of Lehman Brothers would be some of the most extraordinary in the history of financial crashes. It would become clear that Lehman was part of a web of 'shadow' financial institutions that were playing the mortgage market using vast amounts of leverage, which refers to debt undertaken to fund a financial transaction. 'Shadow banking' encompasses financial trans-actions that sit outside the official banking sector.

An investment bank isn't usually considered as being on the front line of mortgage lenders, but Lehman was heavily involved in the mortgage market through other financial activities, including acting as a 'broker-dealer'. Lehman connected borrowers and investors in a repurchase, or repo, market in which firms with excess cash bought the IOUs of firms that needed liquidity, effectively lending their spare cash to other firms, who paid a higher interest rate than the banks.[2] Those firms offered collateral such as mortgages to secure those loans. These transactions created a lot of debt based on a small amount of collateral. In the US, this was limited to 140 per cent of collateral in a bank, but there was no maximum in the UK. So, by trading out of London, American and European banks could go much further with their leveraging – up to 400 per cent in many cases. The IMF estimated there was roughly $4.5 trillion of additional debt cre-ated in this way.[3] This is how the housing crash became a banking crisis. When the housing market collapsed, the collateral held by banks lost its value, which made the staggering level of debt secured on that collateral unsustainable. Lehman was highly leveraged even among investment banks. When it collapsed in September 2008, its role as a 'broker-dealer' sent shockwaves across financial markets and triggered the worst systemic banking crisis in almost a century.

As would be expected with a crisis of this magnitude, its roots go back decades.

Unlike in many other countries, the mortgage market in the US is supported by various government agencies. The US government set up Fannie Mae (Federal Housing Authority) and Freddie Mac (Federal Home Loan Mortgage Corporation) in 1938 and 1970, respect-ively, to make mortgages cheaper and home ownership more attainable for Americans. Fannie Mae created a secondary market for lenders. It did not lend directly to home buyers but it bought mortgages from commercial banks. Through its purchases, Fannie Mae set the standard for 'prime' borrowers – borrowers deemed to be creditworthy; other mortgages were termed 'sub-prime'. This 'originate-to-distribute' model lowered the cost of lending and thus increased home owner-ship from less than 50 per cent of Americans to a pre-crash peak of 69 per cent. Freddie Mac was created to do the same but for the sav-ings and loans discussed in Chapter 2. To give a sense of the scale, these two government agencies supported around half of all mort-gages before the sub-prime crisis.[4]

The 'originate-to-distribute' model led to the securitization of mortgages, a process whereby the originators of the mortgages (the commercial banks) are separated from the institutions that fund them. Securitization increased the funding available for mortgages. The banks that sold the mortgages were repaid by Fannie Mae. To fund those payments, Fannie Mae and Freddie Mac in turn passed on the mortgages to investment banks by selling shares in pools of mortgages known as mortgage-backed securities (MBS). This action by the two government agencies reduced the cost of mortgages further by cre-ating an additional market for them as securities. Unsurprisingly, perhaps, investment banks quickly followed their lead. Thus began the widespread securitization of mortgages, a process that was to become all too familiar decades later.

The 1980s S&L crisis complicated matters, creating a desire to spread risk across a broad set of investors. Securitization seemed to fulfil this need by enabling a large number of banks to own shares of pools of mortgages. Investment banks then created collateralized mortgage obligations (CMOs) that separated mortgage-backed secur-ities into different tiers of riskiness. This 'structured finance' meant that the top tier had first claim on collateral and was deemed to have the lowest risk. Tranches lower down had higher risk of default and early repayment. The top tranches would pay out except if there was collective default, which the credit rating agencies judged to be unlikely, so the CMOs were given the top credit rating of AAA. Just a fifth of CMOs were not given the AAA rating, which made struc-tured finance look safer than the best-performing companies or even entire countries, just a dozen or so of which had an AAA rating.

Securitization spread quickly during the 2000s. With financing costs falling, lenders sought out more borrowers. In addition to reducing the down payment required, mortgage lenders offered a range of products, including interest-only mortgages, adjustable-rate mortgages and very low 'teaser' rates for the first two or three years. The housing market was expanding, with cheaper mortgages and growing demand from aspiring homeowners, who had been encouraged to pursue the American dream of home ownership, with or without a white picket fence. Aspiring homeowners literally bought into this euphoria. If their properties continued rising in value, they would be wealthier and their mortgages would become more affordable since they could refinance on better terms.

Shortly before the housing bubble burst, there was an increase in borrowers described as 'NINJAs': no income, no job or assets. Around half of sub-prime mortgages had incomplete documentation and nearly a third were interest-only mortgages that had been offered to home buyers who had little prospect of meeting even those payments.[5] It wasn't only first-time buyers who were affected. Before the crash, around one-third of new mortgages were not for a first or only home. In the major 'bubble states' of California and Florida, the figure was nearly half.[6]

The exuberant view of the housing market believed that the property market could not decline on a national basis, even though that had happened during the 1930s Great Depression, which, not coincidentally, was also the last time there had been a systemic banking crash in the US. Others believed that, even if house prices were to deflate, the entire housing market would not crash at the same time.

By the summer of 2007, there were about $1.3 trillion invested in sub-prime mortgage-backed securities. Banks had been funding their purchases of mortgage-backed securities not from deposits but by borrowing from wholesale money markets: places in which financial institutions and companies park their cash to be lent out for a short period, ranging from overnight to 270 days, to earn interest. Mortgages had migrated from commercial banks' balance sheets to government agencies to the broader financial markets and were now even funded by wholesale money markets. The euphoria of the housing boom was evident across the financial system.

Economic policy also supported the boom. After the dot com bubble burst and the shock of 9/11 in 2001, the Fed had cut interest rates to cushion that recession. Low interest rates reduced the cost of mortgages. House prices surged. Unsurprisingly, a construction boom ensued. Housing starts hit 2.1 million properties per year, nearly 40 per cent more than was needed to house not only the growth of the US population but the demand for second homes and the replacement of houses due to fires or storms.[7]

When the Fed raised the interest rate from 1 per cent in June 2004 to 5.25 per cent two years later, borrowing costs were initially affected far less than expected. Increasing the cost of mortgages would have tempered the housing boom, but this did not happen. In the aftermath of the Asian financial crisis and related emerging market crises in the late 1990s (as detailed in Chapter 1), the demand for US government debt was high as those central banks built up reserves of safe assets to defend themselves against a future currency crisis. Their actions reduced the cost of borrowing in America since there was strong demand for dollar-denominated debt. This occurred alongside the growth of the shadow banking system that Lehman was part of, which also increased the amount of funds available for mortgages. The housing bubble continued unabated, despite the increase in interest rates.

Like all bubbles, of course, it eventually did burst, as the increase in interest rates finally took hold. The US housing market peaked in 2007. Housing starts began to decline. As the housing market slowed, so did the economy and, even though there wasn't an immediate sharp contraction in GDP growth, the impact on homeowners was stark.

The hardest hit borrowers were those who had made minimal down payments. And there were quite a few of them. The share of sub-prime mortgages increased to one in five of all borrowers by 2006, up from just 6 per cent two years earlier. Because many sub-prime borrowers had made small down payments, once property prices began to decline they ended up in negative equity, their house now being worth less than their mortgage. In addition to the sub-prime borrowers, the increase in borrowing costs for adjustable-rate mortgages meant that low-income homeowners found themselves unable to afford the higher payments each month. Struggling homeowners could either sell their property and hope that their lender would accept a less than full repayment or they could walk away and hand the keys back to the lenders.

When a borrower stopped making payments, investment banks who had bought these mortgages from brokers could ask for a refund. Unsurprisingly, mortgage brokers began to fail as a result,[8] leaving investment banks with tens of billions of dollars of mortgage debt on their books that would not be repaid. In financial terms, they had become 'non-performing' or bad loans.

Banks measured their balance sheets by placing valuations on their assets, so investment banks now wanted to sell mortgage-backed securities but struggled once real-estate prices began to decline, since these assets became harder to value. Hard-to-value assets were harder to sell, so the banks could do little to improve their position. The 'mark-to-market' convention means that firms owning identical securities must value them at the most recent market price. So, once one investment bank became a distressed seller, there was a downward spiral for all mortgage-backed securities holders.

The impact was widespread across the financial system since securitization of mortgages had spread risk far and wide. By grouping different types of mortgages, prime and sub-prime, on property in different locations across the country, investors believed that their risks were not concentrated in one type of borrower or region. But when an entire housing market collapses, then all housing-related assets lose value and securitization does nothing more than spread those losses.

Not everyone lost. One group of investors, including Deutsche Bank, JP Morgan and Goldman Sachs and a number of hedge funds, had built 'big short' positions, buying credit default swaps, or CDSs, which are essentially insurance contracts against default, on mortgage-backed securities. They believed that homeowners would default on their mortgages, so they bought a contract that bet on it. The investors received huge payouts when their bet came home, as Michael Lewis's book *The Big Short* depicts. One investor, Michael Burry, who was played by Christian Bale in the film adaptation, made $825 million from betting against the housing market.

The bust was felt not only in the US. About a quarter of all securitized mortgages were owned by foreign investors. China was the biggest investor in these agency bonds of Fannie Mae and Freddie Mac. Of the $1.7 trillion held by foreigners, China's share accounted for around a third,[9] although these were mainly the relatively safer mortgage-backed securities backed by Fannie Mae and Freddie Mac. By contrast, the riskier assets were owned by European investors, who held just under a third of the total.[10] When it became clear that some of Europe's banks had behaved like their American counterparts, the US sub-prime crisis went global.[11]

With low interest rates in the early 2000s and European banks making money in the US mortgage market, exuberance was almost as evident in Europe. In 2007, the three largest banks in the world (measured by assets) were not American but European: France's BNP Paribas, Germany's Deutsche Bank and the UK's Royal Bank of Scotland (RBS). One reason was that, unlike the US, which had a substantial capital market that funded investments, European borrowers relied on banks for financing. When measured against the GDP of their home nation, European banks loomed large. Irish banks were the biggest, with liabilities that came to 700 per cent of Ireland's national output. In the UK and France, the figure was about 400 per cent of GDP, while it was 300 per cent for Germany and Spain.[12] Moreover, like American banks, Europe's were also reliant on wholesale money markets rather than retail deposits to fund their lending.

When the US housing bubble started to deflate in the summer of 2006, Europe's market soon followed. Throughout the next year, house prices fell markedly in Ireland, Spain and the UK. European homeowners, like Americans, suffered negative equity and started to cut back on spending. The housing crash then led to a recession as households struggled with payments on homes that were worth less than their mortgages, so demand contracted.

Investment banks such as UBS and Bear Stearns began to close their funds as they continued to incur losses on mortgage-backed securities. But when BNP Paribas froze three funds on 9 August 2007 and announced, 'The complete evaporation of liquidity in certain market segments of the US securitization market has made it impossible to value certain assets fairly regardless of their quality or credit rating,' the market was truly shaken.[13] Now that those mortgage assets could not be used as collateral to access funding, liquidity started to dry up. Liquidity's central place in bank operations was described by a bank executive thus: 'It was as if your entire life you had turned the spigot and water came out. And now there was no water.'[14] The European Central Bank was forced to step in to offer much-needed liquidity.

The severity of this crisis for Europe was brought home by the collapse of the UK bank Northern Rock on 14 September 2007. Northern Rock was a mortgage lender that relied largely on wholesale funding to back its loans. About three-quarters of its funding depended on money markets and less than a quarter on deposits.[15] When liquidity in the wholesale money markets dried up, so did Northern Rock's access to funding. It resulted in the first bank run in the UK in 150 years, vividly illustrated by the queues outside its branches when depositors tried to withdraw their savings before the bank collapsed.

In a fractional reserve banking system, one where banks lend most of their funds and keep only a fraction in cash, it's not irrational for depositors to want to get their money out. Government-backed deposit insurance – the amount that would be returned to account holders should the bank collapse – covered up to £30,000 of their savings. It was later increased to £85,000 to prevent future bank runs. That higher level would give assurance to savers that the safety of their money would not depend on the bank's balance sheet. Northern Rock wasn't felled by holding US sub-prime mortgages, and its collapse did not have the potential to bring the entire financial system down. But it was funded by the same wholesale money markets as the US investment banks, and their collapse could, and would, be calamitous.

In the spring of 2008, Bear Stearns was struggling to access funding owing to its substantial exposure to mortgage-backed securities. Bear Stearns at that time was the sixth-largest American investment bank. Still, its investors were concerned about ongoing losses while its creditors were unwilling to renew their loans. On 13 March, Bear was running out of cash to repay its short-term loans. Selling off its portfolio of $200 billion in a fire sale would have forced every US bank to recognize huge losses, so the government had to step in to prevent a collapse both in confidence and, worse, of the market. After $29 billion of Bear's most 'toxic assets' had been taken off its books by the New York Fed, it was acquired by another investment bank, JPMorgan Chase. Bear had effectively been 'rescued' and sold off with the support of the American government.

By contrast, the decision to allow Lehman Brothers to fail that autumn would become the key moment of the sub-prime crisis. Since Lehman was highly leveraged, banks were increasingly unwilling to renew its loans as the company struggled to raise additional capital to address the decline in its net worth, dragged down by the plummeting value of its mortgage-backed securities. As confidence in Lehman collapsed, it faced calls from its lenders to hand over the collateral it had offered. However, that collateral was also the source of its access to funding markets, since Lehman had historically relied on short-term funds to finance its long-term securities. It was now becoming ruinously expensive to refinance the maturing IOUs.

Lehman had been looking to be taken over before its failure. Bank of America was a potential buyer, but it bought Merrill Lynch instead. Merrill shared Lehman's huge exposure to the wholesale money market, without which it could not operate, but Merrill had pursued Bank of America and offered its CEO the chance to realize a business goal that he had long pursued: the creation of a 'universal bank' with both commercial and investment banking. Bank of America paid $50 billion, a third of what Merrill was worth before the crisis. With other major banks struggling or uninterested, the only other potential suitor for Lehman was a UK bank, Barclays.

But the UK was concerned about the health of its own banking sector, and the British PM Gordon Brown and his Chancellor, Alistair Darling, would not allow the takeover without both shareholder approval and support from the US government. Darling had been in regular contact with US Treasury Secretary Hank Paulson and later observed: 'I didn't think he had enough political capital to persuade the Republicans to nationalize another bank.'[16] Indeed, Paulson subsequently struggled to get Congress to pass his crucial bank recapitalization plan, the Troubled Asset Relief Program, which would have injected capital into banks to bolster their balance sheets.

Lehman was soon to run out of money and would shortly fail. US regulators underestimated Lehman's role as a principal 'broker-dealer' in the wholesale money market, and had not classed it as 'too big to fail', a status that would warrant a government rescue and which generally refers to a bank that cannot shut down because it would be too disruptive to economic functions essential to maintain financing in the economy. Lehman's collapse and the crisis it precipitated highlighted the opacity of the shadow banks in the global financial system.

On Monday 15 September 2008, at 1.45 a.m., the 164-year-old Lehman Brothers filed for bankruptcy, the biggest such failure in American history. The fourth-largest US investment bank had gone bust. Images of Lehman employees carrying their belongings in cardboard boxes that were splashed across TV and computer screens have come to symbolize the worst crisis in decades.

In retrospect, the US government's decision not to bail out Lehman would be repeatedly questioned, notably regarding the company's degree of interconnectedness in the shadow banking system as a 'broker-dealer'. That decision has sparked years of debate. Many see it as the trigger for the 2008 global financial crisis. Had Lehman been rescued, could the crash have been avoided? And, even if it had been, would another bank have upended markets in a similar manner in any case?

After Lehman failed, credit markets 'froze'. Banks were unsure who would fail next, so they stopped transacting and liquidity dried up. This 'credit crunch' would affect the wider economy in due course. As risks skyrocketed, the risk premium, which is reflected in interest rates in credit markets, jumped. The cost of borrowing in the inter-bank market increased by a factor of up to forty compared with the rates on the safest assets, US Treasury bills (short-term government debt). Interest rates also surged on higher-risk bonds relative to US Treasury bonds (longer-term government debt).

In this post-Lehman context, the next giant on the brink of toppling wasn't another investment bank but American International Group (AIG), the world's largest insurer. Through its financial products division, AIG held several hundred billion dollars' worth of credit default swaps. Many of these were purchased by firms that were Lehman creditors. When Lehman failed, AIG was left to pick up the bill.

On the day that Lehman failed, AIG's credit rating was downgraded, triggering margin calls from counterparties who wanted their collateral back in case AIG failed too. With dwindling collateral and growing losses on its balance sheet, creditors were no longer interested in lending to AIG. Without rescue, AIG would have failed within days.

The US government had deemed AIG too big to fail because of the repercussions that would have on the rest of the financial system. Its holdings of derivatives, repo and securities activities were larger than Lehman's, and viewed as critical to the functioning of the economy. So, on the day following Lehman's collapse, the Fed declared a Section 13(3) emergency and rescued AIG. In exchange for billions in collateral, the New York Fed offered AIG a credit facility of up to $85 billion. In return, the Fed took a 79.9 per cent holding in the company. AIG's shareholders suffered massive losses.

That day was momentous for another reason, too. The Reserve Primary Fund, one of the oldest money-market funds, informed the Fed that it could not guarantee a payout of a dollar for every dollar invested. It would 'break the buck', which had never happened before. After the failure of Lehman, nervous investors, concerned that even mutual funds were exposed to mortgage-backed securities, pulled half a trillion dollars out and put it into safe assets, such as US Treasury bills and bonds. On 19 September 2008, the US Treasury made the remarkable decision to guarantee, in return for an insurance fee, to stop the run on money market funds. To do so, they would use the Exchange Stabilization Fund, a $50 billion pot set up in the New Deal of the 1930s to manage the US dollar, and quickly repurposed.

The pullback led to what became known as the 'credit crunch'. As investors moved their money into government bonds and troubled banks lent less, there were fewer funds available to businesses. In turn, companies drew down on their credit lines at their banks, which put more pressure on their balance sheets. In Europe, with the freezing of wholesale funding, banks had to recognize their losses, so they also pulled back from lending. This affected not only businesses but also mortgages. The 'credit crunch' and the fallout from Lehman hastened the bursting of housing bubbles on both sides of the Atlantic.

By the summer of 2008, Fannie Mae and Freddie Mac were back-stopping three out of four new mortgages, since the banks were struggling. These two government agencies held mortgage-backed securities totalling some $1.8 trillion, so were effectively insolvent. Both were placed under conservatorship in the autumn.

By 2009, from their peak in 2007, US house prices had fallen by a third. More than 9 million homeowners defaulted on their mortgages and lost their homes. The collapse was even more striking in Ireland, where house prices halved between 2008 and 2012. In the UK, 10 per cent of homeowners were in negative equity when house prices fell by a fifth.

In the early stages of the crash, government officials hoped that banks would help themselves by consolidating through acquisitions. For example, in 2008 the UK's Halifax and Bank of Scotland (HBOS) was sold to Lloyds Bank with encouragement from the British government. Germany's second-largest bank, Dresdner, would merge with its smaller rival, Commerzbank. But it soon became evident that the rescuer put itself at risk of being pulled down by the troubled bank it had acquired.

Given the risks, potential buyers wanted government support. In the US, Japan's Mitsubishi was ready to rescue Morgan Stanley in return for 20 per cent ownership. Warren Buffett was poised to support Goldman with $5 billion. But both offers were dependent on a government backstop.

Fed Chairman Ben Bernanke and Treasury Secretary Hank Paulson knew they needed more funds since this crisis was not only one of liquidity but also, and more challengingly, one of solvency. Recapitalization by injecting money into the banks was required, and that needed Congressional approval of a lot more funds.

The US Treasury had been working on a significant backstop for months. In consultation with Bernanke and the Fed, it decided to ask Congress for up to $700 billion for the Troubled Asset Relief Program (TARP), submitting what Paulson and his Treasury team referred to as a 'break the glass' memo.[17] The proposal was just three pages long but a sizeable ask. Paulson was in a bruising battle with his fellow Republicans to pass the measure, without which the global financial system could fail. Republicans were ideologically opposed to government bailing out and in effect nationalizing banks. Paulson needed Democrat votes in Congress. To secure their support, the measure had been revised to include a commitment that there would be a tax on the financial industry to pay for any losses. Just over a week later, on 28 September, it seemed a deal was imminent that would cover any taxpayer losses by levying a tax on the financial industry. But the bill failed to pass in the House of Representatives the next day. Of the 205 votes in favour, 140 came from Democrats and only 65 from the incumbent Republicans. The shock to financial markets was evident immediately. On 29 September, the Dow Jones index dropped an astounding 778 points and lost $1.2 trillion in the biggest loss on record.

It took more wrangling to reassure Congress that taxpayers would not suffer losses and banks would not be let off the hook before the House voted 263–171 in favour on 3 October. Influenced by the UK's focus on recapitalization in order to restore confidence, the

$700 billion fund was changed from buying toxic assets or giving bank guarantees to recapitalizing banks by injecting capital. Within hours of its passage, President George W. Bush signed it into law.

The news from across the Atlantic wasn't good either. In the UK, the bailout of Northern Rock a year earlier was proving to be only a harbinger of what was to come. UK banks were similarly dependent on the wholesale funding market that had seized up, and both large banks such as RBS and smaller lenders like Bradford & Bingley were suffering. As in America, in Britain the government was trying to persuade 'white knight' banks to come to the rescue. (Spain's Santander bought Bradford & Bingley's branches that September.) It was a similar story in the rest of Europe. The French government was contending with Dexia and the German government with Hypo Real Estate. Fortis, a Belgian-Dutch-Luxembourgeois bank, was around the size of Lehman and under pressure.

The European crisis came to a head on 29 September. The three largest Irish banks, Anglo Irish Bank, the Bank of Ireland and Allied Irish Bank, all needed to be rescued. The next morning the Irish government guaranteed not just the deposits but all of the liabilities of all six major Irish banks for two years. Ireland ended up guaranteeing €440 billion of bank liabilities. To fund the rescues, the government had to borrow a startling 32 per cent of GDP.

Ireland's situation raised significant concerns about smaller economies' ability to contain the banking crisis. The Netherlands, having rescued Fortis, proposed that European states should establish bank rescue funds equal to 3 per cent of GDP, totalling €300 billion. France was supportive. President Nicolas Sarkozy and his finance minister, Christine Lagarde, were persuaded of the need for Europe-wide measures, given the interconnectedness of banks. But Germany was not. It did not want to pay for other countries' bailouts. In early October, European equity markets fell as the lack of measures to match the American efforts roiled investors. The US called an emergency meeting of the G7 and G20 finance ministers on the sidelines of the annual meetings of the World Bank and the IMF on 10 and 11 October.

★

In the UK, RBS was hours from failure. Prime Minister Brown responded by unveiling his bank bailout plan. The British government announced £250 billion to guarantee new debt issued by banks. The Bank of England's special liquidity scheme, under which banks could temporarily swap asset-backed securities for government bills, was extended by £200 billion. The UK's eight major banks could draw on a £50-billion government fund or raise monies themselves to recapitalize. Two banks, RBS and Lloyds TSB-HBOS, received funds directly and ended up with the government as a significant shareholder. The UK government owned 57.9 per cent of RBS after injecting £15 billion, and 43.4 per cent of Lloyds after granting it £13 billion. Barclays and HSBC did not take part in this scheme. Barclays raised capital from individual investors, including Qatar's sovereign wealth fund. HSBC was able to raise funds from the markets since its base of business was largely in Asia, so less affected by the US sub-prime crisis.

Brown's efforts appeared to calm things down, but global markets were still in turmoil. At the G7 finance ministers' meeting there were recriminations, including a general excoriation of the Americans for not rescuing Lehman. The leaders agreed that systemically important financial institutions could not be allowed to fail because they risked bringing down the entire system. The leaders also pledged to get the interbank and securitized assets markets unfrozen and working again.

On the other side of the Atlantic, America's nine major banks were presented with TARP. They were mandated to accept capital from the government in exchange for the government owning preferred shares. The banks would also receive protection from the federal deposit insurance fund for all of their business current accounts as well as guarantees on new debt issuance up to a certain amount. In total, US banks accepted $125 billion from the government.

The Treasury's aim in making TARP universal was to remove the stigma of accepting government funds so that the weaker banks, which had to accept help, would not be picked out and sold off by the market. Simultaneously, the stronger banks knew that in a systemic banking crisis, strength would not matter if financial markets remained frozen, so were willing to participate. Even so, the move wasn't enough to shield Citibank from panicked investors. A month later, the market value of the bank, which held $306 billion in toxic assets on its balance sheet, had dropped to just $20.5 billion, a tenth of its value before the crash. Like other exposed banks, Citibank was struggling to access wholesale markets. So, on 22–23 November, Citi received a further $20 billion from the government, which received preferred shares in return (the US government owned 36 per cent of the bank at one point). Bank of America soon followed suit, the government increasing its shareholding to keep it afloat.

Despite the fact that they were responsible for the global financial crisis of 2008, the American banks ended up recovering more quickly than European ones. TARP recapitalized all the major banks and additional capital injections for Citibank and Bank of America helped to relieve stress in the financial system. Guarantees and other measures also helped. This was in contrast with the less comprehensive efforts of continental Europe. Unsurprisingly, central banks also played a major role, particularly in providing liquidity to unclog credit markets. In a number of respects, the role played by the Fed and other major central banks was simply astounding.

The Fed, at the epicentre of the crisis, offered a number of schemes to support the financial system. In the autumn of 2007, as the crisis was building, its Term Auction Facility gave banks access to short-term funds that they had previously relied on the commercial paper markets to provide. Like other markets, the commercial paper market, which comprised unsecured short-term debt maturing in usually less than 270 days, had frozen. The Fed accepted asset-backed securities and collateralized debt obligations as collateral. At its peak in early 2009, the Term Auction Facility's balance sheet was almost half a trillion dollars.

In the summer of 2008, the Fed established the Term Securities Lending Facility that offered US Treasury bills for twenty-eight days in exchange for mortgage-backed securities. It also provided the Primary Dealer Credit Facility that offered the primary dealers, who were key players in the Fed's open-market operations, access to unlimited overnight liquidity in exchange for a wide range of collateral. The Fed permitted London-based subsidiaries of American banks to access the programme, which helped to support the UK market.

Given the crisis in the commercial paper market, the Fed went further and even lent directly to businesses. It set up the Commercial Paper Funding Facility, which bought top-quality commercial paper. This facility provided $737 billion in short-term lending during the crisis. Since the market for asset-backed securities had also frozen, the Fed in November 2008 set up the Term Asset-Backed Securities Loan Facility. It offered five-year loans to selected borrowers in return for a broad range of collateral such as highly rated consumer credit and small business loans. Given the degree of risk, it is probably just as well that only $71 billion was lent.

Then, in early 2009, the Fed undertook what has been described as 'unorthodox' monetary policy with the launch of quantitative easing. Quantitative easing (QE) is when a central bank prints money to buy assets, such as government bonds, from the owners of those assets, usually companies or banks. Those firms or banks can now spend the cash or invest it. Since it's newly printed money, QE increases the money supply, so there should be more funds available in the economy. Although open-market operations typically involve the central bank buying assets in exchange for cash, the scale of QE and the type of assets the central bank would buy made QE seem less orthodox.

The Fed bought US Treasurys, which is what it would normally do. But it also bought mortgage-backed securities, which was not usual. The Fed bought the higher quality securities backed by the now defunct Fannie Mae and Freddie Mac in order to help that struggling market. Nearly $2 trillion of those securities were on its books by 2010. Reflecting the extent of European banks' involvement in the sub-prime market, more than half of the mortgage-backed securities bought by the Fed were from the balance sheets of European banks.

It was actually the European Central Bank (ECB) that provided the first liquidity support to interbank markets, in August 2007, on account of the extent of European banks' reliance on overnight lending markets. A year later, both the ECB and the Bank of England were offering substantial liquidity support. But what European banks needed were dollars, given their exposure to and reliance on US wholesale markets. The Fed revamped a tool that was established in the 1960s to manage its fixed exchange rate under the Bretton Woods system. Through this, the Fed could lend dollars to the Bank of England via a currency swap line. The way it worked was that the Fed would receive in return a reverse deposit of sterling. The two central banks pledged to reverse the trade on a future date at an agreed exchange rate. The Fed received an interest premium, the cost of which the Bank of England would then pass on to the banks that drew upon this swap line, so deterring banks from using it if they could get dollars from the market. The swap lines had been used intermittently, including after 9/11, but now, in the face of a systemic banking crisis, the Fed expanded them considerably.

Swap lines with the ECB and the Swiss National Bank were established in December 2007. Between September and October 2008, the Bank of Japan, the Bank of Canada, the Reserve Bank of Australia, the Reserve Bank of New Zealand and the central banks of Sweden, Norway, Denmark, Brazil, Mexico, South Korea and Singapore were added. Unlimited access to dollars was now available to European and other central banks that relied on US funding markets. The ECB made the most use of the Fed's swap lines, owing to the dire state of some of its banks. In total, these fourteen central banks engaged in swaps that at one point accounted for over a third of the Fed's balance sheet: the peak was $580 billion in December 2008. The Fed made profits of around $4 billion on its swap lines.[18] This system cemented the Fed as the backstop not only for the US but also for the world economy. Thus, despite the sub-prime crisis being an American bust, the US dollar's place as the world's reserve currency, the currency that other countries want to hold, actually strengthened during this period. For example, China's total purchases of US Treasurys increased during the crisis. It owned $1.46 trillion of Treasurys in 2009, which was up considerably from around $900 billion in

2007,[19] underscoring the importance of the US dollar-denominated instruments as safe assets. Simply put, it had nowhere else to go.

As the fallout from the crisis continued, the European Union soon faced requests for assistance from its member states. On 27 October 2008, Hungary agreed a $25 billion rescue package with the IMF and the EU. That came to an astonishing one-fifth of Hungary's GDP. Soon, other countries beyond and within the EU followed suit: Iceland, Latvia, Ukraine, Pakistan, Armenia, Belarus and Mongolia. The IMF provided precautionary credit to a large number of countries, including in Latin America (Costa Rica, El Salvador, Guatemala) as well as Serbia and Bosnia–Herzegovina. It also established a new flexible credit facility that was precautionary. It offered such support for the first time in an attempt to forestall full-blown and costly rescues. This fund of more than $80 billion was made available to Colombia, Mexico and Poland.

Closer to home for the EU, Austria and Sweden were both under pressure. Austrian banks had liabilities that amounted to more than half of Austrian GDP on account of lending in eastern Europe. Sweden's banks dominated the banking markets of the Baltics. The withdrawal by these banks from the region could lead to a collapse in lending in these countries as they were the biggest lenders. There was an urgent need to act.

Rather than waiting for Brussels, Austria convened the World Bank, the European Bank for Reconstruction and Development (EBRD) and the European Investment Bank (EIB), establishing the Vienna Initiative. These organizations provided €24.5 billion in funds that could be used for bank recapitalization and new lending. With that assurance in place, seventeen pan-European banking groups pledged to maintain their subsidiaries and to continue to lend to central and eastern Europe. The title of a 2012 IMF working paper about this voluntary action was, 'Foreign Banks and the Vienna Initiative: Turning Sinners into Saints?'[20] Banks had been viewed as 'sinners' who caused the crisis, but this paper suggested that they acted like 'saints' in keeping lending going in this region despite their woes, which was essential to the functioning of the smaller European economies.

Even with this bulwark in place, there was another fragile link: the euro peg for EU countries that had not yet joined the single currency. Latvia, Estonia and Lithuania were among those pegged to the euro in anticipation of eventual eurozone membership. But if they could not maintain their peg owing to money leaving the country, then the Vienna Initiative's funds would not be enough. If they devalued, others similarly under pressure, such as Slovakia and Bulgaria, could follow. That could lead to the value of loans held by Sweden's major banks, Swedbank and Nordea, falling and endangering their balance sheets.

These linkages were why the European Commission refused to countenance devaluation in these countries. That is what the IMF usually recommends to struggling economies, which would then typically be followed by debt restructuring. For instance, if Latvia were to let its currency decline by, say, 30 per cent, its exports would be 30 per cent cheaper on world markets. To achieve that competitiveness without devaluation, Latvian companies would have to cut costs by a swingeing 30 per cent, which would result in lower wages and jeopardize people's livelihoods. Instead, Latvia was rescued by a combination of the European Commission, the IMF, the World Bank, the EBRD, Sweden and Denmark. Similar to eurozone members, after receiving a rescue package that totalled a whopping 32 per cent of its GDP, Latvia undertook austerity but maintained its currency peg. Unemployment rose to 30 per cent, a third of teachers lost their jobs and public sector wages were cut by some 35 per cent.

Even as the Fed's actions stabilized the financial system, its injections of trillions of dollars into markets led to investors searching for returns from that cheap cash. Emerging economies that were not drawn into the sub-prime crisis promised higher returns, so investors moved their dollars into those countries. Fund investors increased their investments in emerging markets by more than 50 per cent, from $900 billion in 2008 to $1.4 trillion within six years.[21]

In June 2013, Fed Chairman Ben Bernanke said that, depending on continued positive economic data, the Fed would vote on tapering or scaling back QE by reducing its monthly asset purchases from $85 billion to $65 billion at its next meeting in September. He also said that QE might end by the middle of 2014. Despite signals from the Fed for weeks preceding this announcement, it led to a 'taper tantrum' that summer when investors pulled their money from emerging markets.

The investment bank Morgan Stanley dubbed the countries most exposed to dollar-denominated debt – Brazil, India, Indonesia, South Africa and Turkey – the 'Fragile Five'. These economies had high levels of foreign debt, which made them vulnerable to sudden withdrawals from investors, reminiscent of the emerging markets crisis of the late 1990s discussed in Chapter 1. As a result, these countries raised interest rates to give higher returns to investors to tempt them to stay put. They also imposed capital controls that limited but could not entirely halt the foreign monies leaving their shores.

At the G20 meeting in September 2013, the finance ministers of emerging economies wanted the Fed to take into account the impact of its policies on the global economy. But the Fed's mandate is geared towards the US economy; it would consider the world economy only if it affected America's prospects, which was why the US central bank acted to help stabilize the banks in Europe during the global crisis. It was unlikely that there would be sufficient potential impact from crises in emerging economies to make the Fed act.

Nevertheless, the currencies of some emerging economies, such as India, were stabilized when, on 18 September, the Fed decided not to taper QE and to leave interest rates at rock bottom. The central bank had downgraded its economic forecasts since the spring, and had decided that the economy wasn't yet strong enough to withdraw monetary support. When I interviewed the Indian central bank governor, Chicago economist Raghuram Rajan, in Mumbai for my BBC programme, he had been at the helm only since early September and had been in charge when the rupee had plummeted to a record low against the dollar. By the time we spoke in October, the rupee was heading towards Rs60 against the dollar, strengthening from around Rs70. In addition to the Fed holding steady, Rajan had focused on reforming the banking system and fixing financially distressed financial institutions, which had averted a crisis. He was described as a 'rock star' and even had female fans writing to him. He told me that his wife found that rather amusing for an academic.[22]

That month, there was more central bank action. The Fed made permanent its currency swap lines with the ECB, Bank of England, Bank of Japan, Bank of Canada and the Swiss National Bank. These banks have agreed that this arrangement will continue to serve as a liquidity backstop. Although the swap lines are only among these six, the impact of the dollar liquidity has extended indirectly to other economies. For instance, the Bank of Japan has increased its swap lines with other countries in the region with the knowledge that it can always draw on the Fed. In this way, the Fed's actions resulted in dollars being provided throughout the global economy, which helped to stabilize world markets. Again, despite the sub-prime crisis arising in the US, the dollar's status as the world's reserve currency was strengthened and America's anchoring role in the global system remained intact despite its banking meltdown.

For emerging economies, this was a welcome development, but the global recession that followed the financial crisis was dampening their main export markets, which were still largely America and Europe. The slowdown of emerging markets, notably China, contributed to the end of the commodity price boom – the rapid increase in commodity prices due to the industrialization of emerging markets since the early 2000s, dubbed the 'commodity super-cycle', came to a halt in 2014. The drop in prices dampened the economies of commodity-exporting countries such as Brazil.

With the West slowly recovering and emerging economies entering recession, there was the risk of another global downturn in 2015. This time, it was China in the spotlight. China's financial system was not interlinked with America's in the way that Europe's was. Throughout the financial crisis, China's banking system wasn't impacted, but its export sector suffered from the ensuing great recession, and China's financial markets reacted to both the changed global conditions and slow growth at home.

In June 2015, China's stock market began to slide. Within three weeks, the Shanghai Composite Index entered into a bear market, dropping a whopping 30 per cent. China's stock market is dominated by retail investors and is known to be volatile. The government stabilized the market by asking state-controlled and other investors to support it, but in August there was another fall. The state duly intervened once again. The cycle was repeated in September. By February 2016, the Chinese benchmark index had lost nearly half its value since the previous summer.

Whereas a crisis in the Fragile Five emerging economies wasn't necessarily sufficient to affect the US economy, a crisis in China was of greater concern. On 24 August 2015, the Dow Jones lost 1,000 points as financial markets reacted to the slowdown in the world's second-largest economy. At a press conference a month later, Fed Chair Janet Yellen explained that global factors, notably China, were considered by the central bank in assessing the potential impact on the US economy. After all, like the US, China was an engine of global growth and a 'price maker' in the world economy. Its demand and supply choices affected global prices, as did those of the US, while other economies were largely 'price takers'. This meant that China's economic health would impact global markets in a way that other emerging markets would not. With weaker US growth forecasts, the Fed held steady. At the end of the year, with the US economy on a sounder footing, the Fed did raise interest rates for the first time since 2006, nearly a decade earlier.

Due to Chinese woes, oil prices dropped to $29 per barrel in early 2016, a level that had not been seen since before the commodity boom that began about fifteen years earlier. Commodity markets were nervous that China, the biggest source of demand for oil and numerous other commodities, could slow dramatically while other large emerging economies were in recession. On the supply side, shale oil, largely from the US, was also exerting downward pressure on oil prices.

A great deal hinged on the Chinese government's response. Their interventions to stabilize the financial markets had not been heartening. China's clumsy attempts to support the market revealed the government's inadequacies in managing an increasingly market-based economy, especially when it came to financial markets. Although its financial management did not inspire confidence, China's unleashing of fiscal stimulus and a credit boom were moves more familiar to investors. The result was economic growth, not just in China but in Asia, where its supply chains are. As China recovered, commodity prices rebounded. The threat of deflation – that is, falling prices driven by a collapse in commodity prices and declining demand – receded as China's stimulus boosted both its own growth and that of the world economy.

It wasn't until the end of 2016 that the Fed resumed raising rates. By that point, it seemed that a potential emerging markets crisis, notably a Chinese one, had been avoided and economic growth was slowly getting back to a more stable basis. Unlike the 1930s, which saw a double-dip recession in 1937–38, the 2010s avoided one. It seemed that some lessons from history had been learned – notably, for economic support not to be withdrawn prematurely.

The global financial crisis was in many ways a textbook example of euphoria. Preceding the housing bubble burst was an extraordinary period of sustained belief that prices would keep going up. Investors piled in with more exotic versions of debt. The financial crisis left us with a new vocabulary of acronyms that captured just how much exuberance there was in the US housing market and the myriad ways to make money from it.

The aftermath was just as astounding. No post-war financial crises had crashed the global system, but this one had the potential to do so since US wholesale markets in particular were essential to global financing. In the days after the collapse of Lehman Brothers in September 2008, bankers and many others wondered whether the banks had finally broken the system.

It was extraordinary that, despite being the cause of the crisis, the

US banking system recovered before Europe's. That's where the credibility of the US proved to be so important. And, crucially, its policymakers had learned the lessons of the 1930s. Even though the sub-prime crisis occurred in the US, the dollar's position as the global reserve currency was strengthened rather than weakened as a result. The Fed's role as provider of the liquidity backstop for the world was made evident. The US Treasury and central bank's role in stabilizing the European banking system was instrumental in preventing not just a US financial meltdown but also a global one. Far from being viewed as incompetent for permitting the housing bubble and its associated leverage, US institutions remained trusted.

The Fed also did not prematurely tighten monetary policy and instead kept it supportive – the opposite of what happened in the aftermath of the 1929 Great Crash. The recapitalization of the banks and the swift extension of liquidity were also key. The lessons of the Great Depression had been learned.

# 6   The Euro Crisis of 2010

Following the momentous events of the previous two years, the 2010 euro crisis not only plunged Europe into a recession but was also an existential crisis for the single-currency bloc.

The euro was adopted in 1999 by eleven of the then fifteen European Union (EU) member states and was used as legal tender by twelve countries in 2002 after Greece signed up in 2001. The euro area would eventually expand to include nineteen countries, with most of the remaining members of the EU slated to join when they met certain economic conditions. The exceptions were Denmark and the UK, both of whom opted out.

The countries in the European Monetary Union (EMU) operate under a shared monetary policy set by the European Central Bank. The shared currency wasn't the first effort by European trading partners to seek stable exchange rates. Its predecessor, the Exchange Rate Mechanism, had collapsed in 1992. Nevertheless, the European movement towards greater economic integration continued, as was seen in the Maastricht Treaty of that same year, which established the four freedoms of the single market: the movement of goods, capital, services and people. With cross-border trade and finance growing within the EU, French President François Mitterrand and German Chancellor Helmut Kohl pushed for a form of currency union different from the ERM to further deepen economic integration.

The move to a single currency was greatly influenced by the Belgian-American economist Robert Triffin. His 1960 book *Gold and the Dollar Crisis* criticized the Bretton Woods system of fixed exchange rates that relied on the US dollar's convertibility to gold.[1] He argued that, with ever-growing volumes of foreign-owned dollars and a limited amount of gold reserves, a fixed exchange rate system based on one currency was not sustainable. It was dubbed the Triffin dilemma. The

Bretton Woods system collapsed just a decade later, though the dollar remains the world's reserve currency.

Triffin had sounded his warnings in America. After studying with John F. Kennedy at Harvard University, Triffin worked for a time in the US government. At international meetings he would sometimes appear with the US delegation and at other times with the European delegation. When US Treasury Secretary C. Douglas Dillon pointed this out to JFK, the president replied: 'Relax, Doug! He's our first Atlantic citizen, and we need more of them.'[2]

Post-Bretton Woods, European policymakers continued to view stable exchange rates as important for facilitating trade within the European Economic Community (EEC) or 'Common Market', as the EU was initially known. In search of an alternative, Triffin proposed a European currency unit to his friend the French politician Jean Monnet. Triffin served as an adviser to Monnet's Action Committee for the United States of Europe as well as to the European Commission. Monnet was a founding father of the European Union. He had been a driving force behind the 1950 Schuman Declaration which provided the basis for the European Coal and Steel Community, the precursor of the Common Market. The Declaration stated: 'The solidarity in production will make it plain that any war between France and Germany becomes not merely unthinkable, but materially impossible . . . [T]his proposal will build the first concrete foundation of a European federation which is indispensable to the preservation of peace.'[3]

This effort towards further European integration was continued by French President Valéry Giscard d'Estaing and German Chancellor Helmut Schmidt, both of whom played a crucial role in the formation of the European Monetary System (EMS) in 1978. At its core was the ERM, whereby European currencies were pegged against the German Mark.

After the ERM's collapse in 1992, European politicians revisited the idea of a European currency. Triffin believed that both a single currency and a fixed exchange rate system depended on the same institutions, such as free movement of people and capital, to underpin them. Monnet certainly saw the need for such institutions in support-ing deeper European integration. He famously said: 'Nothing is possible without men, nothing is lasting without institutions.'[4]

The euro came to fruition in 1999, but creating those institutions would turn out to be a rockier proposition. In December 2001 the EU began working on a constitution. It would set up centralized decision-making by majority rule at the EU level and subordinate the various treaties and institutions that made up the EU. It would also set out how the EU could expand as eastern European nations looked to join. The plan met a setback in 2005, when the constitution was rejected by voters in France and the Netherlands, and it fell to Ger-many, which held the rotating presidency of the European Council, to fashion an intergovernmental treaty instead.

The result was the Treaty of Lisbon. In 2007, the treaty was approved by all national legislatures except Ireland's, which finally passed it in 2009 after two referenda. The treaty came into effect in December 2009 and constitutes the basis of the EU in its present form. Under it, the bloc would operate not by centralized decision-making in Brussels but through governments agreeing among themselves. (This unwieldy system meant that the EU would be slow to respond to the euro crisis that arrived the following year, since every decision required a meeting of EU leaders who often disagreed about what to do.) Overseeing the euro is the European Central Bank. The ECB's governing council consists of national central bank governors and an executive council, including the bank's president. The ECB played a vital role in both the build-up to the euro crisis and its eventual resolution.

Germany was particularly concerned that the ECB would print money to buy newly issued European public debt. This was viewed by the Germans as monetizing government debt, which would open the door to potential profligacy by governments and could lead to inflation. The anti-inflation bias of the Bundesbank stemmed from memories of German hyperinflation in the 1920s. Now, as the largest economy in the euro area, Germany's stance affected the ability of the ECB to buy assets in exchange for cash, so it could not initially undertake quantitative easing as the Fed and the Bank of England did. Importantly, in spite of their countries sharing a currency, banks were regulated and supervised at the national level. The decision to adopt a shared monetary policy without a banking union would prove to be problematic during the euro crisis, when the interconnectedness of banks posed a systemic threat.

Despite the strictures, the ECB in effect harmonized the cost of borrowing across the euro area through the way it operated its repurchase, or repo, model. Unlike the Fed or the Bank of England, each of which has one government's debt to hold, the ECB at its inception held little government debt of any of the EU member states. Instead, it managed liquidity through bonds, both public and private. Europe's banks largely bought their governments' bonds and they could exchange them at the ECB for cash on a repurchase basis. How the ECB set the terms for the repo and the size of the 'haircut', which described the amount that would be trimmed off the value for purchasing that debt, would dictate the regulatory requirements of the financial markets of the various eurozone countries. A larger haircut would require a financial institution to hold more capital against certain government bonds, so this mechanism would moderate how much of that sort of debt was held in a portfolio.

The Fed imposes different haircuts in the repo market for different types of bonds. The ECB could have similarly set different haircuts for different countries, imposing tougher conditions on the bonds of more indebted nations. But it didn't. Instead, it decided that a single currency meant the same repo terms for everyone, and therefore it generated similar costs of borrowing for all euro area countries.

This had direct implications for Greece. Before the euro, Greece had faced a higher cost of borrowing than Germany, but after Greece joined the single currency, Greek government debt was treated by the ECB no differently from German bonds, or bunds. Lenders followed suit. Greece's debt service costs fell by more than half as a result of adopting the euro. It wasn't just Greece. Portugal, Spain, Ireland and Italy also enjoyed lower costs of borrowing after they adopted the euro.

Despite the fall in borrowing costs, the eurozone countries initially adhered to the Stability and Growth Pact of the Maastricht Treaty, which was an agreement to keep their budget deficits below 3 per cent of GDP. The pact was first violated by two of the core countries, Germany and France, in the early 2000s, although this was not problematic as their cost of borrowing remained low. But when Portugal and Greece quickly followed in the footsteps of the eurozone's two largest economies, the consequences were far more serious.

Despite the high level of government debt of countries such as Greece, which was around 100 per cent of GDP at the time of euro entry, borrowing increased as the cost of both public and private sector loans fell. Cross-border lending in the eurozone grew dramatically after the cost of borrowing was increasingly harmonized within it. And the lending was all in euros, so there was no risk that exchange rate fluctuations would impact the value of loans. The result was a housing boom in Europe that was larger even than that of the US during the early 2000s. In July 2009, Greece informed the Eurogroup of eurozone finance ministers, then headed by Luxembourg's Jean-Claude Juncker, that its budget deficit might exceed 10 per cent of GDP, well above the Stability and Growth Pact's 3 per cent limit. There was a real prospect that Greece would be unable to service its large budget deficit by further borrowing. In October, after a change in government, Greek Prime Minister George Papandreou of the Panhellenic Socialist Movement Party (PASOK) officially informed the EU that, after revising its figures, the country's budget deficit that year would be a staggering 12.7 per cent of GDP. Greece's overall debt-to-GDP ratio, which was already high at around 100 per cent, would jump to 115 per cent.

In 2010 alone, Greece needed to repay €53 billion, but lenders were concerned about its solvency. The country's creditors were foreign bond holders, who tend to be less forgiving than domestic creditors (as seen during Japan's financial crisis examined in Chapter 3). Of Greece's €293 billion of public debt, about €200 billion was owned by institutions outside the EU, with the remainder split between

European banks and pension and insurance funds. The substantial amounts of Greek debt held by European banks created a problem for the entire European banking system.

One solution for a country facing bankruptcy is to restructure its debt, as discussed in the sovereign debt crises in Chapter 1. Ordinarily, a developing country that could not afford to pay its bills would restructure its debt under an IMF programme. Creditors would either be partially paid or repaid in full over a long period of time, either of which meant losses to the lender. Restructuring Greece's debt would entail similar losses for bond holders. But being within the euro area made that usual avenue all the harder, if not impossible, to negotiate, as Greece was soon to discover. Instead, the eurozone focused initially on a financial rescue.

In early 2010, the scale and terms of a bailout were being debated by eurozone leaders. Other countries, such as Portugal, Ireland and Spain, were also struggling with their growing debt burden after growth collapsed following the 2008 global financial crisis. Collectively, foreign bank lending to these countries was around $2.5 trillion. French and German banks, still weakened by the 2008 crisis, were heavily exposed to the peripheral eurozone countries and their governments were concerned about another hit to their balance sheets.

However, that concern was insufficient for Germany's Chancellor Angela Merkel to support a bailout of Greece. Merkel had been instrumental in the crafting of the Treaty of Lisbon, which had strengthened the 'no bailout' clause of the Maastricht Treaty by ruling out any mutualization of debt. In other words, Germany refused to be responsible for Greece's debt. As already mentioned, fiscal policy in the eurozone was not harmonized; it was up to the taxpayers of each country to settle their own government's debt. In theory, all countries used the same interest rate set by the ECB, but each could set its own tax and spending policies accordingly. In practice, it was not so straightforward.

Greece desperately needed its debt to be restructured, but eurozone leaders were concerned that a sovereign debt default could shake confidence in the single currency. Creditors who are not repaid in full might not lend again at favourable rates; if this were to happen in the eurozone, then European banks as well as pensions and insurance funds would suffer, along with the US mutual funds that had invested hundreds of billions of dollars in European financial institutions.

Not all European countries were greatly concerned about creditors' losses. Germany could see the need for lenders to share the pain. Merkel suggested bringing in the IMF, which would usually be involved in any bailout.[5] Merkel's proposal inflamed many, including the French president Nicolas Sarkozy, who said: 'Forget the IMF. The IMF is not for Europe. It's for Africa – it's for Burkina Faso!'[6] But at the 25 March EU summit, she received US backing. The IMF became involved in the rescues of eurozone countries alongside the EU and the ECB, in what became known as the 'troika'. At Merkel's behest, the troika adhered to the Lisbon Treaty rules, which meant that assistance for Greece would be provided on a voluntary basis from individual EU states and coordinated through the Eurogroup. As it was not a bailout, which was not permitted under the Maastricht Treaty, the loans would not be on a concessional basis, i.e. offered at a very low interest rate. Lender countries would lend at market rates and charge fees. And it would be available only if Greece lost access to bond markets. Yet, it was enough, at least for a while, to reassure bond investors. Greece issued €5 billion of long-term debt at just under 7 per cent yield after receiving this backing from Europe and the IMF.

Matters came to a head in April. The credit rating agency Fitch downgraded Greece's creditworthiness and the yields on its benchmark bonds jumped to 7.4 per cent, which is a huge amount for a government to pay to borrow for ten years. Then, on 22 April, Eurostat, the EU statistics agency, announced that Greece's budget deficit had risen to 13.6 per cent of GDP. It didn't help market confidence that Ireland's deficit was even larger, at 14.3 per cent, as a result of rescuing its banks. The euro crisis was in full swing.

The crisis was apparent in bond markets. Governments fund their spending by selling government bonds. The yield on a bond, expressed as a percentage, is what a country has to pay a creditor to borrow money. If bond investors demand a higher yield, it is because they think there is a risk they won't be repaid. An indicator of a country's riskiness is the 'spread', which is the difference in its cost of borrowing as compared with a safe-haven country such as Germany. The difference in yields between Greek and German bonds jumped to 600 basis points, or 6 per cent. Although there is no hard and fast rule, yields exceeding 7 per cent are generally viewed as unsustainable. Yields on Greek benchmark ten-year debt soared to 9 per cent, a rate that would see any amount borrowed double in just eight years, which effectively meant that Greece could no longer borrow from the bond market. The country was running out of money. On 19 May, €8.9 billion was due to its creditors. It would need to turn to the troika for help.

In early May, the troika announced a rescue package of €110 billion, to be dispensed over three years, €80 billion of which would come from the EU and the rest from the IMF. The terms were challenging. Greece had to cut government spending sufficiently to turn its sizeable budget deficit into a surplus – a turnaround of a mind-boggling eighteen percentage points of GDP. Austerity measures included not only cutting public expenditure but the sale of state assets. As it was out of options, Greece accepted the package. While the measure still needed to be approved by individual European parliaments, the ECB nevertheless continued to accept Greek bonds despite the downgrade, providing a lifeline to a Greek banking system reliant upon continuing access to the eurozone central bank for liquidity to keep money flowing in the economy.

The ECB could have done more if it had been set up differently. It did not follow other central banks like the Fed and the Bank of England in undertaking quantitative easing. The US and UK central banks printed cash and bought government bonds and other assets to increase the amount of money in the economy that could be used for investment and boost growth. Almost regardless of why the central banks were doing it, their bond buying was welcomed by financial markets. Central banks supported the bond market by becoming another buyer during turbulent times. It gave bond investors greater confidence since they were buying US and UK government debt alongside the Fed and the Bank of England.

But that was not how the ECB operated. It was prohibited from monetary financing of government debt, so it did not undertake QE until later on, when the crisis worsened. But at this point, investors were underwhelmed by the ECB, especially when its actions were compared to those of the Fed and the Bank of England.

Financial markets and the euro both fell on the news of the Greek bailout. The euro crisis had exposed the limited support from the central bank as well as the lack of a supranational institutional structure to deal quickly with countries that needed rescuing. The credibility of policymaking is one of the enduring lessons of financial crises throughout history; the eurozone was slow to act and struggled to convince the markets that it was equipped to do so, which prolonged the turmoil.

Not only were markets tanking, there was also fear of contagion from the euro crisis spilling over into the fragile global economy that was still reeling from the US sub-prime crisis. Rather unusually, the Americans were at the EU summit in May. The IMF was again involved. It had not only rescued a developed country, Greece, it had also contributed to a new rescue fund for European nations.

On 9 May 2010, the EU fashioned a rescue fund called the European Financial Stability Facility (EFSF). To prevent any pan-European commitment that obliged countries to share each other's debt, individual governments contributed capital to the EFSF with just a small amount from the EU. Thus, the majority of the money (€440 billion) came from European governments while the European Commission contributed just €60 billion and the IMF put in €250 billion. The EFSF would eventually become the European Stability Mechanism (ESM), the permanent rescue fund dubbed Europe's IMF, based in Luxembourg. It is an example of how the very foundation of the euro was altered and strengthened as a result of the challenge posed by the crisis.

Crucially, having a European rescue fund in place was sufficient to persuade ECB President Jean-Claude Trichet that the central bank should be a buyer of last resort. As governments were funding the rescues, the ECB's role would be to maintain financial stability in bond markets and buy debt to do so if necessary.[7]

The ECB's change of stance helped calm the markets, but not for long. By the summer, the Greek deal was again in doubt after its economy had contracted by 4.5 per cent. As unemployment there jumped to over 10 per cent and incomes fell, tax revenues declined. Doubts grew over the bailout's effectiveness, and the spread between Greek and German bonds blew out to 937 basis points, even larger than in the spring. Still, the troika held firm to its rescue plan.

In an attempt to instil confidence, and following the US lead, stress tests on banks were conducted by the European Banking Authority. Commercial bank ledgers were subjected to a scenario that included a double-dip recession and financial market turmoil. The eurozone leaders, concerned that bond investors would not lend to weaker countries if they were not confident about their banking systems, wanted to reassure markets that the banks could withstand a worsening of the euro crisis.

Many European banks' balance sheets were laden with their governments' debt. This was the so-called 'doom loop'. Since yields are inversely related to the price of a bond, if bond yields rose, then the price of bonds would fall. Such a drop in value of their government debt holdings would further weaken bank balance sheets that were still struggling in the aftermath of the 2008 crisis, raising the prospect that banks would need their governments to recapitalize them. To recapitalize the banks, those governments would need to borrow, which would worsen their budget deficits and lead to investors demanding higher yields in bond markets to lend to those countries. If worsening borrowing conditions also led to credit rating agencies lowering the creditworthiness of government debt, that would further worsen banks' balance sheets. The 'doom loop' would spiral downward in a cycle of weak governments dragging down their banks and their banks in turn worsening their governments' position. In the worst-case scenario the government itself could require a rescue, which was what had happened to Ireland. The stress tests attempted to break that loop by requiring banks to hold sufficient capital to withstand a crisis.

But banking was a national matter, and there was no EU equivalent of the US Treasury, which had worked with the Fed to recapitalize American banks during the global financial crisis and restore confidence. The eurozone's efforts fell short due to its institutional structure.

It was Ireland's experience that epitomized not only the 'doom loop' but the inadequacy of the eurozone stress tests. Ireland had guaranteed all of its banks' debts during the 2008 crisis (a measure that, rather ironically, enabled them to pass the stress tests). Confronted with the prospect of the collapse of the entire banking system, Ireland declared that it would rescue the banks. Its budget deficit would soar to 32 per cent of GDP and its debt-to-GDP ratio, which had previously only been 25 per cent, would jump to nearly 100 per cent as it also struggled with the recession. Ireland was in need of a bailout.

Owing to the 2008 financial crisis, Ireland's budget deficit was already high at 14 per cent of GDP. The government had cut public sector pay by up to 10 per cent and benefits had also been reduced. But more austerity was to come under the rescue programme.

One of the issues that the Irish crisis raised was whether shareholders, who had gained from the boom times, should share the losses during the bust: an investor bail-in instead of a taxpayer bailout. This burgeoning debate came to a quick resolution when Angela Merkel met Nicolas Sarkozy in Deauville on 18 October. They were hosting the Russian president, Dmitry Medvedev. After a stroll on the Normandy beach, Merkel and Sarkozy agreed a set of strictures for the eurozone, consulting neither other euro area countries nor the European Central Bank nor the US before doing so. I recall covering the euro crisis at frenetic pace in the Bloomberg TV newsroom, but that day stood out for their announcement that creditors would be bailed in. Private sector involvement would mean bond holders taking haircuts, so incurring losses. This would reduce the amount of taxpayer funds needed to rescue banks and reduce the size of the budget deficit for the countries involved. Merkel and Sarkozy had, in effect, sanctioned that at least some degree of debt restructuring would apply to future euro area bail-outs from 2013. Ironically, though the debate was triggered by the Greek rescue, holders of Greek bonds had been repaid in full from rescue funds.

This development was as momentous as it was sudden. In the post-war period, creditors expected to get their money back when they lent to an advanced economy. As Sarkozy had earlier implied, debt restructuring was associated with developing countries. Yet the long-simmering debate over debt restructuring in the eurozone was ended without warning. Although, with the extensive daily discussions on Bloomberg TV and elsewhere on financial channels, markets had already contemplated that bail-ins were coming, which helped to soften the shock.

It wasn't the only major decision announced by Merkel and Sarkozy without consultation. The pair also revamped the euro area's stance on budget deficits to mirror that of Germany. They agreed that the Stability and Growth Pact, which was intended to maintain fiscal discipline but struggled to do so from the start, would be overhauled. If a euro area country ran a deficit exceeding 3 per cent of GDP, or debt over 60 per cent of GDP, there would be sanctions that included withdrawal of voting rights, though these would be imposed only by a qualified majority vote.

All this happened while Ireland was being rescued, but too late to be of use, since the Merkel–Sarkozy pact applied to bail-ins only from 2013. Instead, Ireland reached an agreement with the troika on 28 November that did not include private sector involvement. The rescue totalled €85 billion, most of which came from the troika (€63.5 billion) but which also involved loans from other EU members including the UK. On 7 December, Ireland's budget saw another round of austerity measures totalling €6 billion. A bail-in whereby the banks' shareholders accepted a haircut and shared the losses would have reduced the spending cuts.

Ireland became the second euro area country in crisis to be rescued.

Despite the bailouts, the cost of insuring European banks against default surged. Markets were doubtful that the euro crisis could be contained by individual country rescues and remained concerned about widespread European bank failures due to the interconnectedness of bank lending across the euro area.

In March 2011 Portugal's prime minister, José Sócrates, stepped down after failing to pass his budget. A week later, neighbouring Spain's prime minister, José Luis Rodríguez Zapatero, announced that he would not run for re-election so he could focus on Spain's budgetary pressures. In the midst of the euro crisis, governments were cutting spending to try to reduce their budget deficits, ostensibly to avoid being identified as un-creditworthy by markets. These cutbacks in spending were occurring while unemployment had risen above 10 per cent in the euro area. They were also concerned about 'bond vigilantes' who might sell off the bonds of 'struggling' countries, which would restrict their borrowing potential.

In spite of its efforts, on 7 April 2011 Portugal became the third euro area country that needed to be rescued. Since joining the euro, Portugal, like other peripheral countries, had experienced capital inflows that were lent to its companies despite slow economic growth. This increased Portugal's indebtedness, which was 69 per cent of GDP in 2008, above the 60 per cent threshold acceptable for EU countries. As the 2009 great recession hit, its budget deficit grew to 12 per cent of GDP, which was considerably above the Stability and Growth Pact's 3 per cent limit.

As investors fretted about which eurozone countries might struggle to repay their debts, Portugal was in their sights, not least because of its large banking sector. The assets of its three largest banks were equivalent to more than 50 per cent of Portugal's GDP.[8] It was doubtful that the country could afford to rescue them should they fail. Moreover, Portuguese banks also suffered from the 'doom loop'. They held substantial amounts of government debt, around a quarter of their assets, which made them vulnerable to the Portuguese government's rising deficits. Thus, Portugal's yields spiked as bond investors sold off its government bonds, and it was forced to seek a rescue from the troika.

Even as more countries were entering troika programmes, the first eurozone nation to be rescued was experiencing resistance, its economy tanking under the troika's strict terms. On 25 May 2011, Syntagma Square in Athens was occupied by protesters demonstrating against the most recent spending cuts. It wasn't until a month later that the square was cleared after clashes with police.

Greece's debt was not falling as expected; cutting public demand was not stimulating private demand. It soon became clear that Greece was not in a position to return to the markets in 2012. Instead, more help was needed.

While Portugal's rescue was being finalized, Greece was requesting a re-profiling of its debt. It was essentially asking for a restructuring of debt not through a haircut that would reduce the amount to be repaid, but via an extension of the repayment period. The newly minted EFSF, which was the official vehicle that bailed out Ireland and Portugal, could not help. Moreover, it was untested and funded voluntarily. The ECB was already working to stabilize the bond market by buying debt that investors wanted to sell on the secondary market. By early 2011, it owned 15 per cent of Greek debt, which was rated below investment grade. ECB President Jean-Claude Trichet was not keen on debt restructuring as it might cause further shock to the markets.[9]

The ECB also finally introduced different levels of haircut on repos, reflecting the credit status of the countries involved. The ECB's lack of differentiation before the crisis contributed to a convergence in borrowing costs for eurozone countries. This latest move placed the onus firmly on individual countries to maintain the confidence of bond markets. Investors immediately shunned the bonds of the periphery and bought debt issued by the core countries. German bunds were seeing yields fall to close to zero while the spreads with peripheral euro area countries were shooting up.

★

Speculation was growing over the viability of the euro itself. There was much talk of 'Grexit' – the departure of Greece from the eurozone – and eurozone leaders felt that if one country were to leave it would open the door to the disintegration of the entire currency. If Grexit occurred, might other indebted countries follow them through the door? Such contagion, or a cascading loss of confidence, posed an existential crisis for the euro. It's why Grexit was not an option in the view of the eurozone leaders. It led to the eurozone being viewed like 'Hotel California'. The 1976 Eagles' classic includes the lyrics, 'You can check out any time you like. But you can never leave.'

The risk of a banking crisis was also rising because of the 'doom loop'. It highlighted the lack of a banking union in the euro area to underpin the large amount of cross-border exposure, particularly of core-country banks to the smaller, struggling economies. As a result, US money markets, which had been an important source of liquidity for European banks, cut back on lending, slashing their exposure by a mighty 45 per cent in 2011,[10] adding to the pressure on European banks.

The European Council held an emergency meeting on 21 July, but bank recapitalization, which was what the markets were waiting for, was not on the agenda. However, further support for Greece was agreed. It would receive another €109 billion, which was to support it through 2014. Importantly, debt restructuring was also agreed by the ECB, albeit reluctantly. Greece would get more time to repay its debt and at a lower annual interest rate of 3.5 per cent. In return, the ECB would be indemnified for any potential losses. Greek banks would be recapitalized using funds provided by the troika. Notably, there would be private sector involvement, so there would be hair-cuts for debt holders. The eurozone was keen to stress that these measures would be applied only to Greece, because it was insolvent. By contrast, the other rescued countries were deemed to be in need of financial support only. In other words, all other euro area countries were expected to repay both their existing debts and any supporting funds they received in full.

To secure the ECB's support, the EFSF was allowed to buy bonds to reduce the pressure on the central bank. Together, these two entities would try to reduce contagion stemming from the troubles of the periphery that was affecting banks and raising borrowing costs for core countries. By becoming buyers in the bond market, they were aiming to fend off a wider euro area debt sell-off. The EFSF would also be able to establish credit lines for countries not in a rescue programme, such as Spain and Italy. This precautionary credit line approach was one that had been adopted by the IMF during the 2008 global financial crisis to help stabilize economies such as Mexico.

The terms of the private sector involvement had been worked out with the banks via the Institute of International Finance, the trade body for global financial services firms. The agreed haircut for Greece's creditors was a substantial 21 per cent. Even so, Greece would still have a debt level of some 143 per cent of GDP. It was doubtful whether that would be sustainable, but with the ECB's backing, the summer ended with some calm.

It wasn't to last. By September, the costs of avoiding default for Italy and Spain were increasing, reflecting the market's view that this was a growing risk despite ECB support via bond buying. The Bundestag's delay in approving the EFSF's bond market stabilization fund until 29 September, made markets nervous that Germany was not committed to bond buying. It didn't help that Jens Weidmann, the head of the Bundesbank and a former Merkel adviser, had publicly decried it. The ECB's chief economist and German member of the Executive Council, Jürgen Stark, went even further and resigned. The bond markets remained unconvinced.

At the end of September, at the annual IMF meeting in Washington, DC, US Treasury Secretary Tim Geithner warned of a 'cascading default, bank runs and catastrophic risk' if Europe failed to coordinate a collective response that would backstop the markets.[11] His warning was prescient. Within a fortnight there was a bank run on the Franco-Belgian bank Dexia. Despite passing the European Banking Authority's stress test over the summer, just like the Irish banks before their bailouts, Dexia's balance sheet had been severely weakened by the losses stemming from the restructuring of Greek debt. It also failed to hold sufficient liquidity. Dexia was rescued jointly by France and Belgium, which added to those countries' growing budget deficits, once again highlighting the weakness of the euro area institutional structure that lacked a banking union.

The eurozone finally started to contemplate the need for bank recapitalization at its 23 October meeting. To support countries, leaders further expanded the capacity of the EFSF to around €1.2 trillion by leveraging its existing resources and providing insurance to cover losses on private securities instead of directly offering loans. Despite having passed the measure only a month ago, the Bundestag was told by Merkel that it was not enough. The revision was passed by the German parliament on 25 October after Germany's liability was limited to €211 billion.

A day later, European leaders gathered again in Brussels to agree a third rescue package for Greece, which included more debt restructuring. The new Greek package included another €130 billion as well as a 50 per cent haircut on existing debt holders. Altogether, Greece was to receive €240 billion of emergency loans from the troika, which was equal to more than 100 per cent of Greek GDP. Even with this amount, Greece would need to undertake further measures to bring its debt to below 120 per cent of GDP.

With debt restructuring for Greece, recapitalization of banks and a sizeable EFSF to backstop the crisis, it seemed in late 2011 that the eurozone finally had the ingredients to stabilize the situation. Despite appearances, however, the euro crisis was far from over.

Unemployment had now reached nearly 20 per cent in Greece. Anti-austerity demonstrations continued to break out in the capital following the terms of the latest troika programme. The embattled prime minister, George Papandreou, unexpectedly called a referendum on the EU's rescue plan. What had been painstakingly negotiated and passed by European parliaments would now fall under the direct scrutiny of the Greek people. If the referendum failed and the rescue package was rejected, would Greece default? Would it drag down European banks, which were still shaky? Crucially, would a Greece unwilling to accept the troika's terms have to leave the euro area? That could spark a wave of exits from countries dissatisfied with their bail-out conditions and potentially see the end of the eurozone.

The bond markets were worried, and sold off euro area debt. Their nervousness was not limited to Greece. Investors also fled from the debt of the third-largest economy in the euro area, Italy, raising yields on Italian ten-year bonds to over 6 per cent. That was worryingly close to the 7 per cent level that had triggered rescues of other euro area countries. Italian prime minister Silvio Berlusconi let it be known that he refused a precautionary line of credit of €80 billion from the IMF, although did agree to IMF monitoring.[12] His acknowledgement that Italy was on the IMF's watch list was hardly reassuring to markets.

The eurozone leaders were prompted into action. Germany and France wanted to make the referendum not about the Greek rescue package but an in/out decision about eurozone membership. At a press conference in Cannes during the G20 meeting in the first week of November, Merkel and Sarkozy announced that there could be only one question in any Greek referendum. Sarkozy said: 'It's clear that question has to be on the European future of Greece: does Greece want to stay in the euro? We hope it does, but it's up to Greek people to pronounce on that.'[13] He added that the rules must be adhered to, prioritizing the single currency's stability over Greece's membership of it: 'We would rather achieve a stabilization of the euro with Greece than without Greece, but this goal of stabilizing the euro is more important.'[14] The prospect of the currency union's break-up being openly acknowledged alongside Italy's woes led to a broad market sell-off. Italy's benchmark yields exceeded 7 per cent and Greece's shot up to an unprecedented 33 per cent.

The stakes were high. Soon thereafter, Papandreou was replaced as PM by Lucas Papademos, a US-trained economist and former ECB vice-president. Just a week or so later, Berlusconi lost a vote of no confidence and resigned. Mario Monti was appointed by the Italian president to replace him. Like Papademos, Monti was an academic economist, and a former European Commissioner for the Internal Market as well as for Competition. As he did not hold elected office, he was given the honorary position of 'life senator' in order to assume the premiership. Even though there were now two technocrats who were trained economists at the helm, markets remained nervous. If the ECB would not act as a buyer of government bonds except on the secondary market, then, in their view, the euro area required its rescue fund, the EFSF, to be that backstop. But the EFSF needed more firepower if it were to assume that role. This would be another step towards further European integration, which depended on Germany once again. This dilemma was captured by former deputy finance minister Jörg Asmussen, who had taken up the German seat on the ECB Executive Council: 'Either you do what is right for Europe and they crucify you in Germany or . . . you ruin Europe.'[15]

The next push came from Brussels. Herman Van Rompuy, the former Belgian PM who became the first full-time president of the European Council, proposed creating a permanent rescue fund for the euro area, which meant transforming the EFSF. He proposed instead a European Stability Mechanism, which would receive more funding from euro governments and be empowered to break the 'doom loop' by recapitalizing banks directly. This would mean that individual countries would not be felled by rescuing their banks, as had happened in Ireland. But that would mean sharing fiscal obligations among eurozone countries, a move that was resisted by Germany. For German taxpayers to take on the liabilities of other countries was a step beyond what was palatable to the Bundestag. If this was bold, then Van Rompuy's additional call for a new 'eurobond' would certainly take it over the line.

Eurobonds would consist of joint issuance of debt by the eurozone, which would pool liabilities of countries that used the euro. Eurobonds had the potential to make the bond market in the euro area as deep and liquid as that for US Treasurys. But there was a crucial difference: in the eurozone, fiscal policy was separate while monetary policy was shared. In the US, the federal government collected tax revenues and disbursed funds in a federal system that covered all fifty states. Joint issuance of debt would be another step towards greater European integration since the sharing of liabilities was likely to increase calls for oversight of fiscal policy at the eurozone level.

Van Rompuy envisaged that these measures could be passed as secondary legislation, which fell far short of all euro countries needing to agree to treaty change, making this proposal even more unpalatable to Merkel. At this tense time, the UK asked for an opt-out from a proposed EU financial transactions tax. When the request was opposed by Sarkozy and there was no support from Merkel or others, British prime minister David Cameron said that he would block any steps towards closer European integration. Cameron was facing calls from Eurosceptic members of his party who wanted the UK to leave the EU, let alone become more involved in the ongoing euro crisis. This pressure would ultimately lead to Cameron calling the 2016 referendum that was to take the UK out of the EU.

The deal that was agreed included neither eurobonds nor shared bank recapitalization nor an increase in the firepower of the EFSF/ESM. Merkel did concede that the new ESM would be able to intervene in secondary bond markets in return for the adoption of a 'fiscal compact'. This new agreement among the euro countries limited budget deficits to just 0.5 per cent of GDP, and it would be enforced through constitutional amendment and the European Court of Justice. Any country that had a deficit above 3 per cent would be subject to automatic financial sanctions unless a qualified majority of states overruled them. If government debt exceeded 60 per cent of GDP, then the country had to take measures to reduce it. This was essentially Germany's 'debt brake' (*Schuldenbremse*) that enshrined a balanced budget requirement in its constitution so the German economy would not ordinarily run a deficit of more than 0.35 per cent of GDP. Germany had wanted greater fiscal discipline and oversight of member states, and the fiscal compact achieved that aim in return for supporting bond buying.

★

On 1 November 2011, former Bank of Italy governor Mario Draghi became president of the ECB. Draghi had studied at the Massachusetts Institute of Technology, where he earned a PhD in economics at the same time as Fed chairman and Nobel laureate Ben Bernanke and Greek PM Lucas Papademos. To complete the network, Bernanke had shared an office with Bank of England governor Mervyn King.[16]

Later that month, there was a reunion of sorts. Major central banks – the Fed, ECB, Bank of England, Bank of Japan, Bank of Canada and the Swiss National Bank – reopened the dollar swap lines that had been so crucial in 2008 with a lower rate of interest. During the global financial crisis, foreign banks needed to access US dollars to offer their companies when markets were in turmoil. European banks were in this position once again, since there was still no resolution to the euro crisis in sight despite multiple rounds of deliberations.

The ECB once again offered cheap liquidity to eurozone banks. In October, a new long-term refinancing operation provided loans of three years that not only were at cheap rates but also required lower-quality collateral. By the beginning of 2012, 800 banks had taken up half a billion euros of long-term funding. Unsurprisingly, 65 per cent of the banks were from Italy, Spain, Ireland and Greece. The cheap money helped support bond markets as banks profited from buying sovereign debt and earning the difference between the interest rate of 1 per cent charged by the ECB and the higher yields of peripheral countries' bonds. This support was even more important as 2012 got off to a rocky start.

In January, the credit rating agency S&P downgraded seven euro countries, including Portugal, which lost its investment-grade credit rating and was given junk status. Just four eurozone countries held a top AAA rating (Finland, Germany, Luxembourg, the Netherlands) after France and Austria lost theirs. S&P had downgraded the US the previous August after Congress failed to increase the country's debt ceiling until the eleventh hour, which raised the spectre of the US missing interest payments on its debt. The number of top-rated sovereign bonds was decreasing rapidly.

In this tense context, the eurozone declared it had a trillion dollar firewall in February. By raising the EFSF/ESM lending ceiling to €700 billion and counting the €130 billion that had already been given to Greece, euro area leaders could say that they had a backstop of a significant sounding $1 trillion after conversion. But there was no appetite for more funds for Greece, even though its economy had contracted for a third consecutive year, making its level of debt even more unsustainable. Instead, eurozone leaders worked out a further agreement with bond holders of Greek debt. These creditors agreed to take a bigger haircut: 53.5 per cent, which was up from the 50 per cent that had been agreed just the previous October. The remaining Greek debt would then be exchanged for EFSF-backed debt at concessionary rates, which was more secure since it was backed by the eurozone.

By April, the deal was done. It was the largest-ever restructuring of debt for a sovereign nation. Greek creditors agreed to be repaid €107 billion less than they had lent. With the extended repayment timeframe, it meant that there was effectively a 65 per cent haircut on Greek bonds. In December 2012, there was a buyback of the recently issued long-dated bonds. Private creditors took further losses. But the ECB did not. It was exempt from the restructuring. As a result, Greece's debt declined from €350 billion to €285 billion, a 19 per cent reduction. Importantly, the numerous deals also changed whom Greece's creditors were: 80 per cent of its debt was now owed to the EFSF, the ECB and the IMF.

None the less, the IMF's fears still came to pass. The bulk of the money lent to Greece went towards debt repayment. Just 11 per cent of the rescue funds was used to reduce Greece's sizeable budget deficit, illustrating why the IMF would normally not lend to insolvent nations, only to those experiencing a liquidity crisis. Greece was an exception due to the systemic nature of the euro crisis. The collapse of a single member country could have derailed the euro area; contagion from Greek woes might have seen bond markets shunning peripheral eurozone countries and putting European banks at risk owing to the 'doom loop' between banks and their home nations.

Greece's economic circumstances were dire. Before the crisis, its GDP was €240 billion. In 2012, it had shrunk to €191 billion, which made its debt-to-GDP ratio even more unsustainable as the denominator shrank so rapidly. The smaller economy meant unemployment shot up; a staggering one in four Greeks were out of work. It was far worse for young Greeks, of whom an estimated half were unemployed. Unsurprisingly, the May elections saw a collapse of the vote for the government of the PASOK party. Given the miserable circumstances, Grexit was still in the air just as the IMF made a significant revision to its view of austerity.

The IMF revised its assessment of the impact of budget cuts. It had thought that the fiscal multiplier was around 0.5, but now believed that the multiplier was larger than 1.0. So, cutting public spending by €1 would contract GDP by more than €1. It was evident that austerity undertaken by Greece as well as other countries was shrinking their economies as there was no offsetting increase in private spending, which is what a fiscal multiplier of less than 1.0 implied. That dramatically changed the thinking on austerity. But this came late in the day for the euro crisis.

Spain was the next economy in jeopardy owing to its housing bubble. Over 80 per cent of Spaniards owned their homes and many believed in an ever-rising real-estate market. After a decade of heady growth, house prices collapsed by 37 per cent. Hundreds of new houses and apartments went unsold and sat empty. Developers lost their shirts and dragged down the economy with them. More than one in five people lost their jobs, many in the construction sector. Adding to the misery, homeowners remained responsible for their mortgage debt even after their homes were repossessed when they defaulted on payments.[17]

The real-estate boom wasn't fuelled by either large or foreign banks but by Spain's regional mortgage lenders, the *cajas*. The *cajas* had provided around half of all credit in Spain and their lending rapidly grew to account for a staggering 40 per cent of the nation's GDP by 2009.[18] In 2010, during the first phase of the euro crisis, the number of *cajas* had been consolidated from forty-six to seventeen, and their bad loans were taken off their books by the government and put into a 'bad bank', Bankia/BFA. Bankia's balance sheet was huge. At €328 billion, it was equivalent to around 30 per cent of Spanish GDP. Spain attempted to sell shares in Bankia, but investors weren't interested. By early 2012, despite having liquidity support from the ECB, Spanish banks needed recapitalization. Bankia announced in May that it also needed €19 billion. With the banks in trouble, it led to markets selling Spanish government debt. Yields on ten-year benchmark bonds shot up towards the worrying 7 per cent level that had led to bailouts for other eurozone states.

On 25 June, Spain requested €100 billion from the eurozone to recapitalize its banks. The next day, European Commission president José Manuel Barroso, ECB president Mario Draghi, Eurogroup president Jean-Claude Juncker and European Council president Herman Van Rompuy proposed a banking union. It would include a joint crisis fund to recapitalize banks directly.

This approach would avoid lending the money to Spain itself, which would lead to its budget deficit ballooning, as Ireland's had when it borrowed monies in order to bail out its banks. What was needed was a European fund that would directly recapitalize the banks to break the 'doom loop', so that bailing out Spain's banks would not precipitate the need for a rescue of the country as well. The eurozone agreed a procedure different from the one it had used for Ireland. Germany had little choice but to agree, given Spain's importance as the fourth-largest economy in the euro area.

On 28 June, the European Council approved the creation of the banking union that would break the 'doom loop'. The ESM was also revamped. So long as countries were in compliance with the fiscal compact, they could seek the support of the ESM in stabilizing financial markets without troika oversight. A European IMF was born. The European leaders also announced a growth pact for Europe. To boost economic growth, which bond investors were increasingly looking for, the growth pact included €130 billion of investments and tax breaks. Fiscal discipline was one thing; not growing, and therefore shrinking the denominator, was not desirable when markets were looking for stable debt-to-GDP ratios. The problem for Spain, though, was that it wasn't close to meeting the 3 per cent of GDP deficit rule. Its budget deficit was 11.2 per cent, and it was confronted with regional governments asking for help. As a result, bond markets sold off Spanish debt. On 23 July, Spain's benchmark ten-year bond yield jumped above the symbolic 7 per cent level.

As the euro crisis escalated, ECB president Mario Draghi gave his 'whatever it takes' speech. At a Global Investment Conference at London's Lancaster House on 26 July at the start of the 2012 Olympics, he said:

> When people talk about the fragility of the euro and the increasing fragility of the euro, and perhaps the crisis of the euro, very often non-euro area member states or leaders, underestimate the amount of political capital that has been invested in the euro. And so we view this, and I do not think we are unbiased observers, we think the euro is irreversible . . . Within our mandate, the ECB is ready to do whatever it takes to preserve the euro. And believe me, it will be enough.[19]

It was this phrase, 'whatever it takes', that signalled the end of the acute phase of the euro crisis. I was at Lancaster House covering the euro crisis for Bloomberg TV, and the impact of that speech was seen immediately in calmer financial markets. After the speech, bond yields started to come down. Markets, generally speaking, do not bet against a central bank. The ECB was almost an exception due to its rather unusual set-up. Unlike the Fed or the Bank of England, the ECB was constrained in deploying its massive firepower. But when Draghi said that it would do 'whatever it takes', the markets believed him.

The intent was clear, although the details were a little vague. US Treasury Secretary Timothy Geithner visited the ECB afterwards and observed of Draghi's speech: '[H]e decided to add to his remarks, and off-the-cuff basically made a bunch of statements like "we'll do whatever it takes". Ridiculous . . . totally impromptu . . . Draghi at this point, he had no plan. He had made this sort of naked statement.'[20]

Nevertheless, Merkel, Monti and the newly elected French president, François Hollande, issued a joint statement backing the irreversibility of the euro. The Bundesbank was against the idea of the ECB stabilizing bond markets and cast the sole vote against Draghi's new emergency bond-buying programme, Outright Monetary Transactions, at the ECB Governing Council's September meeting. But Merkel and her finance minister, Wolfgang Schäuble, backed Draghi. The risk of Spain itself needing a rescue could precipitate the break-up of the euro if its fourth-largest economy was shut out of markets. Markets could come for its highly indebted third-largest economy, Italy, next; even France wasn't safe.

Therefore, the ECB became the lender of last resort, a role until then played by other central banks. But it was a conditional role. Outright Monetary Transactions would operate to stabilize a country's debt only if it was already subject to an ESM rescue programme. In the end, the measure was never used in the euro crisis. But, as Draghi said, its existence was enough.

Even now, the crisis was not over.

In the summer of 2012, Cyprus became the fifth euro-area country to request a rescue from the eurozone. It had an outsized banking sector, some six and a half times the size of its economy, which was in crisis owing to its holdings of Greek debt. The write-down of Greek debt led to more than €4 billion of losses for banks in Cyprus. To give context, that's more than 22 per cent of Cypriot GDP. Cypriot banks held large amounts of deposits from Russians and other foreigners, which made the ECB reluctant to assist them because most of the benefits would have gone to non-residents.

It took until March 2013 to agree the terms. By this point, the eurozone had pivoted to rescuing the banking system directly from the ESM. Despite the reservations of the ECB, the €10 billion Cypriot bailout was the first full rescue package by the ESM, though the IMF contributed €1 billion to the total.

Rather unusually, the bailout inflicted losses on deposit holders. In addition to the usual measures around austere public finances and downsizing the banking system, Cyprus also placed a tax of 6.75 per cent on all deposits over the deposit insurance limit of €100,000. This 'one-time' levy gave depositors bank stock equal to whatever they paid in taxes. Needless to say, it was challenging to implement since foreigners would prefer to withdraw their deposits than lose nearly 7 per cent of their money. Cyprus had to impose capital controls to prevent money from leaving its borders to avoid this levy, becoming the first European country to deploy capital controls in the modern era. (Capital controls have been used in emerging economies, though sparingly, since they can discourage future investors worried about not being able to get their money out. However, as seen in Malaysia during the Asian financial crisis (Chapter 1), capital controls can moderate destabilizing capital flight. Some form of capital control has even been accepted by the IMF as a tool to be used when facing a systemic crisis.[21]) Creditors also suffered losses since the eurozone was now deploying bail-in measures to reduce the amount of taxpayer funds used in bailing out countries.

Today, the ESM views the Cyprus rescue as a paradigm shift towards bail-ins. A legacy from the euro crisis is the introduction of regulatory capital instruments such as contingent convertibles or CoCos – debt that converts into equity or stock. They are designed to absorb losses during a period of financial stress, so the bank's capital position can be strengthened at a time when lenders may be reluctant to lend. At the global level, bail-in measures have also been applied to systemically important financial institutions, that is, those banks whose failure could lead to a breakdown of the entire financial system. That line was crossed when the euro crisis led to haircuts for creditors, so this more transparent regime is now embedded in regulation for not only European but also other important banks.

The acute phase of the euro crisis may have ended by 2012–13, but the economic consequences lingered on, for Greece in particular. In 2015, Greece was struggling in its sixth consecutive year of recession. Its economy was more than 25 per cent smaller than it had been in

2008, unemployment was still at 25 per cent, roughly a quarter of households lived in poverty and around 100,000 businesses had shut down. In light of the bleak economic circumstances, Greek bond yields began to rise again to unsustainable levels, breaching 8 per cent. But even when Greek bond yields spiked to 26 per cent, the sell-off was contained to Greece. Other eurozone bond yields were stabilized by the ECB, but Greece continued to struggle under the weight of its debt. With contagion now off the table, eurozone leaders were even willing to consider Greece leaving the eurozone or taking a five-year 'time out', as German finance minister Wolfgang Schäuble termed it, in order to restructure its debt and receive aid.[22]

Greece eventually started growing again in 2017 and remains in the euro area due to both its privatization programme that attracted investment and a return of tourism. But, over a decade on, its economy still has not recovered to the level before its 2010 rescue. The other rescued eurozone countries have done better, a key difference being that they did not have the unsustainable debt burden of Greece. Nevertheless, their prime ministers all soon found themselves out of office due to the euro crisis, a fate known as 'Juncker's curse' after the longstanding head of the Eurogroup, Jean-Claude Juncker, who famously stated: 'We all know what to do, but we don't know how to get re-elected once we have done it.'[23]

The crisis began with too much debt that hit European banks at a time when they were still recovering from the 2008 global financial crisis. Although the debt was in different forms – housing in Ireland and Spain, government debt in Greece and Portugal, banks in Cyprus – the result was the same. These countries needed bailouts in order to cope with unsustainable debt levels caused by euphoria after the adoption of the euro.

But what was evident in the euro crisis was that the single currency lacked the very institutions that would imbue creditors with confidence that the euro would survive a systemic financial crisis. Unlike other major central banks, the European Central Bank was not a lender of last resort. The lack of cross-border banking institutions was also problematic, since liabilities crossed borders easily as free-moving capital – one of the four freedoms that defined the EU single market. But there was inadequate cross-border supervision, and the assertion of control by the eurozone also meant that a country such as Greece could not be solely rescued by the IMF. Instead, the 'troika' of the EU, ECB and IMF meant that there was a great deal of decision-making in the hands of Germany in particular, but also France and other eurozone countries over the rescue conditions, which added political strife to a volatile economic crisis.

But lessons were learned during this period, particularly the importance of institutions and credibility when it comes to weathering a crisis. Unlike the financial crashes that came before, to address this crisis a whole set of new institutions and programmes were created, which has transformed the foundations of the single currency.

The government bond-buying programme has made the ECB into a conditional lender of last resort. Banking regulations now include bail-ins, so creditors will suffer losses during a rescue as well as taxpayers. The euro crisis also led to further European integration in the form of a banking union, the ESM (European IMF) and a fiscal compact that bound more closely together the fiscal policies of the euro countries that had previously shared only monetary policy. There are also moves ongoing towards a capital markets union.

The ESM was established as a firewall for the euro area. It also limits to some extent the politics of rescues, at least more so than when the decisions were taken solely by European countries when such a body did not exist. Also, the new single supervisory mechanism of the ECB was set up to reach across eurozone borders and back up the verdicts from its bank stress tests. These measures, particularly the new mandate of the ECB to buy government bonds, were credible enough to stem the crisis.

Although it was certainly an economic crisis, threatening the very existence of the currency, the euro crisis of 2010 was also one in which politics determined its course. This crisis is therefore rather different from those preceding it. Nevertheless, it shares the key elements of euphoria and credibility. The eurozone's lack of institutions equipped to deal with a systemic financial crisis was starkly evident; but the creation of a number of such institutions and new policies appears to have repaired the credibility of the eurozone and ended the crisis. While the debates about 'ever closer Europe' continue, where the euro heads from here will depend on its still-evolving structure.

# 7 The Covid-19 Crash of 2020

The Covid-19 pandemic was the first fully global crisis since the Second World War.[1] Tragically, 1.8 million people lost their lives and around 80 million were infected around the world in the first year alone, according to the World Health Organization (WHO). The pandemic affected every continent on earth, even Antarctica.

The Covid-19 crisis differs from most because it is a crash caused by a lockdown introduced to protect public health. Although there was euphoria in the lead-up to the pandemic, debt wasn't the trigger for the crash. A decade of cheap money since the 2008 global financial crisis had fuelled numerous record highs for stock markets, notably in the US. When economic activity came to a sudden stop, stock markets registered their worst one-day falls in history. Nine of the ten biggest one-day drops of the Dow Jones Industrial Average of US blue-chip stocks occurred during the pandemic crash. In terms of both market falls and economic misery, the Covid-19 crisis was a great crash and a rare one.

There was perhaps one precedent: the great influenza pandemic of 1918, otherwise known as the Spanish flu. The name comes not from where the virus originated but because Spain was a neutral country during a time of wartime press censorship. A number of famous people died from Spanish flu, including sociologist Max Weber, artist Gustav Klimt and Frederick Trump, the grandfather of the future US president. Survivors included the great economist Friedrich Hayek, entrepreneur Walt Disney and US President Woodrow Wilson.[2]

The Spanish flu afflicted a third of the world's population, and had a significant economic impact. Since 1870, the Spanish flu outbreak ranks behind only the Great Depression of the 1930s and the two world wars.[3] The global recession of 1917–21 is estimated to have reduced GDP per capita and consumption of the typical country by

6 per cent and 8.1 per cent, respectively. By comparison, the First World War is associated with an 8.4 per cent drop in GDP per capita and 9.9 per cent fall in consumption.

The first wave of the great influenza pandemic was in the spring of 1918, the second from September 1918 to January 1919 and the third from February 1919 to the end of that year. Some countries experienced a fourth wave, in 1920.[4] A century later, the effects of Covid-19 would follow a similar wave-like pattern.

On 31 December 2019, China alerted the WHO to the spread of a novel coronavirus for which there was no vaccine. Ground zero of the pandemic was the city of Wuhan, whose 11 million inhabitants were placed under quarantine by the Chinese government. The focus of world leaders was the transmission rate of the virus (R). An R of 1 means that, on average, every infected person infects one other person. Anything above this number will lead to rapid spread as the number of victims grows exponentially. As the R number increased and waves of infection gripped entire nations, lockdowns would be introduced to attempt to reduce it to below 1.

On 30 January 2020, the WHO declared a global public-health emergency, only the sixth time it had ever done so. The virus was spreading quickly from China to the rest of Asia, Europe, the Middle East and North America. On 11 February, the WHO named the disease 'Covid-19', a contraction of 'coronavirus disease 2019'. That same day, the official global death toll exceeded 1,000, having quickly surpassed the 774 deaths that occurred during the entirety of the SARS epidemic that began in Asia in February 2003.[5]

With deaths mounting and the speed of transmission increasing, countries imposed restrictive measures and travel bans to try to contain this deadly disease. China's lockdowns and travel restrictions were extended to cover around 760 million people, more than half of its population. On 25 February, San Francisco became the first US city to declare a state of emergency. Later that month, Switzerland banned public gatherings of more than 1,000 people.

Restrictions continued to ramp up around the world. On 6 March, the US Centers for Disease Control and Prevention urged anyone over sixty years of age to stay indoors. That month, several countries closed all their schools and universities, disrupting the education of about a fifth of students around the world.[6]

On 11 March, 'the day everything changed',[7] the WHO upgraded Covid-19 to a global pandemic. Its director-general, Dr Tedros Adhanom Ghebreyesus, said: '[W]e are deeply concerned both by the alarming levels of spread and severity, and by the alarming levels of inaction.'[8] On 9 March, Italy, which had been at the centre of infections in Europe, became the first European country to impose a national lockdown.

That same day, the director of the US National Institute of Allergy and Infectious Diseases, Dr Anthony Fauci, who became a familiar face on TV and computer screens, appeared before Congress after more than 1,000 people in forty of the fifty states had been infected. He warned, 'Bottom line, it's going to get worse.'[9]

Realizing that restrictive measures were insufficient, more countries implemented nationwide lockdowns and shut their borders. On 18 March, Lebanon announced a national lockdown. Greece did the same on 22 March, followed a day later by the UK. By 26 March, nearly one-third of the world's population was locked down.[10]

On 12 March 2020, the day after the WHO declared a global pandemic, stock markets, which had been declining since February, crashed. The Dow Jones Industrial Average of US blue-chip stocks fell by 10 per cent, reversing the longest bull market in history, which had started on 11 March 2009 and ended precisely eleven years later. The US benchmark S&P 500 fell into its fastest bear market on record, dropping by 20 per cent in two days. From their February peaks to the troughs on 23 March, both US benchmarks lost one-third of their value. In a highly unusual move, the New York Stock Exchange suspended trading several times in an attempt to halt the collapse.

Although the size and duration of a market fluctuation can and do vary greatly, the speed and depth of the Covid-19 crash were remarkable. Even against historical comparators, the initial 31.7 per cent decline set records: Spanish flu was estimated to have led to a 26 per cent drop in the return to shares; major wars are typically associated with a 19 per cent decline.[11] The rebound in share values was also rapid and, within a week, markets were up by around 10 per cent as investors reacted positively to the voluminous policies that had been swiftly enacted to support the world's economies. But it was not to last. Markets soon declined again as the number of national lockdowns grew.

The first three months of 2020 saw global stock markets experience their worst quarter since the height of the 2008 crisis. All major US indices had fallen into bear market (down 20 per cent) or correction (down 10 per cent) territory. The picture was equally bad in Europe. The Euro STOXX 600 was down more than 23 per cent. Germany's benchmark DAX index 25 per cent, France's CAC 40 more than 26 per cent, Italy's MIB more than 27 per cent and Spain's IBEX nearly 29 per cent. In London, the FTSE 100 fell by more than 25 per cent, its worst performance since the 1987 stock market crash.

The collapse was not limited to stocks: commodity prices also nosedived when economies shut down. Oil prices fell by more than half in March as lockdowns slashed demand. On 20 April, the benchmark US oil-price, West Texas Intermediate (WTI), crashed into negative territory for the first time ever. Demand for oil had shrunk, and without enough storage space for the surplus it traded as low as minus $40.32 per barrel. As recently as January, Brent Crude, the international marker, had traded above $65 per barrel. It now fell to $15.98, its lowest point since 1999. Prices had dropped by around 40 per cent in a week, but stayed above zero since Brent is a seaborne crude and can easily be shipped to areas of higher demand.

Covid-19 was the first global pandemic in living memory for most of those experiencing it, and the dramatic crashes reflected the uncertainty it provoked. What would happen next? How severe would Covid-19 be? No one really knew.

Two of the first people to describe their symptoms were husband

and wife Hollywood stars Tom Hanks and Rita Wilson, when they told the world they had contracted the coronavirus on 11 March. On 1 April the Wimbledon tennis tournament was cancelled for the first time since the Second World War. Americans were encouraged to wear a face covering in public places. British prime minister Boris Johnson was another victim. On 7 April, he was moved to an intensive care unit and discharged two days later. Such a steady stream of unprecedented announcements reinforced the sense of public uncertainty about just how catastrophic the effects of the virus could become.

We might not have known much about Covid-19 in the early days, but we did know from the Spanish flu that the economic consequences of a global pandemic would be stark. Lockdown measures caused unemployment to shoot up as businesses closed and people stayed at home. More than one in five US companies had ceased trading by April, which was the highest rate of closures on record. During the single week of 16–22 March, more than 3 million Americans lost their jobs, dwarfing the previous one-week high of 695,000 in October 1982 during the global recession. In another three weeks, over 16 million were laid off, more than the 8.6 million who were thrown out of work during the entire 2009 great recession. It was to get even worse. In the first seven weeks of lockdown, more than 33 million Americans filed for unemployment benefits. The unemployment rate rose to 14.7 per cent in April from a near fifty-year low of 3.5 per cent in February. (The closest comparison is the Great Depression, when unemployment was estimated at around 25 per cent in 1933.) To compound the problem, people also left the workforce. The April labour force participation rate, which measures the percentage of the working-age population working or looking for work, dropped to 60.2 per cent, the lowest since 1973.

'The scope and speed of this downturn are without modern precedent, significantly worse than any recession since World War II,' Fed Chairman Jerome Powell warned on 13 March.[12] He was right; the GDP figures were stark. In one of the first releases among the major economies, China reported on 17 April that its economy had shrunk by 6.8 per cent year on year, the first contraction in more than four decades. Its neighbour, Japan, was back in recession.

On 29 April, the US reported that its economy contracted by 4.8 per cent in the first three months of the year, although that did not fully capture the effect of the pandemic, which hadn't really hit until March. US retail sales in April declined by 16.4 per cent, which was a record drop. Consumer spending for a typical household fell by $1,000 per month between January and April, a whopping 31 per cent decline. A day later, the eurozone revealed its worst quarterly contraction on record: 3.8 per cent. Among the euro countries, France experienced a decline in GDP of 5.8 per cent, the biggest since records began in 1949, and fell into recession.

In the UK, the economy contracted by 2 per cent, which was the largest quarterly contraction since the 2008 financial crash. GDP fell by a record 5.8 per cent in March alone. The UK had a stagnant quarter at the end of 2019, so it didn't officially plunge into recession, but that was small comfort. As in the US, the credit-card company Mastercard found that UK consumer spending dropped by over a third in April during the lockdown. Travel spending was down by 50 per cent and there was an unprecedented 97 per cent drop in sales for bars, pubs and clubs, most of which were prohibited from opening their doors. Also like America, the UK saw a huge jump in the number of people claiming unemployment benefit in the early weeks of lockdown, up by 69 per cent to 2.1 million, the fastest rate on record, while average pay fell and recruitment ceased.

By early April, the International Monetary Fund was already estimating that the global economy was set for a contraction, and that both advanced and emerging economies would be in recession. Income per capita would shrink for 170 of its 189 member countries. The contrast with its last pre-pandemic estimate was stark. Then, the IMF had expected prosperity to increase in 160 countries.

Global trade fell by 14.3 per cent for manufactured goods in the second quarter of 2020, which was the biggest decline ever recorded. The impact on emerging market economies, many of which rely on global markets for growth and financing, was concerning. They experienced an unprecedented withdrawal of funds in March and April. Around $100 billion left these countries in March as investors sought to put their money into less risky investments, such as US dollar-denominated assets, the traditional safe haven.[13] By mid-April, investors had withdrawn another $96 billion from emerging market stocks and bonds, dwarfing previous capital outflows, including during the emerging markets crisis of the late 1990s discussed in Chapter 1.[14] As monies flowed out, emerging market currencies such as the Brazilian real, the Mexican peso and the South African rand all lost nearly a quarter of their value against the dollar.

Even while dealing with the Covid-induced crisis, more than a hundred low- and middle-income countries still had to pay $130 billion in debt service in 2020. The G20 group of major economies tried to help by imposing a debt moratorium, though this was of limited effect as it covered only obligations to governments, whereas around half of the debt was owed to private creditors. Unsurprisingly, over ninety countries approached the IMF for help in early 2020.

The economic impact of the pandemic was setting some unwanted records. A day after the S&P 500 plunged into a bear market, the US central bank cut interest rates to essentially zero and restarted quantitative easing to inject cash into the economy. The Fed announced that it would increase its holdings of Treasurys by at least $500 billion and of mortgage-backed securities by at least $200 billion as a result of the cash injections. In the week ending 25 March, the Fed's balance sheet had already expanded to a record $5.3 trillion.

Given the scale of the Covid crash, the Fed announced a series of further actions. The central bank said it would provide funding in the repo market, an important market for firms to access financing, while the New York branch offered overnight loans. The Fed continued to take a series of actions through the summer, including making available an additional $2.3 trillion in loans to provide credit to small businesses and municipalities as well as expanding measures to back corporate debt markets. The Fed even announced it would support the credit needs of businesses via its Commercial-Paper Funding Facility, through which it would lend to companies on a short-term basis. The Fed had pledged close to 20 per cent of US GDP. It was joined by central banks around the world. Those in the G7 countries purchased $1.4 trillion of financial assets in March alone.

On the 15th of that month, the Fed, the ECB and the central banks of Canada, the UK, Switzerland and Japan undertook coordinated action to ensure there was liquidity and access to US dollars via the standing swap line arrangements. The central banks agreed to lower the pricing on the swap lines by twenty-five basis points (0.25 per cent) and also began to offer companies US dollars for eighty-four-day loan periods to help them with managing their dollar liquidity. The Fed also announced that the swaps would be extended to the central banks of Australia, Brazil, Denmark, Mexico, Norway, New Zealand, Singapore and South Korea so that they could tap up to a combined total of $450 billion.

The Fed was going further than it had during the 2008 crisis. At the end of March, with large swathes of the world in some form of lockdown, it began offering dollar liquidity to the global system by allowing foreign central banks to swap Treasury securities for cash.

Central banks around the world responded to the crisis by slashing interest rates, thirty-nine of them doing so during the week of 16 March. The Bank of England cut interest rates twice in just over a week, to 0.1 per cent, breaking its record low set in 2008. It also restarted quantitative easing and enacted a commercial-paper facility that allowed it to lend to companies with the risks indemnified by the government.

On 17 March, at the height of the 'dash for cash' by investors who were selling up and taking their money out of markets, the ECB launched a €750 billion Pandemic Emergency Purchase Programme (PEPP), buying a range of financial assets from the panicked market to 'ensure that all sectors of the economy can benefit from support-ive financing conditions that enable them to absorb this shock'.[15] The ECB also announced that it would increase its QE programme to buy

€120 billion of bonds by the end of the year in addition to its existing commitment to purchase €20 billion a month. Alongside these measures, it offered a new programme of cheap loans to encourage banks to lend to small and medium-sized enterprises.

Its recently appointed president, Christine Lagarde, had been in post for only a few months. Lagarde's appointment in November 2019 was unusual in that she was a lawyer rather than an economist, but she was experienced in handling crises, having been France's finance minister during the euro crisis and then head of the IMF, whose role it is to assist with financial crises worldwide. She turned out to have just the right sort of experience: the ECB's rapid moves to guarantee credit flows to the economy helped markets continue to function and calmed the nerves of the eurozone's businesses and member states.

It wasn't only monetary policy that central banks deployed in force. Significant fiscal resources were also brought to bear by treasury departments across the world. It usually takes time for governments to put together support policies in a crisis but, impressively, there were a number of major fiscal stimuli announced in March. Some form of government help would be offered by every country in the world. The IMF tracked 197 countries' responses and chronicled a range of policies that were geared towards supporting people, jobs, viable businesses and financial stability.[16]

On 27 March, America enacted the Coronavirus, Aid, Relief, and Economic Security (CARES) Act. The largest such fund in history, CARES provided $2 trillion of federal funds to support households and firms. (By comparison, to contend with the 2009 great recession, the American Recovery and Reinvestment Act totalled $800 billion.) Americans started to receive their first round of stimulus cheques in the post by 11 April, although several thousand were delayed by a few days because President Donald Trump wanted his name printed on them.[17]

China planned to spend 3.75 trillion renminbi ($574 billion) to combat Covid and pledged RMB 100 billion ($15 billion) to boost infrastructure. Remarkably, China at its National People's Congress that month decided not to set a GDP growth target for 2020 for the first time since the founding of the People's Republic of China in 1949. Unlike many countries, and despite being the epicentre of the pandemic, China's initial support was less than it spent to address the fallout from the 2008 US sub-prime crisis. In further contrast with the West, the Chinese government's measures focused more on shoring up banks and local governments than on helping households and businesses, though it did double the temporary monthly allowance for low-income families from March to June in order to mitigate the price increases that arose as supply chains were shut down. However, this approach was not surprising since China has a smaller welfare system than other major economies. People save a great deal to prepare for a rainy day rather than rely on the government, which is why China has a much higher savings rate than America and Europe.

In Europe three EU-wide safety nets totalling €540 billion were announced by the European Commission. The first was the Support to Mitigate Unemployment Risks in an Emergency, which provided support for short-time work programmes, keeping workers attached to their employers as full-time workers even when only part-time work was available. The German version of the scheme, *Kurzarbeit*, was widely regarded as the gold standard of protection programmes.[18] The second was the European Stability Mechanism's Pandemic Crisis Support credit line that provided loan-based support to governments. The ESM, which is the region's de facto rescue fund, offered an almost condition-free lifeline. This was in addition to the Coronavirus Response Investment Initiative, which provided €8 billion in immediate liquidity to fund member states' Covid support. The third safety net was the pan-European guarantee fund of the European Investment Bank, which offered €200 billion of financing for EU businesses as well as providing a guarantee to underpin viable businesses.

Individual countries also undertook considerable measures. For instance, on 22 March, the German government announced it would spend €122.5 billion to counter the economic downturn. It also set up a €500 billion bailout fund to take stakes in impacted companies.

Significantly, the government sought to suspend the 'debt brake', a measure in the constitution that limits new government borrowing to just 0.35 per cent of GDP, and moved away from *schwarze Null*, its traditional 'black zero' balanced budget policy.

Germany wasn't the only country heading into new territory to counter the pandemic. The UK enacted a job retention scheme, introducing furlough for the first time in the labour market. Denmark had such a programme, while other European countries had short-time work schemes in their arsenal.

It wasn't a given that the UK would have done so. It didn't during the 2008 global financial crisis, and it wasn't in the spring budget presented by Chancellor of the Exchequer Rishi Sunak on 11 March 2020. I recall when the furlough scheme was announced on Friday, 20 March. Five days earlier, I had appeared before the Treasury Committee of the House of Commons, which was scrutinizing the budget from the previous week. My response when asked whether the government was doing enough to help people was that:

> we should think about programmes like those other governments in Europe have done. I am thinking about Denmark, which has essentially said that, if you keep your workers, the government will pay 75 per cent of workers' pay, while the firm pays 25 per cent, for a three-month period until the beginning of June. Those kinds of measures are intended to ensure that you do not, because of a temporary shock, cause people to lose their livelihoods.[19]

Sunak appeared before the same committee two days later. He was asked whether the UK should look to what other European countries were doing to help people, to which he replied that he was. At the end of that week, he proclaimed: 'Today I can announce that, for the first time in our history, the government is going to step in and help to pay people's wages. We're setting up a new Coronavirus Job Retention Scheme.'[20]

The furlough scheme would pay 80 per cent of a worker's salary up to £2,500 per month to keep them in employment. Furlough was essential in preventing unemployment from rising sharply and ended up supporting around 30 per cent of workers. Although the Chancellor had surely already been looking at options, it felt gratifying to have highlighted the one he chose to implement.

Such large-scale labour market measures aimed to keep people attached to work, which is key in preventing a short-term shock like Covid from damaging the growth potential of an economy over the longer term through hysteresis, a phenomenon that describes people leaving the labour force after losing their jobs or livelihoods because of a loss of skills or motivation. In this, it was only partially successful. Although these policies helped prevent unemployment from spiking, later evidence showed that the pandemic lockdowns still resulted in many workers, especially older ones, dropping out of the workforce. Still, it was a relief, since at the outset of the crisis joblessness would have soared when the economy locked down.

Such unprecedented spending to support economies around the world meant that public debt ballooned. Euro area debt as a share of GDP halted its declining trend since 2014, when it had recovered from the euro crisis, and would rise to about the size of national output. The same would happen in the UK.

Despite the high levels of debt, borrowing costs for advanced economies were falling as investors sought safe assets in the midst of a global crisis. There was expectedly strong demand for US debt, and the US Treasury sold longer term, twenty-year bonds for the first time since 1986 to fund its historic spending packages. The US borrowed at just 1.22 per cent for twenty years after selling $20 billion of bonds. The demand remained high at $50 billion.

The UK even sold bonds with a negative yield for the first time, which reflected investors' views that Britain was highly creditworthy. Although they would be repaid a bit less than what they lent, creditors were confident that they would be repaid, which was worth a great deal during a highly uncertain time. The UK offered £3.8 billion of government debt, or gilts, maturing in three years at a yield of minus 0.003 per cent. Demand was so strong that it could have sold twice as much. The yield on five-year gilts also fell below zero for the first time. Despite the significant amount of borrowing undertaken by the UK to address Covid, its debt continued to hold appeal owing to the British government's credibility, an important factor in determining the aftermaths of financial crises throughout history.

With the lockdowns having proved effective in reducing Covid transmission, manufacturing facilities were reopened in Italy on 4 May as European countries began to relax some restrictive measures. Lifting lockdowns released pent-up demand and monthly GDP figures indicated a return to growth in advanced economies. But there was a great deal of output lost, so the economies were rebounding from a low level. The GDP figures clearly showed the economic cycle following the pattern of restrictions and relaxations.

For instance, the US witnessed the biggest monthly increase in employment of 2.5 million. Leisure and hospitality, sectors that had been largely shut down, represented nearly half of those jobs. The jump almost perfectly mirrored the 2.7 million people who had been on temporary lay-off. A broader unemployment figure that included those in part-time work but wanting full-time jobs also fell slightly, to 21.2 per cent from 22.8 per cent, which was also a record. Worryingly, 40.8 million Americans were still seeking unemployment benefits, the highest rate since the government started tracking data in 1948.

In the UK, the jobs market was stabilized by the furlough scheme. Nearly a third of the workforce had been furloughed in the two months since lockdown. Some 8.4 million people stayed at home but kept their jobs. Another 2 million were receiving support from a separate self-employment scheme. It was a similar picture for the European Union. EU employment subsidy programmes covered 45 million jobs, or one-third of the labour force in Germany, France, Italy and Spain, among others, and have been credited with preventing the sort of job losses seen in the US.

This was a stark contrast between the US and Europe, driven by the differences in their labour markets and the size of their welfare states. In Europe, the emphasis was on job retention, since its labour market is less flexible than in North America where it is easier to hire and fire. In other words, you were more likely to lose your job in the US or Canada, but could also more easily find another one than in Europe, where the larger welfare state provided a social safety net that more generously supported people because it was harder to change jobs. The difference quickly became apparent. Total employment in the second quarter of 2020 fell by 13 per cent in the US and 11 per cent in Canada versus 2.5 per cent across the EU.

Heading into the summer, June saw a flurry of additional government activity to underpin the tentative economic recovery as virus levels remained stable in Europe and America. On the 23rd, the British government eased the lockdown and permitted pubs, restaurants, hairdressers and holiday accommodation to reopen provided they adhered to Covid guidelines, including the introduction of 'social distancing', whereby people were to remain two metres apart. This was a lifeline for the hospitality and other deeply affected industries. To encourage people to return to restaurants and pubs, Rishi Sunak launched the 'Eat Out to Help Out' scheme with an offer of discounted meals, accompanied by reassuring images of Sunak serving a plate of food. The measure was largely popular and added to the Chancellor's standing as he continued to offer support to people and businesses through schemes such as Project Birch, which gave the Treasury greater capacity to handle bespoke bailouts of viable companies that had exhausted all other options.

Even as the Chancellor unveiled further support measures in his summer economic update, with more borrowing to fund them, the Bank of England's QE programme helped keep borrowing costs low despite UK public debt exceeding GDP for the first time since 1963. The head of the UK Debt Management Office, Robert Stheeman, said that yields on government debt would have been 'massively higher' without QE.[21]

France injected more than €8 billion to save the country's motor industry. President Emmanuel Macron said: 'Our country wouldn't be the same without its great brands – Renault, Peugeot, Citroën.'[22]

This was part of France's €100 billion 'France Relance' coronavirus recovery plan. At 4 per cent of GDP, it cost almost three times as much as the one implemented after the 2008 crisis. Macron also wanted the spending to promote the transition to a greener economy, so nearly one-third of the funds went towards green investment. And, in expectation of a slow recovery, France announced that its temporary unemployment scheme to avert lay-offs would last for another year or two.

Germany likewise announced €130 billion in a wide-ranging package of support. Its efforts included a temporary cut to VAT and other measures also aligned with its longer-term strategic growth aims. If the government must spend to support the economy, then the spending ought to achieve its economic goals, specifically the shift to a green economy. The stimulus package included doubling a rebate on electric car purchases and a €50 billion fund to address climate change, innovation and digitization. Germany also pledged to make all fuel stations provide electric-vehicle charging to address concerns that a lack of charging points could hamper the green transition.

July was a landmark moment for the European Union. The EU agreed on a temporary €750 billion recovery fund and a seven-year €1.074 trillion budget. For the first time, the EU would be able to run a deficit to respond to an economic shock like the Covid-19 crisis. It would raise commonly issued debt and make it available to member states. After strong opposition from the 'Frugal Four' of Austria, Denmark, Sweden and the Netherlands, the grant element of the recovery fund was scaled back from €500 billion to €390 billion, which is equal to 3 per cent of EU GDP. But the money was to be distributed to countries without the conditions imposed during the drawn-out Greek debt crisis. Grants could be refused if countries had not drawn up adequate recovery plans, but there would be no national veto over other countries' spending plans. The redistributive nature of the fund meant that the EU would essentially be undertaking emergency fiscal transfers. Although this was not a fiscal union, markets perceived the move as a game changer as it added a fiscal dimension to underpin the monetary union. More importantly, at least in an emergency such as this, the EU was able to issue shared debt, something that had been vehemently opposed by Germany throughout the euro crisis.

The recovery fund came in the nick of time, since the resurgence of the virus was evident by July. Scientists from over thirty countries pointed to evidence of the airborne spread of coronavirus. A Spanish government study of over 60,000 people found that coronavirus antibodies decreased over time, raising questions about the effectiveness of 'herd immunity', a concept that if enough people had the virus, the rate of transmission would slow since they would be largely immune from reinfection.[23] Australia was recording more daily cases than at the peak of its first wave in the spring. The US administration's coronavirus coordinator, Deborah L. Birx, warned: 'What we are seeing today is different from March and April. It is extraordinarily widespread.'[24]

Lockdowns were tightened once more, including in Germany, where the government had reimposed a regional lockdown after an outbreak in a factory. South Africa reinstituted a curfew and a ban on alcohol sales to relieve the burden on hospitals dealing with Covid-19. Californian schools moved to online teaching amidst a rise in coronavirus cases. As a consequence of the tighter restrictions, US jobless claims rose again, the first increase since the spring. Adding to the gloom, second-quarter GDP figures were released showing the worst contractions that most major economies had ever experienced.

National output fell by record amounts: Germany's GDP contracted by 10.1 per cent, France's by 13.8 per cent and Spain's by 18.5 per cent. In fact, Spain's national output had fallen so much that the economy was at the level it had been in 2002. Nearly twenty years of growth had been wiped out in the eurozone's fourth-largest economy. The world's largest economy, the US, reported a stunning 31.7 per cent decline in GDP on an annualized basis, although compared with the preceding three months, which is the metric used by other major economies, the US economy contracted by 9.5 per cent, slightly better than European countries. The UK fared worse. Second-quarter national output fell by a record one-fifth due to an unprecedented 20.4 per cent contraction in GDP in the single month of April. Monthly GDP figures actually showed some growth in May and June following the easing of lockdown. Nevertheless, the UK economy was a fifth smaller than it had been at the end of 2019.

The economic situation also continued to worsen in emerging and developing countries. Argentina defaulted on $65 billion of foreign debt, marking its ninth default. In an effort to stem the rise of poverty, the World Bank announced a $1 billion aid package for India targeted at supporting the urban poor and migrant workers on top of $1 billion that had already been pledged to support the health sector. The UN estimated that an additional 75 to 95 million people would fall into poverty because of Covid, potentially setting back by several years the target of eradicating extreme poverty by 2030.[25]

With the resumption of some economic activity in early summer, the US benchmark stock index, the S&P 500, bounced back to where it had been at the start of 2020. By 8 June, it had erased the historic plunge that saw it lose one-third of its value between 20 February and 23 March. By the end of the month, the US stock market had experienced its best quarter for more than two decades alongside a global stock rally that continued into July.

The economic strain had led to gold hitting record prices. On 27 July it reached $1,944 per troy ounce, zipping past its previous high of $1,921 in September 2011 during the great recession. By August, gold prices passed $2,000, rising by 32 per cent since the start of the year, making it one of the best-performing assets that year. Rather unusually both stocks and gold did remarkably well during the pandemic. Gold is viewed as a safe haven, so investors tend to move their money into it when they're uncertain about other assets such as stocks, which tend to fall when an economy faces recession. During the pandemic, however, investors had put their money into both gold and stocks, perhaps reflecting different views about how the highly volatile situation would play out. Those who were cautious went into gold; those who saw stocks as benefiting from central banks injecting cash into the economy put their money into shares.

There were plenty of investors in the latter camp, and the S&P 500 reached yet another high in August. Even so, fewer than 40 per cent of companies in the US benchmark index were above their level on 19 February at the peak of the market. The five largest stocks, which were all tech companies (Amazon, Alphabet, Apple, Microsoft and Facebook), accounted for one quarter of the rally. They represent more than one-fifth of the index, which is the biggest weighting for the top five since at least 1980. Apple became the first US company to hit a $2 trillion market capitalization, just two years after becoming the world's first trillion-dollar business. Its shares had risen by more than 50 per cent year-to-date, despite worldwide store closures on account of lockdowns. The rapid shift to online shopping and remote work boosted both Apple and technology firms generally. Accordingly, the tech-heavy NASDAQ also hit record highs that summer. It even turned out to be the busiest mergers-and-acquisitions summer on record. Blockbuster deals soared to $456 billion as private equity groups invested in tech companies whose sales were booming because of the pandemic-induced lockdowns.

It was not boom time for all companies, though. Large US corporate bankruptcy filings were running at a record pace and had surpassed the level reached during the 2008 crisis.[26] A record forty-five companies with assets of more than $1 billion had filed for Chapter 11 bankruptcy, which is a common way for distressed companies to restructure themselves. It compared with the thirty-eight companies that failed during the 2008 crisis and was more than double 2019's figure.

Amidst the economic fragility, the chairman of the Federal Reserve, Jerome Powell, said that the US central bank would occasionally allow inflation to exceed its 2 per cent target to make up for past shortfalls. The 'Powell doctrine' changed longstanding policy that had focused on hitting the target, allowing inflation to rise so the economy might grow and create jobs unworried that monetary policy would tighten to control inflation and dampen economic activity. The Fed also signalled that it planned to hold interest rates at historic lows until at least the end of 2023, a year beyond what it had indicated previously.

★

Crucially, there was encouraging news about potential vaccines. On 10 August, Moderna, a biotech company based in Cambridge, Massachusetts, negotiated a deal to supply the US with 100 million doses of its experimental Covid vaccine. A day later, Russia became the first country to approve a vaccine, Sputnik V, although it was widely condemned by scientists as potentially unsafe. The University of Oxford's Jenner Institute and the Oxford Vaccine Group had been working on one since January. In March, they received a further £2.6 million grant from the British government that allowed them to conduct trials and scale up to 1 million doses by the summer. The slimmed-down process and minimal bureaucracy meant that the Oxford University/AstraZeneca vaccine was showing promise even during its ongoing trials, which were due to finish in November.

They were not alone in benefiting from expedited processes. By September, in America, Moderna's Covid vaccine was showing acceptable levels of safety. Johnson & Johnson also announced late-stage testing of its vaccine. With these positive developments, the WHO announced that sixteen major pharmaceutical companies had agreed to scale up manufacturing and ensure that all countries had access to vaccines. The Serum Institute of India, the world's largest vaccine manufacturer by volume, in collaboration with partners like the Bill and Melinda Gates Foundation, would be licensed to produce vaccines including Oxford University/AstraZeneca's, which was to be supplied on a not-for-profit basis during the pandemic and in perpetuity for low- and middle-income countries.[27]

Along with the vaccine good news, the summer weather also saw a decline in coronavirus cases, and major economies showed signs of a rebound in the quarter spanning July, August and September. China reported first. As the pandemic originated there, its economy was affected earlier and thus it recovered sooner. Economic growth in the third quarter was 4.9 per cent, accelerating from 3.2 per cent. After just one negative quarter at the start of the year, the Chinese economy had avoided recession. China even sold its first negative-yielding debt, borrowing for five years at minus 0.45 per cent. Other major economies also registered growth. For Japan, GDP expanded for the first time since 2020, but the economy was still almost 6 per cent smaller than a year earlier.

The US recorded its fastest-ever quarterly growth rate of an annualized 33.1 per cent as it rebounded strongly from its record contraction. GDP increased to $21.2 trillion, which meant that the American economy had nearly recovered to its pre-pandemic level. But the US was still down 10.7 million jobs, including 3.8 million in the leisure and hospitality sector.

The UK also grew by a record 16 per cent quarter-on-quarter as lockdown measures eased. Unlike the US, the level of national output was still about a tenth smaller than it was pre-pandemic. The relief was short lived. As winter fast approached, another wave of Covid-19 would soon push countries back into lockdown.

New variants of Covid-19 were emerging that were more contagious, though less deadly, than the original strains. To avoid the stigma associated with calling them the 'UK variant' or the 'South African variant', the World Health Organization began assigning Greek letters to those variants that might pose a significant threat. Alpha, Beta, Gamma, Delta and Omicron began to fill the headlines, along with neologisms such as 'Deltacron' when people were infected by more than one variant.[28]

The presence of fast-spreading variants caused Argentina to become the fifth country to record over 1 million Covid-19 cases, joining the US, India, Brazil and Russia. Covid had even reached Antarctica, where thirty-six personnel at a Chilean military base had tested positive. There was also concern about the coronavirus spreading from animals to humans in Europe. Denmark culled its entire population of some 17 million mink after a coronavirus mutation spread from them to people. It later had to exhume millions of mink carcasses to avoid water pollution.[29]

In October 2020, second national lockdowns were announced in France, Germany and elsewhere. Italy re-entered lockdown in an effort to head off an expected infection spike over Christmas. To contend with the negative impact of the lockdowns, the ECB increased its Pandemic Emergency Purchase Programme to €1.85 trillion. Just as during the euro crisis, bond markets were supported by the ECB's purchase of debt. As a result, Portugal's benchmark ten-year bond yield fell below zero for the first time – a striking turnaround for Portugal following its rescue in 2011.

In the UK, lockdown restrictions placed different regions into tiers depending on rates of infection. Once again, the British government offered help in the form of cash grants of £2,000 to £3,000 per month to firms that had to shut down and doubled the grants to the self-employed. In an abrupt policy change, the Chancellor also extended to March 2021 the furlough scheme that had been slated to end in October.[30] Just a month earlier, Rishi Sunak had said, 'I can't save every job.'[31] Although there were headlines proclaiming furlough as the government's big success story, Sunak had delayed the announcement of the extension, to the chagrin of businesses.[32] It cost the taxpayer about £6,000 for each furloughed job, or about £69 billion in total, making it the most expensive programme run by the Treasury. But the government had placed two-thirds of the population into the most restrictive lockdown tier, which imposed the closure of pubs and restaurants, so unemployment would have risen sharply without such a scheme. The Chancellor also put in place a replacement for the £65 billion Covid-19 loans programme to support lending by banks to small and medium-sized enterprises. The new recovery loan scheme would carry a guarantee of up to 80 per cent of loans of up to £10 million for viable enterprises that were unable to borrow from banks.

The US also acted, passing a second Covid stimulus package worth $900 billion, which was smaller than the first stimulus but still ranked as the second largest in history. It included sending $600 to each American and grants for small businesses, as well as support for states in the form of expanded unemployment benefits. It came as 140,000 jobs were lost in December, the first monthly loss of jobs since the early stage of the pandemic in the spring.

Despite the economic gloom at year end, markets reached new highs on the back of improving geo-political tensions and, crucially, the approval of the first vaccines for Covid-19. In November, US–China trade talks were on a better footing, and the Trump presidency that had exacerbated the tensions was coming to an end after Democratic candidate and former vice-president Joe Biden had won the election. Rather curiously, the Trump White House had listed ending the pandemic as a top accomplishment.[33]

Importantly, the end of the year and the beginning of 2021 saw a flurry of vaccine approvals. On 2 December, the UK became the first country to approve the Pfizer/BioNTech vaccine. The US was the first to authorize the Moderna version, while the EU also approved the Pfizer/BioNTech. The UK authorized Oxford University/Astra-Zeneca on 30 December, followed by Moderna on 8 January. The vaccines ignited hope that further waves of Covid would not necessarily lead to strict shutdowns and consequent economic downturns around the world.

Just as the vaccines' progress had helped lift markets a few months earlier, their approval saw stocks in the US, China and elsewhere ending the year in bull-market territory (though not in the UK or the rest of Europe). A thirty-year veteran investor in financial markets observed, 'I've never seen anything like it, both the pace of the compression, and then the rebound. Things happened twenty, thirty times faster than ever seen before.'[34]

The US benchmark, the S&P 500, recorded twenty-eight record highs in 2020, while the Dow Jones blue-chip index reached a milestone when it exceeded 30,000. The tech-heavy NASDAQ was up more than 40 per cent, double the 20 per cent rise deemed a bull market. It was likewise for China: its benchmark index, the CSI 300, rose by 27 per cent. Global stocks finished 2020 on a record high following a 16 per cent rally in the final three months of the year. The rise was partly due to tech companies booming. E-commerce giant Amazon had a tremendous year delivering goods when people had to stay at home, but its 79 per cent increase in value made it only the 100th best performer in global stock markets. Number one was Tesla, which had seen its shares increase by a staggering 787 per cent, taking its valuation from $75 billion at the start of 2020 to $669 billion by the end of the year.

In contrast, the FTSE 100 ended 2020 with its worst performance since the 2008 financial crisis, down 14 per cent. That the UK benchmark index continued a run of underperformance may be due to the UK's deep Covid recession, its relative lack of tech companies and the ongoing uncertainty over Brexit as the UK's transitional EU arrangements were coming to an end in January 2021. It was later confirmed that the UK economy contracted by 11 per cent in 2020, the biggest fall in national output since 1709 and the worst among G7 countries. Continental Europe fared better. Its largest economy's stock market, Germany's DAX, eked out gains for the year, helping the pan-European STOXX 600 to be down by just 1.6 per cent in 2020.

The asset that outpaced all others in both gains and losses was cryptocurrency. Called the 'mother all bubbles', the price of Bitcoin rose by 300 per cent in 2020.[35] It jumped from around $14,000 on 3 November 2020 to a record high of $34,000 on 3 January 2021. But such volatility also saw prices drop by as much as a fifth in a day in the first week of the new year.

At the start of 2021, US stocks hit yet more highs. On 7 January, the Dow, S&P 500 and NASDAQ all exceeded previous records. The Dow passed 31,000, the S&P 500 ended up at its milestone above 3,800, while the NASDAQ finished well above 13,000. US markets were rising as the new Biden administration committed to spending more on pandemic relief. They were joined by emerging-market stocks, which entered a bull market in the first weeks of 2021, rising by 20 per cent. By 10 February, global stocks were at all-time highs and had more than recovered their pandemic losses, driven by expectations of a more robust economic recovery in the coming year.

The markets might have recovered quickly from their dramatic losses, but economies did not, and that's why the pandemic can be called a great crash.

In November 2020, Zambia became the first country to default on its debt. It wouldn't be the last. The IMF estimated that 60 per cent of low-income countries were at risk of debt distress, meaning they might not be able to pay their debts and would require a rescue.[36]

By contrast, advanced economies were able to borrow to fund their Covid support programmes, which aided their recovery. This was despite the rapid increase in government debt that had just begun to stabilize after the 2008 global financial crisis. The average public debt level was around 80 per cent of GDP before the pandemic. For the EU, that was far above the 60 per cent maximum set in the Maastricht Treaty. For the UK, debt as a percentage of GDP had tripled since 2001. Due to Covid-19, debt rose further and reached record levels of about 100 per cent of GDP for both the UK and the EU.

Advanced economies spent about 9 per cent of GDP in 2020 on the pandemic, which was roughly double that of emerging and developing economies. The advanced economies had more capacity to borrow, while developing economies had less, which hampered their ability to address the crisis even though their economies contracted by twice as much as advanced economies on average.[37] Although major economies had largely recovered to pre-pandemic levels by the beginning of 2022, the rest of the world, with less access to vaccines and less room to borrow, did not fare as well. The global economy cannot fully recover until all economies are able to cope with Covid-19.

It is challenging to draw many lessons from a financial crash that was caused by a global pandemic. But it provides yet more evidence that there's no boom without a bust.

Euphoria drove the eleven-year bull market for US stocks that ended in March 2020. In 2019 alone, the Dow Jones registered twenty-two record highs. The run-up in share prices was buoyed by a decade of cheap money from central banks that were contending with the slow economic recovery after the 2008 crisis. The pandemic then led to more cash being injected by central banks around the world along with deeper interest rate cuts, which bolstered the market's recovery.

During the lockdowns, the stock market was also propelled by technology, e-commerce and pharmaceutical companies, which had received massive boosts from widespread stay-at-home orders and from funding that had poured into vaccine research and production.

Mobile technology popularized in the last decade had made e-commerce available in the way envisioned by the dot coms two decades ago. As tech stocks soared, there were concerns about a bubble bursting. In the end, it was a pandemic that led to the biggest one-day crashes in history, but with cheap money and a shift to more online sales and work, US stocks had not only recovered but set new records shortly after the historic crash.

The discrepancy between the stock markets and the economies was stark. This is a familiar pattern; previous recoveries that were fuelled by cheap money led to stocks increasing sharply in value while the economy slowly rebuilt itself. The 2008 crisis is a recent case in point.

That's not the only commonality. The second trait that the Covid crash shares with other crises is the importance of credibility. The ability of countries like the US, the UK, China, Japan, Germany, France and even recently rescued countries such as Portugal to borrow at record low rates reflected a belief in their governmental institutions. Despite high debt levels and the economic damage, creditors were willing to lend cheaply to these countries.

Being able to spend to support the recovery matters for the aftermath, and less developed countries fared badly, finding it harder to borrow to support their economies and to access vaccines, a state of affairs that will prolong not only their own recovery but also the world's. Two years on, the global economy has not recovered; indeed, the WHO estimates that its 70 per cent vaccination rate target won't be met by the end of 2022.

The aftermath of the Covid-19 pandemic will be determined by the availability and efficacy of vaccines and also the effectiveness of governments in preventing permanent economic damage by keeping people in work. In terms of how to support the global economic recovery, government spending should continue to be tailored to jobs. To prevent hysteresis, government support should focus on employment to try to prevent discouraged workers from leaving the labour force. The extension of various furlough schemes in Europe into the recovery period targets this issue. This will be harder for developing countries that are fiscally constrained.

By contrast, for advanced economies, the recovery spending can also be designed to support longer-term aims such as greener growth and address longstanding challenges such as low productivity. The IMF changed its emphasis during Covid-19 to encourage countries that can afford to do so to borrow to invest, shifting the focus from fiscal discipline to promoting economic growth that can take advantage of low interest rates. In its October 2020 *World Economic Outlook*, the IMF estimated that, during periods of high uncertainty such as a global pandemic, 1 per cent of GDP spent on public infrastructure will generate 2.7 per cent in GDP growth and raise employment by 1.2 per cent after two years as well as boost private investment.[38] That translates into between two and eight jobs for each $1 million invested in traditional infrastructure. But, if it is spent on green infrastructure, such as renewable energy or R&D, there would be a bigger impact of five to fourteen jobs created by every $1 million invested by the state. The lower capital stock and higher technological component of green investments could generate a larger return than traditional infrastructure. In addition, public spending could also help the economy adjust to technological shifts and operate more efficiently. For instance, building more digital infrastructure could provide better access to faster broadband that would enable remote working and e-commerce. Improved transport links would help with hybrid working and deliveries of online shopping.

In short, creating jobs, supporting greener growth and boosting productivity would focus the extraordinary amounts of government spending on both near-term needs and longer-term aims. And that would help ensure a better aftermath from the most extraordinary of crashes.

# 8   The Next Great Crash?

Each financial crisis is different from the one that came before, and no one can predict with certainty when the next great crash will arrive. The only fact beyond doubt is that there will be one. Yet throughout this book we have seen that lessons can be drawn from financial crises that might be useful when another one appears on the horizon. Applying the lessons we've learned so far, it is China that certainly warrants attention.

Prior to Covid-19, China's was the only major economy to grow consistently for four decades. It has never had a great crash. (It is open to debate just how forthcoming China would be about reporting a financial crisis, but if a systemic crash were to occur there on the scale of Japan's real-estate crash or the 2008 global financial crisis, even China's closed system would not be able to conceal it.) None the less, China's is one of the more challenging economies to analyse, not only because of its opacity – even its GDP figures are often debated – but also because its financial system still has great portions of state ownership, while many other parts that are not owned by the state outright are effectively state-controlled.

This is a legacy of 1949, when the Chinese Communist Party under Mao Zedong founded the People's Republic of China and introduced a centrally planned economy. The state made all the decisions in what was termed the 'command economy'. The situation changed somewhat in 1979, when Mao's successor, Deng Xiaoping, introduced sweeping market-oriented reforms that transformed China into a transition economy in which market forces were allowed to determine what got produced and how it was sold, albeit still under varying degrees of state control.

This makes the absence of a Chinese financial crisis even more unusual. Transition economies, such as those in the former Soviet Union, had crashed spectacularly in the early 1990s when they transformed into capitalist and democratic systems. Known as 'transformational recessions', the decade-long downturns in eastern and central Europe, Russia and elsewhere in the former Soviet bloc devastated those countries' economies and their financial sectors. Russia ended that decade with a lower standard of living and higher rates of poverty than at the start.

However, no country can defy the cycle of boom and bust indefinitely, and China is unlikely to be an exception. There are a number of potential triggers. For example, its gigantic, highly indebted property sector could implode. Its system of lending outside the formal banking system, known as shadow banking, could collapse. There could be a major stock market crash. Such events are not without precedent: China had a local shadow banking crisis in 2014 as well as a stock market crash in 2015. Neither episode was disastrous, but both highlight the weaknesses in the country's financial system as well as the large amount of debt that exists there, all of which would make a property crash concerning.

Since the turn of the century, China has seen a euphoric property boom, house prices rising at a rate unprecedented for a major economy.[1] Until the 1990s, housing had been allocated by a worker's employer, typically a state-owned enterprise. The latter part of that decade saw the privatization of the housing market, which then grew exponentially. The owners of the state-allocated housing were permitted to buy their homes at preferential rates, which kicked off the growth of the real-estate market.

The period during which China opened up to the world saw massive migration from the countryside to the cities as rural workers were brought in to work in factories producing for export, and they all needed housing. Urban workers could sell their housing units, bought at preferential rates, to migrants and trade up to new and more expensive flats.

Although limited mortgages were offered by the state-dominated banking system, especially to first-time buyers, most purchases were financed with cash. China is a high-saving economy, and the housing market was experiencing euphoria, believing that prices could only continue to go up. Property seemed to provide both a secure store of value and a much higher rate of return than bank deposits and volatile investments such as stocks. There were few avenues of financial diversification open to the average Chinese citizen since foreign investment was restricted, so bricks and mortar became the preferred holding. China's home ownership rate today is a remarkable 90 per cent, one of the highest in the world. Owning a home is also culturally valued. Potential spouses will be viewed more favourably if they own a property. A survey of Chinese mothers even revealed that four in five would object to their daughter marrying a non-homeowner.[2]

As people demanded properties and made home improvements, the housing market boomed. Housing expenditure alone accounted for as much as 10 per cent of GDP.[3] Despite 10 million housing units being built every year, the demand for housing in cities was growing even more rapidly, pushing up prices. One restriction on the supply of new housing is the fact that land in China is largely state-owned. Land sales are an important source of revenue for local governments when they auction the land to developers or construct apartments as partners. Although there is no lack of land, there are frequently hostile reactions from farmers and existing residents that prevent it from being built on and constrain supply. Ill-advised construction by local governments across the vast nation has also resulted in the strange paradox of China having both a shortage of housing and millions of unoccupied apartments built in the wrong areas. There are so-called 'ghost cities' in more far-flung provinces such as Inner Mongolia.

The exuberant assumption that prices would continue to increase was validated for twenty years, but China's growth began to slow in the late 2010s as the economy approached upper-middle-income level. This is a phenomenon that occurs in all developing countries: as income growth adjusts and urban migration slows, it follows that the demand for housing will also slow, causing prices to increase less rapidly or even decline and spelling trouble for developers.

At present, it seems that the Chinese are still largely in the euphoric thrall of the house-price optimism that has characterized housing bubbles throughout history and around the world. Those first state-subsidized homeowners and other early purchasers remain in a good position, but rising house prices have meant that aspiring homeowners, the very people in the middle class that the government wants to support, are finding it difficult to get on the housing ladder. This is one reason that the Chinese government is concerned about improving 'common prosperity', which aims to enable people to more equitably enjoy the fruits of economic growth, including housing.

There are doubts about the ability of the Chinese government to manage a controlled deflation of the housing market. When a potential bust is considered in the context of an underdeveloped financial system that is already laden with debt, the risk of a great crash is both clear and rising.

Chinese banks have been recapitalized by the state several times, notably in the late 1990s and early 2000s. This was to improve their balance sheets before foreign banks entered the domestic market after China joined the World Trade Organization (WTO) in 2001 and agreed to open up swathes of its services markets. A lingering problem was that the bad debts removed from the balance sheets of the four state-owned commercial banks remained in the Chinese financial system, held by an asset-management company also owned by the state. This meant that any assessment of the banking system must include the legacy of bad debt since those liabilities would need to be counted when assessing China's indebtedness, and its ability to weather a financial crisis.

The bad debts that have weakened Chinese state-owned banks have been accumulated over decades from state-owned enterprises. Their growth was due to the inefficient operations of these firms, which dominated most sectors of the economy until the 2000s. Since they were owned by the state, they had little incentive to be efficient and no cost constraint (the 'soft budget constraint' problem, in economic jargon). When market-oriented reforms began in 1979, there was growing consumer demand, so state-owned firms asked for more inputs to sell more output, with little regard to cost. Managers earned more if they generated more revenue, but they were heedless of costs because the funds for investment came from the state and even their workers were allocated to them based on a plan that bore no relation to firms' individual productivity. State-owned enterprises such as China National Petroleum and SAIC Motor took the easy option of asking for more capital and labour to increase output, rather than producing more efficiently using what they had, which is much harder to do.

This explains the strong growth of the Chinese economy in the 1980s even though state-owned enterprises were loss-making. By the early 1990s, around two-thirds of state-owned firms were losing money.[4] This led to a massive reform in the mid-1990s that got rid of most of the state-owned enterprises, bringing the number down from 10 million to under 300,000 by the end of that decade. But the Chinese banks that had financed these state-owned firms still had to be recapitalized before foreign competitors entered China in the early 2000s.

The debt problems worsened after the 2008 global financial crisis. China's underdeveloped financial market did not trade in the complex securities that brought down large segments of the Western banking system, but shadow banking was allowed to grow to support the weakened economy. Shadow banking is the slightly sinister name for those non-bank financial institutions that perform banking functions without a banking licence. It's a murky sector that includes trusts, leasing companies and insurance companies as well as payday loan companies and loan sharks. By the 2010s, the financial system in China was facing a triple threat of debt. It was not only funding the fast-growing property market while still carrying a legacy of state-owned-enterprise debt but also having to deal with new debt from shadow banking.

The Chinese stock market has some unusual features too. China's two stock exchanges were launched just over three decades ago, in

Shanghai in 1990 and Shenzhen in 1991, with trades permitted in 1993. In late 2009, Shenzhen created a NASDAQ-style market called the Growth Enterprise Board, aimed at listing smaller companies. At the end of 2019, China's stock market became the second largest after that of the United States.

Rather strangely, around two-thirds of the shares in listed companies on Chinese exchanges were non-tradable in the 1990s, which meant that share prices were dictated by the state rather than by supply and demand. Also, the categorization of shares as 'individual', 'government' or 'legal persons' (state-owned firms), each with its own trading restrictions, was problematic. Due to these unusual features, and being largely closed to foreign investors, listed firms were insulated from feeling the full discipline of the market. Corporatization – that is, the transformation of state-owned enterprises into companies owned by shareholders – in the early days of the reforms had failed to generate the expected improvement in corporate governance.

But private investors in China have few places to invest, owing to capital controls restricting how much money leaves its shores, so they invest in Chinese stocks as well as housing. This preponderance of retail investors can make Chinese equities volatile. The market rose rapidly during the 1990s and then lost about 50 per cent of its value in the early 2000s before growing quickly once again. During the depths of the US sub-prime crisis, in the first half of 2009, the Shanghai stock market rose by over 80 per cent in about seven months. In 2014–15 it rose by 150 per cent before crashing. This 'roller-coaster' trajectory, evident throughout its short history, shows how risky Chinese markets are compared with others.

The continued existence of non-tradable shares contributed to the volatility. Chinese investors who wanted to invest in companies had no option other than to buy shares, even though they could not sell them. Being able to trade shares is a normal feature of stock markets, one without which funds can't flow efficiently. The Chinese authorities announced in August 2005 that state-owned enterprises would be allowed to sell shares controlled by the state, amounting to nearly

$270 billion of assets. Although the process was slow at first, the percentage of non-tradable shares had dropped to around 19 per cent of the total by the end of the 2010s. Promisingly, private firms jumped from representing just 8 per cent of listed firms in 2010 to account for about half a decade later,[5] but the other 50 per cent of companies whose shares are traded on the two stock exchanges are still subsidiaries of large state-owned enterprises. In summary, these reforms helped improve liquidity in the market, but ongoing state control means that a lot of firms are not operating as efficiently as would be expected of companies listed on a major stock exchange.

The underdevelopment of China's stock market is reflective of the state of its wider financial system. This is not atypical of emerging economies, but China is unusual in being simultaneously both an emerging market and one of the world's biggest economies owing to its large population. On a per capita basis, China is not a rich country of the type usually associated with developed financial markets, but a middle-income economy where such institutions are still evolving. Nevertheless, the sheer size of its economy raises expectations as to how its markets should function. It certainly makes apparent the risk that a financial crisis will affect the world, given China's place in the global economy.

The expected opening of China's markets after it joined the World Trade Organization in 2001 hastened the development of its financial system. The expectations of international financial markets in terms of corporate governance and reporting requirements helped fuel reforms. For instance, permitting fund management companies, developing investment banking services and liberalizing some aspects of the currency are all aimed at deepening financial markets in China.

In some ways, the development of capital markets, such as creating a fund management industry, is less burdened by the legacy of central planning since such markets simply did not exist before 1979. It was easier to develop a new industry than to reform the existing banking system. The banking sector has had to cope with the complicated relationships that drive lending in a partially marketized economy, in which loans are sometimes made to state-owned enterprises rather than on a strictly commercial basis. The mindset from the centrally planned period hampered the development of a commercial credit culture. When interest rates were first liberalized in October 2004, for example, Chinese banks found it difficult to use rates to price for risk since they had not needed to do so under central planning. Early attempts to control risk led to bankers being fired if they lent to a company that went bankrupt. State-owned enterprises could not go bust, since they were owned by the government, so they remained favoured by bankers. It was no wonder that private firms found it hard to obtain credit from the state-owned commercial banks and turned to shadow banking.

Gradual reforms have introduced more market factors into decision-making, but other problems, including the lack of capital and currency convertibility, remain to be solved. Given China's weight in the global benchmark MSCI Emerging Markets Index, the inability to move portfolio capital freely due to capital controls and currency restrictions is an obstacle that China has been attempting to remove by gradually liberalizing its capital account, recognizing that the lack of convertibility of the currency will stymie the development of a liquid capital market.

The Chinese authorities view the opening up of capital markets in tandem with exchange rate reform. The Asian crisis highlighted the dangers of a combined currency and financial crisis. 'Hot money' flows coupled with underdeveloped financial markets were important ingredients in the third-generation crises discussed in Chapter 1. With a fixed exchange rate and increasingly liberalized lending, China may be at risk in the future. Knowing it has an underdeveloped, state-dominated financial market, the government has moved slowly on making the renminbi tradable and opening up its capital account.

The weaknesses of Chinese markets caused by the incomplete nature of its reforms became evident in the 2010s when not one but two crises threatened the financial system. The first was triggered by the 2008 global financial crisis. The ensuing 2009 great recession led to one-quarter of workers in China's export sector losing their jobs as demand collapsed in America and Europe. The government encouraged Chinese companies to grow by selling instead to the home market in order to both stimulate the domestic economy and create jobs. Some financed that expansion by borrowing from shadow banks.

The shadow banking problem originated with the state-owned banking sector, which accounts for nearly all official lending. There has been little scope for private banks to operate. Two decades after China had opened up the banking sector as part of its WTO obligations, foreign banks accounted for less than 3 per cent of its total assets. As private firms sought funds that the formal banking system, which predominantly lent to state-owned firms, was reluctant to provide, unlicensed lending grew. Since it needed economic growth to happen quickly, the Chinese government turned a blind eye to shadow banking, which quickly took off.

To prevent a recession, the central government also launched a stimulus package of RMB4 trillion ($586 billion), focused largely on spending to build infrastructure. It fell to local governments to implement most of it. Because China doesn't have a well-established bond market where local governments can issue debt and borrow to fund their spending, some of them, too, turned to shadow banks. Around half of local government debt was accumulated after the global financial crisis.[6] According to China's National Audit Office, the share of local government debt in the form of bank loans dropped from 79 per cent before the crisis to 23 per cent after 2008. Around 28 per cent was borrowed from shadow banks while the remaining 49 per cent or so was in the form of IOUs or deals whereby developers or contractors bore the initial costs up front to build on land owned by local governments. Local governments made revenues from selling development rights to property companies or building blocks of flats. These links between the property sector and local governments meant that each had the potential to drag down the other. If the debts were to go bad it could trigger a local financial crisis that could spread across the country if large numbers of localities were in a similar position.

In 2014, China suffered a shadow banking crisis in one of its provinces. When large sums of unofficial loans suddenly went unpaid, I visited Wenzhou in Zhejiang province to film a report on the subject for my BBC programme. Wenzhou has been at the forefront of China's experiments with private industry since reforms had begun four decades earlier. As a result, its average income was double that of China as a whole. But the dominance of private firms also meant that an astounding 89 per cent of households and 59 per cent of firms had borrowed money privately, rather than from officially licensed banks.[7]

I visited Zhejiang Brothers Printing Company, which prints playing cards. Its CEO, Zhou Feng, was paying 24 to 30 per cent interest on short-duration loans to be repaid in three to five days. He explained:

> We still prefer to use shadow banking as a channel to get money to solve business problems as it's efficient and quick, though the rate is much higher than the banks['] . . . If the money can't arrive on time, we may have trouble. For instance, if we don't have the loan to buy the materials, we will fail to deliver the order and lose the business.[8]

I spoke to one shadow banker who charged interest rates of up 100 per cent and lent on average RMB6 million per month, which was about £600,000. He didn't think the state could get on top of the problem: '[They] can never get rid of the borrowing in the society. So shadow banking will exist forever. They can only ban the very high-rate loans but can't ban all shadow banking. It's like gambling. Though gambling is banned in China, many people play cards or mahjong [a Chinese tile-based game] to gamble.'[9]

When a whole network of shadow banking debt threatened to come crashing down, it resulted in a quiet rescue by the local government. Shadow bankers themselves borrow to fund their loans, and I met a number of people who had lost everything after lending to shadow bankers in hopes of high returns but had no recourse when the money disappeared. Given the devastation, the Chinese government even offered an amnesty to get these murky loans registered and brought into the light of the formal banking system. I was there at the registration centre on the first day of this scheme. Unsurprisingly, not one shadow banker or borrower turned up.

That particular crisis was contained locally, but it might easily have become a national one. It opened a window onto how quickly debt in China had grown in just a few years. The level of debt matters because, if China does have a financial crisis due to a real-estate bust, whether the government can afford to rescue the banks and the property companies will be key to how it plays out.

In 2021, China's debt-to-GDP ratio approached 300 per cent, on a par with the US and the eurozone. However, there are doubts as to whether even that high figure captures the extent of indebtedness in China since, by definition, it's hard to count shadow banking loans with any degree of precision. Estimates range from 15 per cent to a perilous 70 per cent of GDP.[10] Clearly concerned, the Chinese government has been clamping down on shadow banking since the end of the 2009 great recession.

Shadow banking is only one potential cause of a financial crisis. Another is stocks, and the Chinese government's response to the country's stock market crash of 2015 made investors doubt the credibility of their financial sector reforms.

In contrast to other major markets, where institutional investors (with their relative abundance of information) are the biggest players, in China retail investors account for around 85 per cent of trades. A feature of a market dominated by small traders is 'herding' behaviour: individuals assume that others have better information, so when they see selling, they also sell and vice versa. The result is an extremely volatile market in which rumour and emotion play an oversized role. For instance, the state-owned train maker, CRRC, saw its shares skyrocket that year as retail investors speculated on Weibo, China's equivalent of Twitter, that CRRC would benefit from China's investments in infrastructure abroad even though no foreign rail contract had ever been signed.[11] An American investment banker based in Shanghai observed, 'Remember during the dot-com boom when everyone from the taxi driver to your grandmother was investing and making money? People quitting their jobs to be day traders? That is exactly what it is like in China. I have staff that quit their jobs to do day trading.'[12]

On the back of exuberant trading, China's stock market became the best performing in the world, rising by more than 150 per cent year-on-year in June. But by early July, the market had crashed into bear-market territory, losing around 30 per cent of its value. After extensive government interventions that prevented the selling of shares and even froze trading for the bulk of the market, prices rebounded, but a month later, on 24 August, it fell 8.5 per cent, followed by a 7 per cent drop the next day. This volatility continued through to early 2016.

The Chinese stock market crash was a financial crisis but not a great crash since it did not trigger a recession, largely because fewer than 10 per cent of Chinese households participate in the stock market, and equities comprise less than 15 per cent of household assets. But, given that China is the most populous nation on earth with over 1.4 billion people, even a small fraction of Chinese households experiencing losses at least on the face value of their shareholdings still amounts to tens of millions of people who are affected. The retail investors who play the stock market had mostly been betting relatively small amounts and largely hadn't lost their shirts. Nevertheless, there was sufficient cause for concern for the government to act, albeit clumsily.

As China's stock market fell that summer of 2015, the government also decided to devalue the renminbi, not once but twice, on consecutive days. The immediate effect was to compound the worries in global markets by adding currency instability on top of financial instability. Chinese exports had plummeted by more than 8 per cent compared with 2014, since the Chinese currency had risen due to being pegged to a US dollar strengthened by America's recovery from the sub-prime crash. China's devaluation sent shockwaves through financial markets. Stock markets around the world fell, including in Europe, where the London market lost about 2 per cent of its value.

Markets were worried that this could ignite a currency war in which other countries would also devalue, destabilizing global trade. As it had in the stock market, the government intervened with some heavy-handed stabilization measures, imposing strict capital controls and spending about $320 billion of reserves to maintain the value of the currency peg.[13]

The 2015 stock market and currency episodes raised questions about the Chinese government's management of its increasingly market-oriented economy. In Chapter 5 we saw how China's wobbles slowed the US central bank's move to raise interest rates. It is becoming increasingly apparent that how the Chinese government manages its financial sector reforms to prepare for a crisis matters not just for China but also for the global economy.

China now faces the sort of housing bubble that has felled economies in the past. The country's second-biggest property developer, Evergrande, has debts of $305 billion. The largest developer, Country Garden, is not as indebted but has seen its share price plummet owing to the concerns about the property sector. Evergrande's debt is equal to 2 per cent of China's GDP, an enormous sum, considering that China has the second-largest economy in the world. It owes billions to offshore bond holders, has missed several key bond interest payments and has been deemed essentially in default by international rating agencies.

Evergrande's liabilities are the highest of any publicly traded real-estate management or development company anywhere.[14] Much of its debt is held by Chinese banks and other institutions, though foreign investors are also creditors. At various points in 2021, Evergrande bond notes were trading at 25 to 50 cents on the dollar. In other words, creditors expected to receive only 25 to 50 per cent of what they had lent to the property company.

Worryingly, Evergrande is but one of many developers that are highly leveraged. Chinese property developers had total outstanding debts of RMB33.5 trillion ($5.24 trillion) at the end of 2021, equivalent to roughly a third of China's GDP.[15] Like Evergrande, several have missed offshore bond payments. If debt defaults grow, then so does the chance of a financial crash should developers go bankrupt and drag down the banks. Property sector loans account for more than a quarter of Chinese bank lending, which is why the banking regulator has been scrutinizing their balance sheets to assess the risks to the banking system.[16]

Unsurprisingly, Evergrande and other troubled developers have been unable to complete many of the homes they have already sold. Evergrande alone is liable for an estimated 1.4 million pre-sold units to buyers. The woes of the property sector have both a human cost and a direct impact on China's economy given the outsized role of the sector, accounting for 29 per cent of national output once related services are included.[17] On a quarterly basis, China's economic growth slowed to just 0.2 per cent between July and September 2021, during the height of Evergrande's revelations about its predicament. Together with a strict Covid lockdown that quarter, confidence in the economy was significantly dented which in turn depressed spending by firms and consumers. As of the time of writing, the government had created a real-estate fund of RMB300 billion ($44.4 billion) to contain the budding crisis amidst protests by thousands of Chinese mortgage holders unhappy to continue paying for housing that may never be built.

Ironically, it was the Chinese government that had orchestrated the deflation of the property sector. This was part of President Xi Jinping's focus to create 'common prosperity' centred on the so-called 'Three Mountains': housing, health care and education. The government was seeking to manage expectations around the slowdown of the economy. After decades of nearly double-digit growth rates during which people had seen their incomes double every seven to eight years on average, the economy was now slowing as it approached upper-middle-income status. Given the slower growth, the government's plan was to make housing as well as education and health care more affordable by spreading the benefits more evenly via measures such as a property tax on the most expensive housing and on second homes. The property sector's woes are a consequence of the Chinese government's attempts to reduce inequality.

China's major cities regularly ranked among the least affordable places in the world to own a home. The price-to-income ratio in Beijing, Shanghai and Shenzhen all exceeded a multiple of 40, as compared with 22 in London and 12 in New York.[18] It's a longstanding issue. Even a decade ago, the price of a two-bedroom, two-bathroom apartment in China's Tier 1 cities was equivalent to $600,000, some thirty times higher than average income. The cost per square foot ranged between $600 and $800, which was three to four times the average cost in comparable US cities.[19]

Affordability was not the only concern, the government was also worried about the negative impact the large amount of debt and the outsized property sector would have on the economy. The real-estate market was likely to deflate in any case under the weight of its debts, but regulatory action to reduce leverage was certainly a contributing factor. The government tried to reduce debt levels by imposing 'red lines' that placed limits on ratios of (1) liabilities (excluding advanced proceeds) to total assets, (2) net debt to equity and (3) cash to short-term debt. The measures were intended to cut the amount of debt that Evergrande and other property developers were taking on. In 2021 the government clamped down, so precipitating the property crisis.

The early signs of its 'Three Mountains' policy are not promising. Its crackdown on property companies may be well intentioned, but it has arrived a tad late. China has allowed mounting debt to fuel a sizeable bubble with the potential to drag down the banking system. Since China is too big to bail out, the key question is whether it can afford to rescue its property sector without devastating its economy for years to come.

Some crucial indicators are there. China's debt was high even before the pandemic, at a level similar to the US and EU, but differs in a key aspect, in that the biggest share is corporate rather than government loans. The sizeable debts of property developers and other leveraged companies could trigger a banking crisis if those loans go bad. Importantly, however, China's debt is nearly all domestically owned. The Japanese experience discussed in Chapter 3 indicates that domestic creditors are likely to stay put and accept government measures, unlike foreign creditors, who have a tendency to call in loans and quickly depart a country in crisis. And, like Japan, a great crash in China could similarly lead to a decade or more of economic stagnation following a rescue of its banks by the state.

It is also likely to be devastating in different ways, since no two crises are ever entirely alike. But, although the systemic global effect of a Chinese crisis may be mitigated by the fact that the creditors are largely domestic, there would still almost certainly be a significant impact on both international trade and developing countries whose debt is owed to Chinese banks.

China has been one of the twin engines of world economic growth, alongside the US, since the 1980s, but the sub-prime crisis that hobbled the US economy revealed how important was China's role. Although its economy is smaller than that of the US, China has contributed more to global growth since the 2008 financial crisis than any other country, according to the IMF.[20] In the 2000s, the US and China generated as much output as the rest of the world combined.[21]

What are the potential consequences of a dramatic slowdown in China's economic growth due to a financial crash? The main areas of global impact would include not only commodities (China is the world's largest consumer) and capital goods (China is one of the largest buyers in the world), but also a wide range of imported consumer goods, reducing the profits of multinational companies around the world.

As Chinese demand for raw materials and commodities declined, so would oil imports from the Middle East and Africa, so reducing those countries' economic growth. China is the most important trading partner for great swathes of Sub-Saharan Africa, particularly commodity exporters like Nigeria. China has even surpassed the US as the largest trading partner for Latin America, which has traditionally been seen as the US's backyard and therefore most susceptible to the economic fortunes of its northern neighbour. That is less the case now that Latin American exports to China have grown to account for a record 3 per cent of regional GDP.

The European Union is China's largest trading partner, and China is the second largest trading partner of the EU after the US. A slowdown in China would severely affect Europe, as was evidenced in Germany when profit warnings were issued by companies such as BMW as their sales in China slowed during the 2015 stock market turmoil. Exports from the United States to China, by contrast, are less than 1 per cent of US GDP, but that doesn't mean that American multinationals will be unaffected. The US behemoth Apple sells more iPhones in China than it does in America, for example.

A Chinese crisis would reverberate throughout global financial markets. Even though China's stock market is largely closed to foreign investors, the impact on multinational companies would be reflected in equity markets worldwide. The London Stock Exchange lists a significant number of such stocks, and when China's market tanked in 2015, UK shares experienced their worst one-day fall to that point since the 2008 financial crisis.

China's financial system isn't yet integrated with the rest of the world in the way America's was in 2008, but it is becoming increasingly connected through developments such as the Hong Kong Stock Connect programmes that link China's domestic bourses to one of the most open and global stock exchanges. Chinese markets are also connected to global markets through the renminbi-trading hubs that are located around the world, including in London and Singapore. As China promotes the use of its currency internationally and integrates its financial system with the rest of the world, the risk of contagion from a crisis grows. This is especially the case for countries that have borrowed from Chinese banks.

In 2016, China's banking system had become the largest in the world. A year later, China became the world's largest official creditor, bigger than either the IMF or the World Bank.[22] Chinese bank lending accelerated with the Covid-19 pandemic because developing economies needed cash. Of the 185 countries tracked by the Bank for International Settlements, Chinese banks had lent to all but ten.[23] Though the amounts involved represented only 7.5 per cent of cross-border bank lending, they were concentrated in emerging markets. For instance, as part of its Belt and Road Initiative that saw China invest in infrastructure across Asia and Africa, it lent $300 million to Sri Lanka to construct the Hambantota International Port on its southern coast, and $3.6 billion to Kenya to build a railway linking its capital to the sea. In 133 countries, Chinese bank loans accounted for more than a quarter of their foreign borrowing. There are sixty-three countries that owe more to Chinese banks than to any other country.[24] Should China suffer a financial crisis, then those countries will be significantly affected when loans dry up. As Chinese banks expand their global footprint, the potential fallout from a crash will only grow.

China's heavily indebted property sector has the potential to create a great crash. The Chinese housing market has been characterized by exuberance as developers and investors saw rising house prices as never ending. They accumulated more and more debt to build, even as some homes sat empty and all were becoming increasingly unaffordable.

The bubble of China's property sector has been deflating; whether it will burst, resulting in a huge crash, is yet to be determined. A property sector collapse could trigger a Chinese banking crisis, with all that implies for the global economy. Were that to happen, a bank rescue should be easier, given that China owns the banking system, but the result nevertheless is likely to be prolonged economic stagnation.

As we have seen from a century of financial crises, the credibility of institutions is crucial. How well might China's perform in a crisis? The clumsy handling of the 2015 stock market crash dented confidence in the government. Nevertheless, that crisis did not crash the economy or have lasting consequences. Despite China's economy being rather unusual, a crash there would still be likely to exhibit the traits of previous crises: euphoria, credibility and an aftermath that is determined by the first two factors.

There are four lessons that might help. First, although it's almost impossible to manage euphoria, as it seems to be human nature to pile into rising markets, the Chinese government can regulate the amount of debt taken on to fund such exuberant beliefs. The People's Bank of China can 'lean against the wind', using macroprudential tools – measures designed to ensure the stability of the financial system as a whole – that require banks to lend less when the housing market looks bubbly. This counter-cyclical policy works to push back against rising collateral values linked to rising house prices that enable developers to accumulate unsustainable levels of debt. The central bank already uses the reserve ratio requirement to mandate banks to deposit more money with the central bank when it wants to rein in lending. It was the government's three 'red lines', constraining the developers, that triggered the emerging property crisis. If the central bank acted instead, it could have leaned against the debt bubble earlier on and tried to deflate it slowly. Using more market-based tools such as the ones set out above rather than administrative diktats would instil more confidence in the development of China's regulatory system.

History has taught us that banks need to hold sufficient capital and liquidity. The Chinese banking system is dominated by four state-owned commercial banks, which have already been recapitalized over the past few decades. Because of the opacity of their books, it is challenging to determine how much of their balance sheets, and those of local government's state-owned banks, are weighed down by the legacy of state-owned enterprises, shadow banking, and property lending. With the looming risk of a property crisis, it should be a matter of urgency to ensure banks can withstand a crash in housing. After all, it is banking crises that have resulted in the deepest recessions throughout history. With state ownership, the widespread expectation is that the Chinese government would recapitalize the banks again. But what's unknown is the cost of unwinding the debt built up from years of property-market euphoria.

China's banks have lent to many developing countries, and a second lesson derives from how the US sub-prime financial crisis nearly dragged down the European banks. Despite ongoing geo-economic tensions with the United States and Europe over trade, tech, competition and China's links with Russia, these major economies need to ensure they are able to work together quickly to prevent a Chinese great crash becoming a global one. For instance, China is already part of the global standards body governing the capital requirements of systemically important banks. In a crisis, it might need to work with Western governments to come up with alternative funding, potentially from the IMF, to ensure that a cessation of Chinese lending doesn't tip low-income countries into crisis.

A third lesson from three generations of currency crises is that a financial crisis can trigger an exchange rate crisis. China has a controlled currency that is not freely tradable as well as a relatively closed capital account, so it is in a different position from many emerging markets. However, 'hot money' still flows in and out of China, since capital controls are porous, so the government should bolster its credibility by reforming the regulatory system, and not just its reserves, in case there should be a sell-off of the Chinese currency. History shows that reserves can be depleted, and when there's disbelief in the government's position, that is what usually leads speculators to bet against a currency. So long as China maintains a fixed exchange rate, it is at risk. Since very little Chinese debt is foreign-currency denominated, and since foreign investors still hold little market share in domestic lending, this risk is not yet great, but it could become so should Chinese markets open up further.

The aftermath of a Chinese crash, like others, will depend on the cause of the crisis and the credibility of policymakers in addressing it. The government may be able to deflate the property bubble gradually and recapitalize faltering real-estate companies, but if the bubble bursts and those firms go bust, taking down the banking system, then China could end up suffering a crash similar to the one that occurred in Japan in the early 1990s. Even though the aftermath will probably play out differently, the fourth and final lesson is that

China can learn from the mistakes made in Japan. It should act quickly to restore confidence in its financial system as well as doing all it can to avoid a deflationary mindset and expectations of slow growth from taking hold in both the domestic and business sectors, so inducing a recessionary downward spiral from which it could take decades to recover.

# Epilogue

An enduring insight from financial crises is the importance of recognizing the risk posed by rising levels of debt fuelled by euphoria. Another is that policymakers can resolve a crisis only if their actions are viewed as credible. We've also seen that the aftermaths of crises vary greatly. How a country fares depends not only on the cause of the crash but also on how it is resolved.

All financial crises are due to too much debt in some shape or form, but not all of them lead to a country needing to be rescued or a slow economic recovery. The more debt-fuelled a crisis is, the worse the economic outcome. A differentiating factor is whether it is predominantly a banking crisis or another sort of crash. In the case of the most frequent source of crises, stock market crashes, investors are not usually borrowing from banks, so, although they might lose their shirts, there is not always a wider economic impact. At the other end of the scale, the effects of a banking crisis, which can be accompanied by a property-market crash, are much worse.

A banking great crash is followed by a process of deleveraging, during which firms and households are repaying debt and not spending. At the same time, banks are rebuilding their balance sheets, so are reluctant to lend.[1] The result is a 'credit crunch', which can lead to a deep recession. When credit does not flow through the economy, recovery from the crisis stalls as financing for mortgages and investments are stymied. In eighteen post-war banking crises, the aftermath was a slow economic recovery. National output declined for roughly two years, falling by 9 per cent on average. Unemployment rose by seven percentage points over four years. Asset prices dropped steeply: house prices plunged, while equity prices declined by an average of 55 per cent over three and a half years.[2]

Housing market crashes can lead to banking crises. If the level of indebtedness is so high that it brings down the banks, then it will lead to a serious crisis as seen in the US and Japan. But, unlike Japan's, other housing busts in the early 1990s – in Scandinavia, for example – did not leave lingering scars and those economies grew well that decade.

A currency crisis also does not necessarily lead to a prolonged economic downturn, as it could be caused simply by the actions of speculators like George Soros. A fall in the exchange rate can occur without leading to massive instability. In the aftermath of the European Exchange Rate Mechanism devaluations, for example, European countries experienced a decade of strong growth fuelled by the resulting increase in the competitiveness of their exports. But if a currency crisis results in a sovereign debt crisis, the outcome can be devastating, as was seen in the emerging market crises of the 1980s and 1990s that necessitated rescues of those countries by the IMF.

For the euro area, the 'doom loop' between the states and banks led to bailouts of entire countries and banking systems. Emerging economies are especially at risk from this type of crisis, particularly if they owe a large amount of debt to foreign creditors, but, as we have seen, even more advanced economies such as Greece and Ireland are not immune.

Even though stock market crashes occur regularly, fortunately these do not always drag down the economy. (The Great Depression and the dot com crash are, of course, notable warnings against complacency.) All recessions include a stock market fall, but not all recessions are caused by a stock market crash. Since 1970, there have been fifteen US bear markets, and eleven of those have coincided with recessions, including six of the past seven bear markets.[3]

Looking across these financial crises through history, we can draw some key lessons.

The first set relates to euphoria. Since banking crises lead to deep recessions, it is important to ensure that banks have sufficient capital to weather a bust in asset markets, be that housing or bonds. This requires not only effective regulation but also risk management by financial institutions so they can monitor debt and leverage and adjust their lending when they are on the rise. This was a lesson that was not learned from the 1929 Great Crash. In 2008, the entire banking systems in the US and Europe almost imploded because banks were insufficiently capitalized to withstand a collapse in the American housing market and did not hold enough liquidity when credit markets seized up. Since then, banks have been stress tested and must now hold adequate levels of capital and liquidity as well as have resolution plans so that, if they fail, they can do so in a way that does not bring down the economy.

A related lesson is for economic policy to be counter-cyclical in order to stem rising levels of debt. Major central banks now have macroprudential tools that enable them to 'lean against the wind'. They can, for example, limit loan-to-value ratios of mortgages when the housing market looks bubbly, to reduce lending and therefore the level of debt on banks' balance sheets. Rather than allowing debt to rise with house prices (since rising property values increase the value of collateral), macroprudential policy can 'lean' against a rising market. This is a shift from when Federal Reserve chairman Alan Greenspan decided it wasn't feasible to determine if the dot com boom driving strong economic growth during the late 1990s was a bubble or a fundamental shift in e-commerce, a cautious approach that dated back to 1955, when then Fed chairman William McChesney Martin described the Fed raising interest rates to dampen the economy as being like 'the chaperone who has ordered the punch bowl removed just when the party was really warming up'.[4] Central bankers are now more inclined to take away the punch bowl instead of letting the bubble burst and dealing with the consequences.

A further lesson is the need for supranational regulatory supervision, since lending easily crosses borders internationally, and even more so within the EU single market. There is a greater role for global bodies like the Financial Stability Board to set capital requirements as well as the EU's banking union to supervise the activities of major banks.

The second trait of crises, the importance of credibility, offers numerous lessons, particularly drawn from the currency crises that have affected advanced and emerging economies alike. In a system of fixed exchange rates, even holding ample reserves that can be deployed to buy currency to support the peg might not be sufficient to prevent a collapse of the exchange rate in the face of speculation. But it helps. After the Asian financial crisis, emerging markets built up their reserves in the early 2000s for just this reason.

However, reserves are finite, and if defending the value of a currency requires raising interest rates to attract buyers, then that's where credibility comes to the fore. The 1992 ERM crisis showed that the UK, Spain and other European countries were ultimately unwilling to raise interest rates during a recession to maintain a currency peg. It wasn't credible that policymakers would value the exchange rate more than the damage from higher unemployment. Higher rates mean higher returns to buyers of the currency, but it also means a higher cost of borrowing, which dampens demand just when the economy needs support during a recession. Monetary policies that prioritize maintaining an exchange rate can lack credibility. The lesson is for policymakers to ensure that their choice of exchange rate systems is clearly compatible with their economic aims. For instance, the UK's adoption of a floating rate signals that its monetary policy is geared at managing the domestic economy's ups and downs rather than maintaining any particular value of the pound.

Another lesson relating to credibility derives from the third-generation crisis (Chapter 1) that was characterized by contagion. The Asian financial crisis spread to Turkey, Russia and Latin America when investors pulled their money out of emerging markets as an investment class. To stem the 'hot money' outflows that triggered the currency crisis, capital controls were imposed by Malaysia during its acute phase in the late 1990s. That might be a helpful crisis management tool, but, given the porous nature of borders, it is by no means a perfect one. Investors might also be wary of returning to a country that does not allow them to move their money out.

As a preventive measure, governments need to differentiate their country to show they are financially robust and avoid being caught up in a general sell-off by investors of their holdings in emerging economies as a group. Investors themselves have become more discerning, as seen in the 2013 'taper tantrum' when the Fed's signal that it would taper its QE programme led to a sell-off of only some emerging economies. They fled from the 'Fragile Five' economies of Brazil, India, Indonesia, South Africa and Turkey, all of which had high levels of dollar-denominated debt, but stayed put in others. The lesson for governments is to not become over-indebted and to present their fiscal positions clearly so as to avoid being caught up in an indiscriminate sell-off.

A lack of credibility is also how, in 2010, a banking crisis in Europe led to a sovereign debt crisis when bond investors sold off the debt of weaker countries, notably Greece. That led to an existential debate about the single currency. The crisis was eventually ended by the creation of new institutions and political pledges about the future of the euro, which worked because they were viewed as credible by financial markets.

The final lesson concerns the aftermath of a crisis, the nature of which is determined both by its cause and by the credibility of the actions taken by policymakers. So, if policymakers can learn from history by regulating debt levels and rapidly deploying credible tools to address a crisis, then they might just be able to prevent the next crash from becoming a global meltdown.

It's not only policymakers who can learn from what has come before; we can all apply our understanding of euphoria, credibility and aftermath to better position ourselves for the next inevitable crash.

First, be wary of euphoria and avoid piling into rising markets by borrowing too much. It's tough to stand on the sidelines of an exuberant market, but it would be worse to feel so euphoric that we overborrow and can't afford to repay our debts when the inevitable bust happens. It is difficult to differentiate between an upward trajectory and a bubble, but since all markets, bubbly or not, will deflate, the lesson remains the same: borrow with caution. Invest instead for the long term, since markets will rise again. And here's the hard part, try not to sell at the bottom of the market or retire then. Drawing down a lump sum from your pension or buying an annuity would lock in any loss in asset value that reduces your income in retirement, so seek professional advice and look carefully at how the market is behaving before doing so.

Second, it is certainly challenging to identify when the next crash might occur, but we can look for evidence of credible policies to determine how it could play out. When too much debt in a market is causing its growth to slow, that is a sign of a potential crash. Whether it becomes a crisis depends on whether policymakers can orchestrate a managed deflation of the market and cushion any impact on the economy. For instance, are regulatory measures in place to reduce the amount of borrowing in a rising market? Does government policy support keeping people in work and viable businesses afloat, so that a deep recession is less likely to follow a crisis?

Third, it's important to bear in mind that financial markets have crashed regularly for centuries and the aftermaths have varied considerably, so it's best to prepare our finances in anticipation that the next crisis is never far away. The old advice to 'save for a rainy day' captures this well. For the business community, there are also lessons to be learned. Firms such as Amazon that were running tight ships despite the dizzying heights of the market not only survived but thrived in a crisis. A crash inevitably separates the strong from the weak, and a well-placed company that continues to invest prudently might even end up in a better position at the end of one.

At the time of writing, double-digit inflation due to the Russia–Ukraine war that began in February 2022 was causing a severe cost of living crisis throughout the world as both countries are major commodity exporters. The rapid rise in energy and other commodity prices has driven up inflation and depressed economies at the same time, reminiscent of the 1970s when there was high inflation alongside a stagnant economy ('stagflation').

Central banks have raised interest rates to try to dampen inflationary pressures. Increasing the cost of borrowing has led to declining share prices: the US stock market fell into bear-market territory, dropping by more than 20 per cent between the first and the third quarters of the year. This was not an instance of euphoria leading to a bubble that burst. The market crash was due to tighter credit conditions and the expectations of investors that a recession would follow from the shock to global supply prices that has pushed up the cost of production and squeezed disposable incomes for consumers. Recession leads to lower sales, and that's been reflected in companies' share prices. So, the stock market and the economy are both falling due to an external shock. Although it is not a financial crash, the second trait of such crises, the importance of credible monetary policies, remains an important factor in determining how the crisis will impact the economy.

A lesson from the 1970s is that raising interest rates to control inflation can tip the economy into a downturn. Fed chairman Paul Volcker brought down inflation, which had reached nearly 15 per cent, by raising US interest rates to as high as 20 per cent in 1981, triggering an American and a global recession. The monetary policy worked, as inflation dropped to 5 per cent a year later, but at the cost of a high unemployment rate that had reached 11 per cent. Today, central banks are again trying to dampen inflation but not by so much that it leads to a repeat of the early 1980s. This is, needless to say, a difficult task. Just like the 1970s energy shocks, the Russia–Ukraine war is beyond the control of central banks, but their actions can influence how the cost-of-living crisis affects the people and businesses.

Developing countries are still trying to recover from the Covid-19 pandemic, and a number of them are being rescued by the IMF, so there have already been some sovereign debt crises. But, there will surely be more pain to come before the full aftermath of the current energy crisis can be assessed.

The final great crash in this book also offers up some reflections for us all for the future.

Perhaps because the Covid-19 crisis was so unusual, it offers the most novel lessons. There are, of course, the important lessons about managing the economic impact of a global pandemic, including the rapid deployment of income support for people and of liquidity help for businesses. But the lockdowns also led to a sudden stop to the way we work, shop and go to school. This was accompanied by wholesale adoption of technologies that enabled working from home and accelerated e-commerce along with other online activities. As a result, we are facing a potential 'great reset' with at least three dimensions: well-being, fairness and greening the economy.

We're getting glimpses of a great reset that uses this pause to change the course of the economy. Deploying technology, it's possible to grow the economy in a qualitatively different way. Perhaps the most dramatic shift has been in the way that we work. More flexible working can reconfigure the work–life balance. Even though technologies like Zoom were available before the pandemic, their widespread adoption during the lockdowns has continued after it. (Just as if only one party has a telephone, the technology doesn't work if you're the only one with the Zoom app!) Changing business practices to embrace remote working enabled by technology can increase productivity for individual firms and thus the economy. Adoption is essential for innovations to have an economy-wide impact. This is harder to do than it appears. We live surrounded by technology and yet still face slow economic growth. This is known as the Solow paradox after the great economist Robert Solow, who observed: 'You can see the computer age everywhere but in the productivity statistics.'[5] Even so, the pandemic might well prove to have accelerated technology adoption, which could be key to improving productivity, our living standards and the well-being of those who have enjoyed greater autonomy in their working day.

Secondly, policies that increase fairness are another much-needed reset. Government support for jobs and livelihoods was seen in pretty much every country around the world. Countries like the UK, which had never had a furlough scheme, adopted one quickly as large swathes of the economy went into lockdown. In the European Union, the introduction of collective borrowing to fund the EU budget, in order to allow struggling states to offer direct support for their citizens, was something that the eurozone members had not done during the euro crisis a decade earlier. Although the US typically will send cheques to Americans to boost their income during recessions, the repeated direct support offered by it and other countries has stimulated discussions about a universal basic income, whereby everyone regardless of their income receives money each month from the government to sustain their basic standard of living.

Given the high levels of inequality in the years preceding the pandemic, government spending to maintain employment levels and incentivize businesses to provide good jobs could be an important change in governments' conceptualization of economic growth going forward. People have seen the benefit of having a basic level of income support when times were tough. This varies greatly from country to country, but the welfare role of the state has been highlighted in the pandemic and future measures to increase fairness may continue to be viewed favourably.[6]

Thirdly, a greener economy would be an important part of a great reset. Pollution levels dropped sharply under lockdown travel restriction, but soon picked up again. In the midst of a focus on public health, there was concern that the environment would fall by the wayside. But 2021 witnessed renewed interest, with the new Biden administration taking the US back into the Paris Climate Change Accord and global efforts continued at the COP26 climate summit, which was held in the UK that November. Growing in a greener way was also highlighted by the IMF as generating greater returns, including jobs from public investment in green infrastructure.

Ultimately, greening the economy will require a wide range of stakeholders who press for a paradigm shift. In addition to legal and regulatory measures, broad societal changes are also required, much as when the welfare state was created in the early twentieth century. When there's widespread acceptance of the need for change, formal measures are not just passed but, importantly, accepted. For a de jure measure to be effective, there has to be de facto compliance. The importance of formal and informal institutions in setting the 'rules of the game' has been well known since the great economist Douglass North established the school of thought known as New Institutional Economics.[7] Sometimes a regulation or tax will run ahead of public opinion, while others fall behind. But lasting change requires societal acceptance, which only comes about when people are persuaded of the cause. So, simply changing laws or imposing regulations is not enough. Any climate measure will need the support and buy-in of stakeholders, not just in the public sphere but also the private sector.

An example of how norms are shifting is the trend towards incorporating environmental, social and governance (ESG) considerations in business, which was also strengthened rather than weakened by the pandemic. Prompted by regulatory requirements, many companies are incorporating ESG, particularly new environmental goals, into their strategies. Firms have signed up to support the 2030 Sustainable Development Goals through the UN Global Compact and are setting their own net-zero carbon-emissions targets, which are sometimes more ambitious than those of their home governments. There is also a growing number of ESG ratings of companies by specialist and financial firms. Although imperfect, this focus helps investors select well-rated companies and screen out those that do not abide by environmental as well as social and governance standards. Such actions complement formal measures, such as legislation to achieve net zero, and enhance their effectiveness.

There is a risk that these efforts are just a new version of the corporate social responsibility that has been criticized for paying lip service to causes. But the change in social norms appears to reflect a societal shift in preferring environmentally responsible businesses. It seems to be what customers and employees increasingly demand and expect. Plus, those who are running or investing in companies are themselves people who may want to do their part.

This is the crux of how a paradigm shift or a reset occurs: the consensus as to what is acceptable changes. A century ago, it was the unacceptable levels of poverty and inequality that led to the creation of the welfare state. Today, it is the destruction of our planet.

In order to reach a new consensus, we as individuals have an important part to play in executing these lessons from history and recognizing that our sustained effort is important, because progress is not linear and there can be backtracking by governments and companies. We can discuss in public and social forums our own actions, such as recycling and the importance of net zero, which stress the value of a greener economy. We can vote for politicians who will implement policies that address climate change and promote equality and better opportunities for all. We can choose not to buy from companies that do not treat their employees fairly or abide by environmental commitments. Through our collective efforts, we could precipitate a great reset to improve our well-being, insist on fairer policies from governments and hold companies to account for their environmental and social impact.

After the devastation of the pandemic, a great reset could be a way of growing out of the Covid-19 crisis into a happier, fairer and greener twenty-first-century world. That may be the most satisfying lesson to draw from a century of great crashes.

# Acknowledgements

There are so many people to thank. First, I am deeply grateful to my publisher, Daniel Crewe, at Viking/Penguin Random House. He is everything a top publisher should be. I feel very fortunate to have his longstanding and patient support. I have also benefited from his insightful editing of the manuscript. I also want to convey my gratitude to his colleague, Celia Buzuk, at Penguin Business. I am very thankful for all her encouragement and her impressive ability to liven up the text. And I would like to acknowledge the entire team at PRH, including Ellie Smith, without whom such a book could not exist. Their professionalism and kindness are greatly appreciated.

I would like to give my heartfelt thanks to my literary agent, Will Francis, at Janklow & Nesbit (UK). He is simply the best in the business. I am immensely grateful to be represented by him and to have been able to work with such a talented individual over so many years.

I would also give a huge thanks to my copy-editor, Trevor Horwood. I marvel at his ability to rephrase or tweak a sentence to make it clearer and more effective in conveying what I am trying to say. It's been wonderful to have his help in editing and checking the text.

I am also grateful to the UK Treasury for the opportunity to serve on the Independent Review Panel on Ring-Fencing and Proprietary Trading from 2021 to 2022. As the economist on the six-person panel that reviewed the UK banking regulatory system a decade on from the 2008 crisis, I gained a great deal of perspective and knowledge that has improved my understanding of financial crashes.

This book has benefited from my broadcasting work at the BBC and Bloomberg TV. It was thanks to wonderful colleagues at both companies that I was able to cover some of these great crashes. I may have fronted the programmes as a TV and radio presenter, but they get on air because of the hard work of the teams behind the scenes. I am very thankful and have learned so much about broadcasting, financial markets and how to get the best out of interviewees.

And I want to thank my family, particularly Graeme, who is simply one of the best economists. Without their support, none of this would be possible.

Finally, I want to thank all of you who have picked up this book. Only through common endeavour will we learn the lessons from history so as to try to avoid repeating its worst mistakes.

# Notes

## Introduction: The Great Crash of 1929

1 J. K. Galbraith, *A Short History of Financial Euphoria*, New York: Whittle Books in association with Viking, 1993, p. 13.

2 Gary Richardson et al., 'Stock Market Crash of 1929', Federal Reserve History, 2013, www.federalreservehistory.org/essays/stock-market-crash-of-1929.

3 Robert Z. Aliber and Charles P. Kindleberger, *Manias, Panics, and Crashes: A History of Financial Crises*, 7th edn, Basingstoke: Palgrave Macmillan, 2015, p. 201.

4 Linda Yueh, *The Great Economists: How Their Ideas Can Help Us Today*, London: Viking, 2018, p. 95.

5 Gary Richardson, 'The Great Depression: 1929–1941', Federal Reserve History, 2013, www.federalreservehistory.org/essays/great-depression.

6 Richardson et al., 'Stock Market Crash of 1929'.

7 Aliber and Kindleberger, *Manias, Panics, and Crashes*, p. 137.

8 Ibid.

9 Melvyn Bragg, 'John Steinbeck's Bitter Fruit', *Guardian*, 21 November 2001, accessed 15 August 2022, www.theguardian.com/books/2011/nov/21/melvyn-bragg-on-john-steinbeck.

10 Michael Gou et al., 'Banking Act of 1932', Federal Reserve History, 22 November 2013, www.federalreservehistory.org/essays/banking-act-of-1932.

11 William L. Silber, 'Why Did FDR's Bank Holiday Succeed?' *Economic Policy Review*, 15(1) (2009), 19–31, www.newyorkfed.org/research/epr/09v15n1/0907silb.html.

12 Patricia Waiwood, 'Recession of 1937–38', Federal Reserve History, 2013, www.federalreservehistory.org/essays/recession-of-1937-38.

13  Richardson, 'The Great Depression: 1929–1941'.

14  Kimberly Amadeo, 'Black Monday in 1929, 1987, 2015, and 2020', *The Balance*, 26 January 2022, accessed 17 July 2022, www.thebalance.com/what-is-black-monday-in-1987-1929-and-2015-3305818.

## Chapter 1: *Three Generations of Currency Crises*

1  Sandra Kollen Ghizoni, 'Creation of the Bretton Woods System, July 1944', Federal Reserve History, 2013, www.federalreservehistory.org/essays/bretton-woods-created.

2  Ivo Maes with Ilaria Pasotti, *Robert Triffin: A Life*, Oxford: Oxford University Press, 2021, p. 145.

3  Paulina Restrepo Echavarria and Praew Grittayaphong, 'Bretton Woods and the Growth of the Eurodollar Market', Federal Reserve Bank of St. Louis on the Economy blog, 22 January 2022, accessed 30 August 2022, www.stlouisfed.org/on-the-economy/2022/january/bretton-woods-growth-eurodollar-market.

4  Aliber and Kindleberger, *Manias, Panics, and Crashes*, p. 202.

5  Trade Association for the Emerging Markets (EMTA), 'The Brady Plan', accessed 14 October 2022, www.emta.org/em-background/the-brady-plan/.

6  Phillip Inman, 'Black Wednesday 20 Years On: How the Day Unfolded', *Guardian*, 13 September 2012, accessed 19 August 2022, www.theguardian.com/business/2012/sep/13/black-wednesday-20-years-pound-erm.

7  Paul Krugman, 'Devaluing History', *New York Times*, 24 November 2010, accessed 19 August 2022, https://archive.nytimes.com/krugman.blogs.nytimes.com/2010/11/24/devaluing-history/.

8  Dani Rodrik, 'Globalization's Wrong Turn: And How It Hurt America', *Foreign Affairs*, 98(4) (2019), pp. 26–33, p. 26.

9  Chris Wright, 'Asia '97: The Financial Crisis That Left Its Mark for Good', *Euromoney*, 9 May 2019, accessed 19 August 2022, www.euromoney.com/article/b1f7pksth48x10/asia-97-the-financial-crisis-that-left-its-mark-for-good.

10 Maggie Farley, 'Malaysia Leader, Soros Trade Barbs', *Los Angeles Times*, 22 September 1997, accessed 18 July 2022, www.latimes.com/archives/la-xpm-1997-sep-22-fi-34969-story.html.

## Chapter 2: The US Savings and Loan Crisis of the 1980s

1 Associated Press, 'Obama Accuses McCain of Smear Tactics', NBC News, 5 October 2008, accessed 18 July 2022, www.nbcnews.com/id/wbna27034817.

2 Robert D. McFadden, 'Charles Keating, 90, Key Figure in '80s Savings and Loan Crisis, Dies', *New York Times*, 2 April 2014, www.nytimes.com/2014/04/02/business/charles-keating-key-figure-in-the-1980s-savings-and-loan-crisis-dies-at-90.html.

3 Lawrence J. White, *The S&L Debacle: Public Policy Lessons for Banks and Thrift Regulation*, New York and Oxford: Oxford University Press, 1991, p. 59.

4 Ibid.

5 Michael Corbett, 'Oil Shock of 1973–74', Federal Reserve History, 22 November 2013, www.federalreservehistory.org/essays/oil-shock-of-1973-74.

6 Steven Kettell, 'Oil Crisis', *Encyclopedia Britannica*, 31 January 2020, www.britannica.com/topic/oil-crisis.

7 White, *The S&L Debacle*, p. 64.

8 Ibid., p. 70.

9 Ibid. p. 77.

10 James R. Barth, Susanne Trimbath and Glenn Yago, 'The U.S. Savings and Loan Crisis in Hindsight 20 Years Later', in *The Savings and Loan Crisis: Lessons from a Regulatory Failure*, The Milken Institute Series on Financial Innovation and Economic Growth, vol. 5, Boston, MA: Springer, 2004, pp. 179–250, p. 185.

11 Ibid., p. 186.

12 Aliber and Kindleberger, *Manias, Panics, and Crashes*, p. 89.

13 Tom Nicholas and Matthew G. Preble, 'Michael Milken: The Junk Bond King', Harvard Business School Case 816-050, March 2016, revised May 2021, www.hbs.edu/faculty/Pages/item.aspx?num=50852.

14  Aliber and Kindleberger, *Manias, Panics, and Crashes*, p. 155.

15  Ibid., p. 156.

16  Ibid., p. 90.

17  Ibid., p. 156.

18  White, *The S&L Debacle*, p. 99.

19  Ibid., p. 103.

20  Kitty Calavita, Robert H. Tillman and Henry N. Pontell, 'The Savings and Loan Debacle, Financial Crime, and the State', *Annual Review of Sociology*, 23 (1997), 19–38, www.jstor.org/stable/2952542, pp. 23-4.

21  White, *The S&L Debacle*, p. 109.

22  Ibid., p. 109.

23  Ibid., p. 110.

24  Aliber and Kindleberger, *Manias, Panics, and Crashes*, p. 29.

25  White, *The S&L Debacle*, p. 139.

26  Ibid., p. 147.

27  Ibid., p. 151.

28  David Mason, 'Savings and Loan Industry, US', *EH.net Encyclopedia*, ed. Robert Whaples, 10 June 2003, http://eh.net/encyclopedia/savings-and-loan-industry-u-s/.

## Chapter 3: Japan's Real-Estate Crash of the Early 1990s

1  World Bank, *World Development Report: The Challenge of Development*, Washington, DC, 1991, https://openknowledge.worldbank.org/handle/10986/5974.

2  Alice H. Amsden and Ajit Singh, 'The Optimal Degree of Competition and Dynamic Efficiency in Japan and Korea', *European Economic Review*, 38(3–4) (1994), 941–51.

3  Ajit Singh, 'International Competitiveness and Industrial Policy', in Irfan ul Haque, ed., *International Competitiveness: Interaction of the Public and the Private Sectors*, Washington, DC: World Bank, 1990, pp. 41–4, p. 41.

4  Jeffrey Frankel, 'The Plaza Accord, 30 Years Later', NBER Working Paper 21813, 2015, www.nber.org/papers/w21813.

5 Christopher Wood, *The Bubble Economy: Japan's Extraordinary Speculative Boom of the '80s and the Dramatic Bust of the '90s*, London, Sidgwick & Jackson, 1992, p. 53.

6 Ibid., p. 117.

7 AP News, 'Susumu Ishii, Former Underworld Boss at Center of Scandal, Dead at 67', 3 September 1991, accessed 14 July 2022, https://apnews.com/article/0526cb865863c5a82566cb93e4a1d885.

8 *Chicago Tribune*, 'Japan Bank Woes Take Ominous Turn', 30 October 1994, accessed 14 July 2022, www.chicagotribune.com/news/ct-xpm-1994-10-30-9410300273-story.html.

9 Michael Hirsh, 'Finance Minister, Bank Heads Announce Resignation in Clean Sweep', AP News, 4 October 1991, accessed 14 July 2022, https://apnews.com/article/bcb726865da3f947535b2de9689fc7ff.

10 Leslie Helm, 'Japanese Bank Says It Loaned Billions to Scandal Figure', *Los Angeles Times*, 15 August 1991, accessed 14 July 2022, www.latimes.com/archives/la-xpm-1991-08-15-fi-843-story.html.

11 Claudia Dziobek and Ceyla Pazarbasioglu, 'Lessons from Systemic Bank Restructuring: A Survey of 24 Countries', IMF Working Paper WP/97/161, 1997.

12 Kiyohiko G. Nishimura and Yuko Kawamoto, 'Why Does the Problem Persist? "Rational Rigidity" and the Plight of Japanese Banks', RIETI Discussion Paper Series 02-E-003, March 2002, p. 14.

13 Jennifer A. Amyx, *Japan's Financial Crisis: Institutional Rigidity and Reluctant Change*, Princeton: Princeton University Press, 2004, p. 183.

14 Ibid.

15 *Nihon Keizai Shimbun*, 21 October 1998.

16 *Nihon Keizai Shimbun*, 12 October 2001.

17 Amyx, *Japan's Financial Crisis*, p. 1.

## Chapter 4: The Dot Com Crash, 2000–2001

1 Abby Miller, 'No More Checks from CyberRebate', DNM News, 29 May 2001, accessed 16 September 2022, www.dmnews.com/no-more-checks-from-cyberrebate/.

2 Robert J. Shiller, *Irrational Exuberance*, Princeton: Princeton University Press, 2000.

3 David Goldman, '10 Big Dot.com Flops', CNN Money, 10 March 2010, accessed 25 May 2022, https://money.cnn.com/galleries/2010/technology/1003/gallery.dot_com_busts/.

4 Amazon, 'Amazon.com Announces Investment in Pets.com', 29 March 1999, https://press.aboutamazon.com/news-releases/news-release-details/amazoncom-announces-investment-petscom.

5 Brad Stone, 'Amazon's Pet Projects', *Newsweek*, 21 June 1999, p. 56.

6 Ibid.

7 Ibid.

8 Pui-Wing Tam and Mylene Mangalindan, 'Pets.com's Demise: Too Much Litter, Too Few Funds', *Wall Street Journal*, 8 November 2000, p. B1+.

9 Goldman, '10 Big Dot.com Flops'.

10 Brett Trueman, M. H. Franco Wong and Xiao-Jun Zhang, 'The Eyeballs Have It: Searching for the Value in Internet Stocks', *Journal of Accounting Research*, 38 (2000), 137–62.

11 Ibid.

12 Andrew Chen, *The Cold Start Problem: Using Network Effects to Scale Your Product*, New York: Random House Business, 2021.

13 Jennifer Thornton and Sunny Marche, 'Sorting Through the Dot Bomb Rubble: How Did the High-Profile E-tailers Fail?' *International Journal of Information Management*, 23 (2003), 121–38.

14 Andrew Hill, 'IPOs and the Ghost of Pets.com's Sock-Puppet', *Financial Times*, 19 February 2014, accessed 25 May 2022, www.ft.com/content/db124a89-98bf-3474-97e3-83df3cf6b5ee.

15 John Kay, *The Foundations of Corporate Success: How Business Strategies Add Value*, Oxford: Oxford University Press, 1993, p. vi.

16 Yueh, *The Great Economists*; Charles Mackay, *Memoirs of Extraordinary Popular Delusions and the Madness of Crowds*, 2nd edn, vol. 1, London: Office of the National Illustrated Library, 1852.

17 Aart Kraay and Jaume Ventura, 'The Dot-Com Bubble, the Bush Deficits, and the US Current Account', in Richard H. Clarida, ed., *G7 Current Account Imbalances: Sustainability and Adjustment*, Chicago: University of Chicago Press, 2007, pp. 457–95.

18 Ibid.

19 Jacob Schlesinger, 'How Alan Greenspan Finally Came to Terms with the Market', *Wall Street Journal*, 8 May 2000, accessed 18 May 2022, www.wsj.com/articles/SB95774078783030219.

20 Ibid.

21 Ibid.

22 J. Bradford DeLong and Konstantin Magin, 'A Short Note on the Size of the Dot-Com Bubble', NBER Working Paper 12011, 2006, www.nber.org/papers/w12011.

23 Ibid.

24 Schlesinger, 'How Alan Greenspan Finally Came to Terms with the Market'.

25 Thornton and Marche, 'Sorting Through the Dot Bomb Rubble'.

26 Brent Goldfarb and David A. Kirsch, *Bubbles and Crashes: The Booms and Busts of Technological Innovation*, Stanford: Stanford University Press, 2019.

27 Thornton and Marche, 'Sorting Through the Dot Bomb Rubble'.

28 Alex Fitzpatrick, 'A Judge Ordered Microsoft to Split. Here's Why It's Still a Single Company', *Time*, 5 November 2014, https://time.com/3553242/microsoft-monopoly/.

29 Ibid.

30 Pierre Azoulay et al., 'Research: The Average Age of a Successful Start-up Founder is 45', *Harvard Business Review*, 11 July 2018, https://hbr.org/2018/07/research-the-average-age-of-a-successful-startup-founder-is-45.

31 Thornton and Marche, 'Sorting Through the Dot Bomb Rubble', p. 126.

32 Ibid.

33 Ibid., p. 127.

34 Erika Matulich and Karen Squires, 'What a Dog Fight! TKO: Pets.com', *Journal of Business Case Studies*, 4(5) (2008), 1–5, https://core.ac.uk/download/pdf/268109951.pdf.

35 Thornton and Marche, 'Sorting Through the Dot Bomb Rubble'.

36 Ibid.

37 Ruth Simon, 'Margin Investors Learn the Hard Way That Brokers Can Get Tough on Loans', *Wall Street Journal*, 27 April 2000, p. C1.

38  Antonio Gledson de Carvalho, Roberto B. Pinheiro and Joelson Oliveira Sampaio, 'The Dotcom Bubble and Underpricing: Conjectures and Evidence', Federal Reserve Bank of Cleveland Working Paper 16–33, 2016.

39  Goldfarb and Kirsch, *Bubbles and Crashes*.

40  Thornton and Marche, 'Sorting Through the Dot Bomb Rubble'.

41  Ibid.

42  Evelyn Cheng, 'Nasdaq Closes Above 5k for First Time Since March 2000; Dow, S&P at Records', CNBC, 2 March 2015, www.cnbc.com/2015/03/02/us-stocks-open-narrowly-mixed-ahead-of-data.html.

43  Danny Fortson, 'The Great Tech "Revaluation" Has Just Begun', *Sunday Times*, 22 May 2022, accessed 22 May 2022, www.thetimes.co.uk/article/the-great-tech-revaluation-has-only-just-begun-92l8vh9rx.

44  Noel Randewich and Lewis Krauskopf, '20 Years After Dot-Com Peak, Tech Dominance Keeps Investors on Edge', Reuters, 18 February 2020, accessed 25 May 2022, www.reuters.com/article/us-usa-stocks-dotcombust-graphic-idUSKBN20C1J7.

45  Ibid.

46  Goldfarb and Kirsch, *Bubbles and Crashes*.

47  Kevin L. Kliesen, 'The 2001 Recession: How Was It Different and What Developments May Have Caused It?' *Federal Reserve Bank of St. Louis Review*, 85 (5) (2003), 23–38, https://files.stlouisfed.org/files/htdocs/publications/review/03/09/Kliesen.pdf.

48  Ibid.

49  Ibid.

50  Ibid.

51  David S. Langdon, Terence M. McMenamin and Thomas J. Krolik, 'U.S. Labor Market in 2001: Economy Enters a Recession', *Monthly Labor Review*, US Bureau of Labor Statistics (February 2002), 3–33, www.bls.gov/opub/mlr/2002/02/art1full.pdf.

52  Yueh, *The Great Economists*.

53  Randewich and Krauskopf, '20 Years After Dot-Com Peak'.

54  Richard Milne, 'Klarna CEO Says Fintech Will Focus Less on Growth and More on "Short-Term Profitability" ', *Financial Times*, 26 May 2022,

accessed 1 June 2022, www.ft.com/content/b5b7d26c-2407-4845-8276-ef5da20f778a.

55 Yueh, *The Great Economists*.

56 Fortson, 'The Great Tech "Revaluation" Has Just Begun'.


## Chapter 5: The Global Financial Crisis of 2008

1 BBC Radio 4, 'What Next for the Credit Crunch?', 15 September 2008, accessed 13 September 2022, http://news.bbc.co.uk/1/hi/business/7612607.stm.

2 Aliber and Kindleberger, *Manias, Panics, and Crashes*, p. 325.

3 Manmohan Singh and James Aitken, 'The (Sizable) Role of Rehypothecation in the Shadow Banking System', IMF Working Paper WP/10/172, July 2010.

4 Adam Tooze, *Crashed: How a Decade of Financial Crises Changed the World*, London: Allen Lane, 2018, p. 46.

5 Andrew Haughwout et al., 'Real Estate Investors, the Leverage Cycle, and the Housing Market Crisis', Federal Reserve Bank of New York Staff Reports, 514, September 2011.

6 Ibid.

7 Aliber and Kindleberger, *Manias, Panics, and Crashes*, p. 316.

8 Ibid., p. 321.

9 Herman M. Schwartz, *Subprime Nation: American Power, Global Capital, and the Housing Bubble*, Ithaca, NY: Cornell University Press, 2009, pp. 101–4.

10 Daniel O. Beltran, Laurie DeMarco and Charles P. Thomas, 'Foreign Exposure to Asset-Backed Securities of U.S. Origin', International Finance Discussion Papers 939, Board of Governors of the Federal Reserve System, 2008, Table 6: line 6.

11 Carol Bertaut et al., 'ABS Inflows to the United States and the Global Financial Crisis', *Journal of International Economics*, 88(2) (2012), 219–34.

12 Torsten Ehlers, Steven Kong and Feng Zhu, 'Mapping Shadow Banking in China: Structure and Dynamics', BIS Working Paper 701, February 2018, www.bis.org/publ/work701.pdf.

13  *New York Times*, 'BNP Paribas Suspends Funds Because of Subprime Problems', 9 August 2007.

14  Neil Irwin, *The Alchemists: Three Central Bankers and a World on Fire*, New York: Penguin, 2014, p. 2.

15  Hyun Song Shin, 'Reflections on Northern Rock: The Bank Run that Heralded the Global Financial Crisis', *Journal of Economic Perspectives*, 23(1) (2009), 101–19, p. 102.

16  Alistair Darling, *Back from the Brink: 1000 Days at Number 11*, London: Atlantic Books, 2011, pp. 121–2.

17  Tooze, *Crashed*, p. 180.

18  Ibid., p. 214.

19  Ibid., p. 241.

20  Ralph De Haas et al., 'Foreign Banks and the Vienna Initiative: Turning Sinners into Saints?', IMF Working Paper WP/12/117, 2012, www.imf.org/external/pubs/ft/wp/2012/wp12117.pdf.

21  IMF, *Global Financial Stability Report*, Washington, DC, April 2015.

22  Linda Yueh, 'The Limits of Star Power', BBC News, 29 October 2013, accessed 13 September 2022, www.bbc.co.uk/news/business-24723411.

## Chapter 6: The Euro Crisis of 2010

1  Robert Triffin, *Gold and the Dollar Crisis: The Future of Convertibility*, New Haven: Yale University Press, 1960.

2  Maes, *Robert Triffin*, pp. 136–7.

3  Ibid., pp. 151–2.

4  Ibid., pp. 154.

5  Tooze, *Crashed*, p. 333.

6  George Papaconstantinou, *Game Over: The Inside Story of the Greek Crisis*, Athens: Papadopoulos Publishing, 2016, Chapter 8.

7  Tooze, *Crashed*, p. 343.

8  Ricardo Reis, 'The Portuguese Slump and Crash and the Euro Crisis', *Brookings Papers on Economic Activity*, 46(1) (2013), 143–210, p. 177.

9  Tooze, *Crashed*, p. 387.

10  Ibid., p. 379.

11  Philip Aldrick, 'Multi-Trillion Plan to Save the Eurozone Being Pre-pared', *Daily Telegraph*, 24 September 2011, accessed 4 April 2022, www.telegraph.co.uk/finance/financialcrisis/8786665/Multi-trillion-plan-to-save-the-eurozone-being-prepared.html.

12  Tooze, *Crashed*, p. 410.

13  Angelique Chrisafis, 'Euro Stability More Important than Greece, Says Angela Merkel', *Guardian*, 3 November 2011, accessed 8 April 2022, www.theguardian.com/business/2011/nov/03/euro-stability-more-important-greece.

14  Ibid.

15  Peter Spiegel, 'If the Euro Falls, Europe Falls', *Financial Times*, 15 May 2014.

16  Tooze, *Crashed*, p. 418.

17  Suzanne Daley, 'In Spain, Homes are Taken but Debt Stays', *New York Times*, 27 October 2010.

18  Amalia Cárdenas, 'The Spanish Savings Bank Crisis: History, Causes and Responses', IN3 Working Paper Series, Fundació per a la Universitat Oberta de Catalunya, 2013.

19  Mario Draghi, Speech at the Global Investment Conference in London, 26 July 2012, www.ecb.europa.eu/press/key/date/2012/html/sp120726.en.html.

20  Peter Spiegel, 'Draghi's ECB Management: The Leaked Geithner Files', *Financial Times*, 11 November 2014.

21  Anton Korinek, Prakash Loungani and Jonathan D. Ostry, 'A Welcome Evolution: The IMF's Thinking on Capital Controls and Next Steps', VoxEU.org, 8 April 2022, https://voxeu.org/article/imf-s-thinking-capital-controls-and-next-steps.

22  *Der Spiegel*, 'Schauble's Push for Grexit Puts Merkel on Defensive', 17 July 2015.

23  *The Economist*, 'The Quest for Prosperity: Europe's Economy Has Been Underperforming. But Whose Fault is That?', 17 March 2017.

## Chapter 7: The Covid-19 Crash of 2020

1  Organisation for Economic Co-operation and Development (OECD), *OECD Economic Outlook*, December 2020, www.oecd-ilibrary.org/economics/oecd-economic-outlook/volume-2020/issue-2_39a88ab1-en.

2  Robert Barro, José Ursúa and Joanna Weng, 'Coronavirus Meets the Great Influenza Pandemic', VoxEU.org, 20 March 2020, https://voxeu.org/article/coronavirus-meets-great-influenza-pandemic.

3  Ibid.

4  Ibid.

5  Caroline Kantis et al., 'Updated: Timeline of the Coronavirus', Think Global Health, an initiative of the Council in Foreign Relations, 16 September 2022, www.thinkglobalhealth.org/article/updated-timeline-coronavirus.

6  Ibid.

7  Laurel Wamsley, 'March 11, 2020: The Day Everything Changed', NPR, 11 March 2021, accessed 15 September 2022, www.npr.org/2021/03/11/975663437/march-11-2020-the-day-everything-changed.

8  Ibid.

9  Ibid.

10  Kantis et al., 'Timeline of the Coronavirus'.

11  Barro, Ursúa and Weng, 'Coronavirus Meets the Great Influenza Pandemic'.

12  Jim Zarroli, 'Stocks 2020: A Stunning Crash, Then a Record-Setting Boom Created Centibillionaires', NPR, 31 December 2020, accessed 8 October 2022, www.npr.org/2020/12/31/952267894/stocks-2020-a-stunning-crash-then-a-record-setting-boom-created-centibillionaires.

13  Bilge Erten, Anton Korinek and José Antonio Ocampo, 'Managing Capital Flows to Emerging Markets', VoxEU.org, 11 August 2020, https://voxeu.org/article/managing-capital-flows-emerging-markets.

14  Ibid.

15  European Central Bank (ECB), 'ECB Announces €750 Billion Pandemic Emergency Purchase Programme (PEPP)', press release, 18 March 2020, www.ecb.europa/eu.

16  IMF, 'Fiscal Monitor Database of Country Fiscal Measures in Response to the COVID-19 Pandemic', IMF Fiscal Affairs Department, 2021, accessed 21 September 2022, www.imf.org/en/Topics/imf-and-covid19/Fiscal-Policies-Database-in-Response-to-COVID-19.

17  Lisa Rein, 'In Unprecedented Move, Treasury Orders Trump's Name Printed on Stimulus Checks', *Washington Post*, 14 April 2020, accessed 20 September 2022, www.washingtonpost.com/politics/coming-to-your-1200-relief-check-donald-j-trumps-name/2020/04/14/071016c2-7e82-11ea-8013-1b6da0e4a2b7_story.html.

18  IMF, 'Kurzarbeit: Germany's Short-Time Work Benefit', 15 June 2020, accessed 13 April 2022, www.imf.org/en/News/Articles/2020/06/11/na061120-kurzarbeit-germanys-short-time-work-benefit.

19  Treasury Committee, 'Oral Evidence: Spring Budget 2020', 16 March 2020, https://committees.parliament.uk/oralevidence/190/html/.

20  Rishi Sunak, 'The Chancellor Rishi Sunak Provides an Updated Statement on Coronavirus', HM Treasury, 2020, www.gov.uk/government/speeches/the-chancellor-rishi-sunak-provides-an-updated-statement-on-coronavirus.

21  Philip Aldrick, 'Bank of England Rode to Government's Rescue as Gilt Markets Froze', *The Times*, 30 April 2020, accessed 13 April 2022, www.thetimes.co.uk/article/bank-of-england-rode-to-government-s-rescue-as-gilt-markets-froze-w8dkqvvkg.

22  France24, 'Macron Announces Plan to Rescue French Auto Industry', 26 May 2020, www.france24.com/en/20200526-macron-announces-plan-to-rescue-french-auto-industry.

23  Jessie Yeung et al., 'July 6 Coronavirus News', CNN, 7 July 2020, accessed 20 September 2022, https://edition.cnn.com/world/live-news/coronavirus-pandemic-07-06-20-intl/h-f3005c39fdd5e19c7fd68148baef68e8.

24  Veronica Stracqualursi, 'Birx Warns US is "in a New Phase" of Coronavirus Pandemic with More Widespread Cases', CNN, 2 August 2020, accessed 20 September 2022, https://edition.cnn.com/2020/08/02/politics/birx-coronavirus-new-phase-cnntv/index.html.

25  United Nations (UN) Economic and Social Council, *Progress Towards the Sustainable Development Goals: Report of the Secretary-General*, New York, 2022.

26  Patrick Mathurin, Ortenca Aliaj and James Fontanella-Khan, 'Pandemic Triggers Wave of Billion-Dollar US Bankruptcies', *Financial Times*, 20 August 2020, accessed 14 April 2022, www.ft.com/content/277dc 354-a870-4160-9117-b5bodece5360.

27  University of Oxford, 'Facts About COVID-19 Vaccines', Vaccine Knowledge Project, 9 June 2022, accessed 20 September 2022, https:// vk.ovg.ox.ac.uk/vk/COVID19-FAQs#Q6.

28  Linda Geddes, 'Omicron WHAT? A User's Guide to COVID-19 Variant Names', Gavi Vaccines Work, 15 July 2022, www.gavi.org/ vaccineswork/omicron-what-users-guide-covid-19-variant-names.

29  James Hookway, 'Denmark to Dig Up Millions of Dead Mink After Botched Covid-19 Cull', *Wall Street Journal*, 21 December 2020, accessed 20 September 2022, www.wsj.com/articles/denmark-to-dig-up-millions-of-dead-mink-after-botched-covid-19-cull-11608558671.

30  George Parker and Sebastian Payne, 'Rishi Sunak Extends Furlough Scheme to End of March', *Financial Times*, 5 November 2020, www.ft. com/content/8f9371a7-e8e2-4a73-b1b6-d2330bb224a3.

31  Isabel Togoh, ' "I Can't Save Every Job" Warns British Chancellor with Plan to Help Millions of Furloughed Workers', *Forbes*, 24 September 2020, www.forbes.com/sites/isabeltogoh/2020/09/24/i-cant-save-every-job-warns-british-chancellor-with-plan-to-help-millions-of-furloughed-workers/.

32  Michiel Willems, '2021 in Review: Furlough is Government's Big Success Story, but Rishi Sunak's £69bn Lifesaver Comes at a Price', *City A.M.*, 27 December 2021, www.cityam.com/2021-in-review-furlough-is-governments-big-success-story-but-rishi-sunaks-69bn-lifesaver-comes-at-a-price.

33  Tommy Beer, 'White House Lists "Ending" Covid-19 Pandemic as Trump Accomplishment', *Forbes*, 27 October 2020, accessed 20 September 2022, www.forbes.com/sites/tommybeer/2020/10/27/white-house-lists-ending-covid-19-pandemic-as-trump-accomplishment/?sh=178725 991034.

34  Graeme Wearden, ' "I've Never Seen Anything Like It": 2020 Smashes Records in Global Markets', *Guardian*, 30 December 2020, www.the

guardian.com/business/2020/dec/30/ive-never-seen-anything-like-it-2020-smashes-records-in-global-markets.

35 Ryan Browne, 'Bitcoin Hits Fresh Record High Near $42,000, Climbing 40% So Far This Year', CNBC.com, 8 January 2021, www.cnbc.com/2021/01/08/bitcoin-btc-price-hits-41k-up-40percent-so-far-in-2021.html.

36 IMF, *World Economic Outlook, July 2022: Gloomy and More Uncertain*, Washington, DC, 2022.

37 IMF, 'Fiscal Monitor Database'.

38 IMF, *World Economic Outlook, October 2020: A Long and Difficult Ascent*, Washington, DC, 2020.

## Chapter 8: The Next Great Crash?

1 Kenneth Rogoff, 'Can China's Outsized Real Estate Sector Amplify a Delta-Induced Slowdown?' VoxEU.org, 21 September 2021, https://voxeu.org/article/can-china-s-outsized-real-estate-sector-amplify-delta-induced-slowdown.

2 Shang-Jin Wei and Xiaobo Zhang, 'Relationship Between the Chinese Housing and Marriage Markets', VoxDev, 5 July 2017, https://voxdev.org.topic.macroeconomics-growth/relationship-between-chinese-housing-and-marriage-markets.

3 Aliber and Kindleberger, *Manias, Panics, and Crashes*, p. 375.

4 Yueh, *The Great Economists*.

5 Tianlei Huang and Nicolas Veron, 'The Advance of the Private Sector Among China's Largest Companies Under Xi Jinping', VoxEU.org, 7 July 2022, https://voxeu.org/article/advance-private-sector-among-china-s-largest-companies-under-xi-jinping.

6 Xin Zhou and Kevin Yao, 'China Local Government Debt Audit Finds $84 Billion Problem', Reuters, 4 January 2012, accessed 27 July 2022, www.reuters.com/article/uk-china-debt-idUKTRE8030Mo20120104.

7 People's Bank of China, *Wenzhou Private Lending Market Report*, 21 July 2011.

8   Linda Yueh, 'The Shadowy Threat from China's Lenders', BBC News, 6 March 2014, accessed 4 May 2022, www.bbc.com/news/business-26335304.

9   Ibid.

10  Ehlers, Kong and Zhu, 'Mapping Shadow Banking in China'.

11  Gabriel Wildau, 'Retail Investors Bear Brunt of China's Stock Rout', *Financial Times*, 7 July 2015, www.ft.com/content/7a5341ce-2476-11e5-9c4e-a775d2b173ca.

12  Mark Fahey and Eric Chemi, 'Three Charts Explaining China's Strange Stock Market', CNBC, 9 July 2015, www.cnbc.com/2015/07/09/three-charts-explaining-chinas-strange-stock-market.html.

13  Karen Yeung, 'China's 2015 Yuan Reform Sent Shock Waves Through Financial Markets, Now It's "Learning Its Lesson"', *South China Morning Post*, 12 August 2021, www.scmp.com/economy/china-economy/article/3144769/chinas-2015-yuan-reform-sent-shock-waves-through-financial.

14  Thomas Hale et al., 'Evergrande Bondholders Yet to be Paid as Crucial Debt Deadline Passes', *Financial Times*, 7 December 2021, www.ft.com/content/6906eacc-ece2-4b66-9096-96d364e0917d

15  Martin Farrar, 'China Evergrande Shares Fall Sharply After $2.6bn Asset Sale Collapses', *Guardian*, 21 October 2021, accessed 29 July 2022, www.theguardian.com/business/2021/oct/21/china-evergrande-shares-fall-sharply-after-26bn-asset-sale-falls-through.

16  Engen Tham and Ziyi Tang, 'China Regulator Launches New Probe into Banks' Property Loan Exposure', Reuters, 18 August 2022, www.reuters.com/business/finance/exclusive-china-regulator-probes-banks-property-loan-portfolio-sources-2022-08-18/.

17  Rogoff, 'Can China's Outsized Real Estate Sector Amplify a Delta-Induced Slowdown?'

18  Ibid.

19  Aliber and Kindleberger, *Manias, Panics, and Crashes*, p. 374.

20  Steven Barnett, 'China: Size Matters', IMF Blog, 26 March 2014, https://blogs.imf.org/2014/03/26/china-size-matters/.

21  Ibid.

22 Sebastian Horn, Carmen Reinhart and Christoph Trebesch, 'China's Overseas Lending', *Journal of International Economics*, 133 (2021), 1–32, https://doi.org/10.1016/j.jinteco.2021.103539.

23 Eugenio Cerutti, Catherine Koch, and Swapan-Kumar Pradhan, 'Banking Across Borders: Are Chinese Banks Different?', BIS Working Paper 892, October 2020, www.bis.org/publ/work892.pdf.

24 World Bank, 'Debt Service Suspension Initiative', 10 March 2022, www.worldbank.org/en/topic/debt/brief/covid-19-debt-service-suspension-initiative.

## Epilogue

1 Luc Laeven, Angela Maddaloni and Caterina Mendicino, 'Monetary Policy, Macroprudential Policy and Financial Stability', ECB Working Paper Series 2647, 2022.

2 Carmen Reinhart and Kenneth Rogoff, 'Recovery from Financial Crises: Evidence from 100 Episodes', NBER Working Paper w19823, 2014.

3 Ruchir Sharma, 'There is Another Act to Come in this Market Drama', *Financial Times*, 6 June 2022, accessed 6 June 2022, www.ft.com/content/53c7a5a4-e183-493c-8d62-be0c79123f24.

4 William McChesney Martin, 'Address Before the New York Group of the Investment Bankers Association of America', 19 October 1955, https://fraser.stlouisfed.org/title/statements-speeches-william-mcchesney-martin-jr-448/address-new-york-group-investment-bankers-association-america-7800.

5 Yueh, *The Great Economists*, p. 271.

6 A similar reset was seen in the early twentieth century which saw the widespread creation of the welfare state that transformed capitalism, which was featured in Yueh, *The Great Economists*.

7 Ibid., Chapter 11.

# Bibliography

Agenor, Pierre-Richard, Otaviano Canuto and Michael Jelenic, 'Avoiding Middle-Income Growth Traps', *Economic Premise*, 98 (2012), Washington, DC: World Bank, p. 1, http://siteresources.worldbank.org/EXTPRE MNET/Resources/EP98.pdf

Aldrick, Philip, 'Bank of England Rode to Government's Rescue as Gilt Markets Froze', *The Times*, 30 April 2020, accessed 13 April 2022, www. thetimes.co.uk/article/bank-of-england-rode-to-government-s-rescue-as-gilt-markets-froze-w8dkqvvkg

———, 'Multi-Trillion Plan to Save the Eurozone Being Prepared', *Daily Telegraph*, 24 September 2011, accessed 4 April 2022, www.telegraph. co.uk/finance/financialcrisis/8786665/Multi-trillion-plan-to-save-the-euro zone-being-prepared.html

Aliber, Robert Z. and Charles P. Kindleberger, *Manias, Panics, and Crashes: A History of Financial Crises*, 7th edn, Basingstoke: Palgrave Macmillan, 2015

Amadeo, Kimberly, 'Black Monday in 1929, 1987, 2015, and 2020', *The Balance*, 26 January 2022, accessed 17 July 2022, www.thebalance.com/ what-is-black-monday-in-1987-1929-and-2015-3305818

———, 'When Did the Stock Market Crash? Stock Market Crashes, Corrections, and Dips in History' *The Balance*, 4 January 2022, www. thebalance.com/when-did-the-stock-market-crash-4158559

Amazon, 'Amazon.com Announces Investment in Pets.com', 29 March 1999, https://press.aboutamazon.com/news-releases/news-release-details/ amazoncom-announces-investment-petscom

Amsden, Alice H. and Ajit Singh, 'The Optimal Degree of Competition and Dynamic Efficiency in Japan and Korea', *European Economic Review*, 38(3–4) (1994), 941–51

Amyx, Jennifer A., *Japan's Financial Crisis: Institutional Rigidity and Reluctant Change*, Princeton: Princeton University Press, 2004

AP News, 'Susumu Ishii, Former Underworld Boss at Center of Scandal, Dead at 67', 3 September 1991, accessed 14 July 2022, https://apnews.com/article/0526cb865863c5a82566cb93e4a1d885

Associated Press, 'Obama Accuses McCain of Smear Tactics', NBC News, 5 October 2008, accessed 18 July 2022, www.nbcnews.com/id/wbna27034817

Azoulay, Pierre, Benjamin F. Jones, J. Daniel Kim and Javier Miranda, 'Research: The Average Age of a Successful Start-up Founder is 45', *Harvard Business Review*, 11 July 2018, https://hbr.org/2018/07/research-the-average-age-of-a-successful-startup-founder-is-45

Baldwin, Richard, ed., *The Great Trade Collapse: Causes, Consequences and Prospects*, VoxEU e-book, 27 November 2009, https://voxeu.org/article/great-trade-collapse-what-caused-it-and-what-does-it-mean

Balke, Nathan S. and Mark A. Wynne, 'Are Deep Recessions Followed by Strong Recoveries? Results for the G-7 Countries', *Applied Economics*, 28(7) (1996), 889–97

Barnett, Steven, 'China: Size Matters', IMF Blog, 26 March 2014, https://blogs.imf.org/2014/03/26/china-size-matters/

Barro, Robert and José Ursúa, 'Macroeconomic Crises Since 1870', *Brookings Papers on Economic Activity*, 30(1) (2008), 255–350

Barro, Robert, José Ursúa and Joanna Weng, 'Coronavirus Meets the Great Influenza Pandemic', VoxEU.org, 20 March 2020, https://voxeu.org/article/coronavirus-meets-great-influenza-pandemic

Barth, James R., *The Great Savings and Loan Debacle*, Washington, DC: The AEI Press, 1991

Barth, James R. and Robert E. Litan, 'Preventing Bank Crises: Lessons From Bank Failures in the United States', in Gerard Caprio, Jr., William C. Hunter, George G. Kaufman and Danny M. Leipziger, eds, *Preventing Bank Crises: Lessons From Recent Global Bank Failures*, EDI Development Series, Washington, DC: World Bank, 1998

Barth, James R., Susanne Trimbath and Glenn Yago, 'The U.S. Savings and Loan Crisis in Hindsight 20 Years Later', in *The Savings and Loan Crisis: Lessons from a Regulatory Failure*, The Milken Institute Series on Financial Innovation and Economic Growth, vol. 5, Boston, MA: Springer, 2004, pp. 179–250

BBC Radio 4, 'What Next for the Credit Crunch?', 15 September 2008, http://news.bbc.co.uk/1/hi/business/7612607.stm

Beer, Tommy, 'White House Lists "Ending" Covid-19 Pandemic as Trump Accomplishment', *Forbes*, 27 October 2020, accessed 20 September 2022, www.forbes.com/sites/tommybeer/2020/10/27/white-house-lists-ending-covid-19-pandemic-as-trump-accomplishment/?sh=178725991034

Beltran, Daniel O., Laurie DeMarco and Charles P. Thomas, 'Foreign Exposure to Asset-Backed Securities of U.S. Origin', International Finance Discussion Papers 939, Board of Governors of the Federal Reserve System, 2008

Bertaut, Carol, Laurie Pounder DeMarco, Steven Kamin and Ralph Tryon, 'ABS Inflows to the United States and the Global Financial Crisis', *Journal of International Economics*, 88(2) (2012), 219–34

Bikhchandani, Sushil and Sunil Sharma, 'Herd Behavior in Financial Markets: A Review', IMF Working Paper WP/00/48, 2000, www.imf.org/external/pubs/ft/wp/2000/wp0048.pdf

Bragg, Melvyn, 'John Steinbeck's Bitter Fruit', *Guardian*, 21 November 2001, accessed 15 August 2022, www.theguardian.com/books/2011/nov/21/melvyn-bragg-on-john-steinbeck

Browne, Ryan, 'Bitcoin Hits Fresh Record High Near $42,000, Climbing 40% So Far This Year', CNBC.com, 8 January 2021, www.cnbc.com/2021/01/08/bitcoin-btc-price-hits-41k-up-40percent-so-far-in-2021.html

Calavita, Kitty, Robert H. Tillman and Henry N. Pontell, 'The Savings and Loan Debacle, Financial Crime, and the State', *Annual Review of Sociology*, 23 (1997), 19–38, www.jstor.org/stable/2952542

Cárdenas, Amalia, 'The Spanish Savings Bank Crisis: History, Causes and Responses', IN3 Working Paper Series, Fundació per a la Universitat Oberta de Catalunya, 2013

Carvalho, Antonio Gledson de, Roberto B. Pinheiro and Joelson Oliveira Sampaio, 'The Dotcom Bubble and Underpricing: Conjectures and Evidence', Federal Reserve Bank of Cleveland Working Paper 16-33, 2016

Casanova, Cathérine, Eugenio Cerutti and Swapan-Kumar Pradhan, 'The Global Footprint of Chinese Banks', VoxEU.org, 24 November 2021, https://voxeu.org/article/global-footprint-chinese-banks

———, 'The Growing Footprint of EMDE Banks in the International Banking System', *BIS Quarterly Review*, December 2018

Cerutti, Eugenio, Catherine Koch and Swapan-Kumar Pradhan, 'Banking Across Borders: Are Chinese Banks Different?', BIS Working Paper 892, October 2020, www.bis.org/publ/work892.pdf

Chen, Andrew, *The Cold Start Problem: Using Network Effects to Scale Your Product*, New York: Random House Business, 2021

Cheng, Evelyn, 'Nasdaq Closes Above 5k for First Time Since March 2000; Dow, S&P at Records', CNBC, 2 March 2015, www.cnbc.com/2015/03/02/us-stocks-open-narrowly-mixed-ahead-of-data.html

*Chicago Tribune*, 'Japan Bank Woes Take Ominous turn', 30 October 1994, accessed 14 July 2022, www.chicagotribune.com/news/ct-xpm-1994-10-30-9410300273-story.html

Chrisafis, Angelique, 'Euro Stability More Important Than Greece, Says Angela Merkel', *Guardian*, 3 November 2011, accessed 8 April 2022, www.theguardian.com/business/2011/nov/03/euro-stability-more-important-greece

Corbett, Michael, 'Oil Shock of 1973–74', Federal Reserve History, 22 November 2013, www.federalreservehistory.org/essays/oil-shock-of-1973-74

Daley, Suzanne, 'In Spain, Homes are Taken but Debt Stays', *New York Times*, 27 October 2010

Darling, Alistair, *Back from the Brink: 1000 Days at Number 11*, London: Atlantic Books, 2011

De Haas, Ralph, Yevgeniya Korniyenko, Alexander Pivovarsky and Elena Loukoianova, 'Foreign Banks and the Vienna Initiative: Turning Sinners into Saints?' IMF Working Paper WP/12/117, 2012, www.imf.org/external/pubs/ft/wp/2012/wp12117.pdf

DeLong, J. Bradford and Konstantin Magin, 'A Short Note on the Size of the Dot-Com Bubble', NBER Working Paper 12011, 2006, www.nber.org/papers/w12011

*Der Spiegel*, 'Schäuble's Push for Grexit Puts Merkel on Defensive', 17 July 2015

Draghi, Mario, Speech at the Global Investment Conference in London, 26 July 2012, www.ecb.europa.eu/press/key/date/2012/html/sp120726.en.html

Dziobek, Claudia and Ceyla Pazarbasioglu, 'Lessons from Systemic Bank Restructuring: A Survey of 24 Countries', IMF Working Paper WP/97/161, 1997

Echavarria, Paulina Restrepo and Praew Grittayaphong, 'Bretton Woods and the Growth of the Eurodollar Market', Federal Reserve Bank of St. Louis on the Economy blog, 22 January 2022, accessed 30 August 2022, www.stlouisfed.org/on-the-economy/2022/january/bretton-woods-growth-eurodollar-market

*The Economist*, 'The Quest for Prosperity: Europe's Economy Has Been Underperforming. But Whose Fault is That?', 17 March 2017

Ehlers, Torsten, Steven Kong and Feng Zhu, 'Mapping Shadow Banking in China: Structure and Dynamics', BIS Working Paper 701, February 2018, www.bis.org/publ/work701.pdf

Erten, Bilge, Anton Korinek and José Antonio Ocampo, 'Managing Capital Flows to Emerging Markets', VoxEU.org, 11 August 2020, https://voxeu.org/article/managing-capital-flows-emerging-markets

European Central Bank (ECB), 'ECB Announces €750 Billion Pandemic Emergency Purchase Programme (PEPP)', press release, 18 March 2020, www.ecb.europa/eu

European Stability Mechanism (ESM), 'Crisis in Cyprus: "No Negotiating Power, No Credibility"', *Safeguarding the Euro in Times of Crisis: The Inside Story of the ESM*, Luxembourg: ESM, 2019, www.esm.europa.eu/publications/safeguarding-euro/crisis-cyprus-no-negotiating-power-no-credibility

Fahey, Mark and Eric Chemi, 'Three Charts Explaining China's Strange Stock Market', CNBC, 9 July 2015, www.cnbc.com/2015/07/09/three-charts-explaining-chinas-strange-stock-market.html

Farley, Maggie, 'Malaysia Leader, Soros Trade Barbs', *Los Angeles Times*, 22 September 1997, accessed 18 July 2022, www.latimes.com/archives/la-xpm-1997-sep-22-fi-34969-story.html

Farrar, Martin, 'China Evergrande Shares Fall Sharply After $2.6bn Asset Sale Collapses', *Guardian*, 21 October 2021, accessed 29 July 2022, www.theguardian.com/business/2021/oct/21/china-evergrande-shares-fall-sharply-after-26bn-asset-sale-falls-through

Fitzpatrick, Alex, 'A Judge Ordered Microsoft to Split. Here's Why It's Still a Single Company', *Time*, 5 November 2014, https://time.com/3553242/microsoft-monopoly/

Fortson, Danny, 'The Great Tech "Revaluation" Has Just Begun', *Sunday Times*, 22 May 2022, accessed 22 May 2022, www.thetimes.co.uk/article/the-great-tech-revaluation-has-only-just-begun-92l8vh9rx

France24, 'Macron Announces Plan to Rescue French Auto Industry', 26 May 2020, www.france24.com/en/20200526-macron-announces-plan-to-rescue-french-auto-industry

Frankel, Jeffrey, 'The Plaza Accord, 30 Years Later', NBER Working Paper 21813, 2015, www.nber.org/papers/w21813

Friedman, Milton, 'Monetary Studies of the National Bureau', in *The National Bureau Enters Its 45th Year*, 44th Annual Report of the National Bureau of Economic Research, 1964, pp. 7–25

Galbraith, J. K., *A Short History of Financial Euphoria*, New York: Whittle Books/Viking, 1993

Gaspar, Vitor, Paulo Medas and Roberto Perrelli, 'Global Debt Reaches a Record $226 Trillion', IMF Blog, 15 December 2021, https://blogs.imf.org/2021/12/15/global-debt-reaches-a-record-226-trillion/

Geddes, Linda, 'Omicron WHAT? A User's Guide to COVID-19 Variant Names', Gavi Vaccines Work, 15 July 2022, www.gavi.org/vaccineswork/omicron-what-users-guide-covid-19-variant-names

Ghizoni, Sandra Kollen, 'Creation of the Bretton Woods System, July 1944', Federal Reserve History, 2013, www.federalreservehistory.org/essays/bretton-woods-created

Glasner, Joanna, 'EToys Epitaph: "End of an Error"', *Wired*, 8 March 2001, accessed 27 May 2022, www.wired.com/2001/03/etoys-epitaph-end-of-an-error/

Goldfarb, Brent and David A. Kirsch, *Bubbles and Crashes: The Booms and Busts of Technological Innovation*, Stanford: Stanford University Press, 2019

Goldman, David, '10 Big Dot.com Flops', CNN Money, 10 March 2010, accessed 25 May 2022, https://money.cnn.com/galleries/2010/technology/1003/gallery.dot_com_busts/

Gopinath, Gita, 'Reopening from the Great Lockdown: Uneven and Uncertain Recovery', IMF Blog, 24 June 2020, https://blogs.imf.org/2020/06/24/reopening-from-the-great-lockdown-uneven-and-uncertain-recovery/

Gou, Michael, Gary Richardson, Alejandro Komai and Daniel Park, 'Banking Act of 1932', Federal Reserve History, 22 November 2013, accessed 17 September 2022, www.federalreservehistory.org/essays/banking-act-of-1932

Greene, Stephen, 'Emergency Banking Act of 1933', Federal Reserve History, 2013, accessed 17 August 2022, www.federalreservehistory.org/essays/emergency-banking-act-of-1933

Hale, Thomas, Sun Yu, Hudson Lockett and William Langley, 'Evergrande Bondholders Yet to be Paid as Crucial Debt Deadline Passes', *Financial Times*, 7 December 2021, www.ft.com/content/6906eacc-ece2-4b66-9096-96d364e0917d

Haughwout, Andrew, Donghoon Lee, Joseph Tracy, and Wilbert van der Klaauw, 'Real Estate Investors, the Leverage Cycle, and the Housing Market Crisis', Federal Reserve Bank of New York Staff Reports, 514, September 2011

Helm, Leslie, 'Japanese Bank Says It Loaned Billions to Scandal Figure', *Los Angeles Times*, 15 August 1991, accessed 14 July 2022, www.latimes.com/archives/la-xpm-1991-08-15-fi-843-story.html

Hill, Andrew, 'IPOs and the Ghost of Pets.com's Sock-Puppet', *Financial Times*, 19 February 2014, accessed 25 May 2022, www.ft.com/content/db124a89-98bf-3474-97e3-83df3cf6b5ee

Hirsh, Michael, 'Finance Minister, Bank Heads Announce Resignation in Clean Sweep', AP News, 4 October 1991, accessed 14 July 2022, https://apnews.com/article/bcb726865da3f947535b2de9689fc7ff

Hookway, James, 'Denmark to Dig Up Millions of Dead Mink After Botched Covid-19 Cull', *Wall Street Journal*, 21 December 2020, accessed 20 September 2022, www.wsj.com/articles/denmark-to-dig-up-millions-of-dead-mink-after-botched-covid-19-cull-11608558671

Horn, Sebastian, Carmen M. Reinhart and Christoph Trebesch, 'China's Overseas Lending', *Journal of International Economics*, 133 (2021), 1–32, https://doi.org/10.1016/j.jinteco.2021.103539

————, 'China's Overseas Lending and the War in Ukraine', VoxEU.org, 8 April 2022, https://voxeu.org/article/china-s-overseas-lending-and-war-ukraine

Huang, Tianlei and Nicolas Veron, 'The Advance of the Private Sector Among China's Largest Companies Under Xi Jinping', VoxEU.org, 7 July 2022, https://voxeu.org/article/advance-private-sector-among-china-s-largest-companies-under-xi-jinping

Inman, Phillip, 'Black Wednesday 20 Years On: How the Day Unfolded', *Guardian*, 13 September 2012, accessed 19 August 2022, www.theguardian.com/business/2012/sep/13/black-wednesday-20-years-pound-erm

*International Banker*, 'The Savings and Loan Crisis (1989)', 29 September 2021, accessed 24 January 2022, https://internationalbanker.com/history-of-financial-crises/the-savings-and-loan-crisis-1989/

International Monetary Fund (IMF), 'Fiscal Monitor Database of Country Fiscal Measures in Response to the COVID-19 Pandemic', IMF Fiscal Affairs Department, 2021, accessed 21 September 2022, www.imf.org/en/Topics/imf-and-covid19/Fiscal-Policies-Database-in-Response-to-COVID-19

————, *Global Financial Stability Report*, Washington, DC, April 2015

————, 'Kurzarbeit: Germany's Short-Time Work Benefit', 15 June 2020, www.imf.org/en/News/Articles/2020/06/11/na061120-kurzarbeit-germanys-short-time-work-benefit

————, 'Policy Responses to Covid-19', Policy Tracker, 2021, www.imf.org/en/Topics/imf-and-covid19/Policy-Responses-to-COVID-19

————, *World Economic Outlook, July 2022: Gloomy and More Uncertain*, Washington, DC, 2022

————, *World Economic Outlook, October 2020: A Long and Difficult Ascent*, Washington, DC, 2020

Irwin, Neil, *The Alchemists: Three Central Bankers and a World on Fire*, New York: Penguin, 2014

Jonung, Lars, 'Lessons from the Nordic Financial Crisis', 2010, Prepared for the AEA Meeting in Denver, Colorado, January 2011, based on Chapter 12 in Lars Jonung, Jaakko Kiander and Pentti Vartia, eds., *The Great Financial Crisis in Finland and Sweden. The Nordic Experience of Financial Liberalization*, Cheltenham: Edward Elgar, 2009

Kane, Edward J., 'The Role of Government in the Thrift Industry's Net Worth Crisis', in George J. Benston, ed., *Financial Services: The Changing Institutions and Government Policy*, Englewood Cliffs, NJ: Prentice-Hall, 1983, pp. 156–84

Kantis, Caroline, Samantha Kiernan, Jason Socrates Bardi and Lillian Posner, 'Updated: Timeline of the Coronavirus', Think Global Health, an initiative of the Council in Foreign Relations, 16 September 2022, accessed 20 September 2022, www.thinkglobalhealth.org/article/updated-timeline-coronavirus

Kay, John, *The Foundations of Corporate Success: How Business Strategies Add Value*, Oxford: Oxford University Press, 1993

Kettell, Steven, 'Oil Crisis', *Encyclopedia Britannica*, 31 January 2020, www.britannica.com/topic/oil-crisis

Kliesen, Kevin L., 'The 2001 Recession: How Was It Different and What Developments May Have Caused It?' *Federal Reserve Bank of St. Louis Review*, 85(5) (2003), 23–38, https://files.stlouisfed.org/files/htdocs/publications/review/03/09/Kliesen.pdf

Korinek, Anton, Prakash Loungani and Jonathan D. Ostry, 'A Welcome Evolution: The IMF's Thinking on Capital Controls and Next Steps', VoxEU.org, 8 April 2022, https://voxeu.org/article/imf-s-thinking-capital-controls-and-next-steps

Kose, M. Ayhan and Naotaka Sugawara, 'Understanding the Depth of the 2020 Global Recession in 5 Charts', World Bank Blogs, 15 June 2020, https://blogs.worldbank.org/opendata/understanding-depth-2020-global-recession-5-charts

Kraay, Aart and Jaume Ventura, 'The Dot-Com Bubble, the Bush Deficits, and the US Current Account', in Richard H. Clarida, ed., *G7 Current Account Imbalances: Sustainability and Adjustment*, Chicago: University of Chicago Press, 2007, pp. 457–95

Krugman, Paul, 'Devaluing History', *New York Times*, 24 November 2010, accessed 19 August 2022, https://archive.nytimes.com/krugman.blogs.nytimes.com/2010/11/24/devaluing-history/

Laeven, Luc, Angela Maddaloni and Caterina Mendicino, 'Monetary Policy, Macroprudential Policy and Financial Stability', ECB Working Paper Series 2647, 2022

Langdon, David S., Terence M. McMenamin and Thomas J. Krolik, 'U.S. Labor Market in 2001: Economy Enters a Recession', *Monthly Labor Review*, US Bureau of Labor Statistics, February 2002, 3–33, www.bls.gov/opub/mlr/2002/02/art1full.pdf

McFadden, Robert D., 'Charles Keating, 90, Key Figure in '80s Savings and Loan Crisis, Dies', *New York Times*, 2 April 2014, www.nytimes.com/2014/04/02/business/charles-keating-key-figure-in-the-1980s-savings-and-loan-crisis-dies-at-90.html

Mackay, Charles, *Memoirs of Extraordinary Popular Delusions and the Madness of Crowds*, 2nd edn, vol. 1 (London: Office of the National Illustrated Library, 1852)

Maes, Ivo, with Ilaria Pasotti, *Robert Triffin: A Life*, Oxford: Oxford University Press, 2021

Martin, William McChesney, 'Address Before the New York Group of the Investment Bankers Association of America', 19 October 1955, https://fraser.stlouisfed.org/title/statements-speeches-william-mcchesney-martin-jr-448/address-new-york-group-investment-bankers-association-america-7800

Mason, David, 'Savings and Loan Industry, US', *EH.Net Encyclopedia*, ed. Robert Whaples, 10 June 2003, http://eh.net/encyclopedia/savings-and-loan-industry-u-s/

Mathurin, Patrick, Ortenca Aliaj and James Fontanella-Khan, 'Pandemic Triggers Wave of Billion-Dollar US Bankruptcies', *Financial Times*, 20 August 2020, accessed 14 April 2022, www.ft.com/content/277dc354-a870-4160-9117-b5b0dece5360

Matulich, Erika and Karen Squires, 'What a Dog Fight! TKO: Pets.com', *Journal of Business Case Studies*, 4(5) (2008) 1–5, https://core.ac.uk/download/pdf/268109951.pdf

Miller, Abby, 'No More Checks from CyberRebate', DNM News, 29 May 2001, accessed 16 September 2022, www.dmnews.com/no-more-checks-from-cyberrebate/

Milne, Richard, 'Klarna CEO Says Fintech Will Focus Less on Growth and More on "Short-Term Profitability"', *Financial Times*, 26 May 2022, accessed 1 June 2022, www.ft.com/content/b5b7d26c-2407-4845-8276-ef5da20f778a

*New York Times*, 'BNP Paribas Suspends Funds Because of Subprime Problems', 9 August 2007

Nicholas, Tom and Matthew G. Preble, 'Michael Milken: The Junk Bond King', Harvard Business School Case 816-050, March 2016, revised May 2021, www.hbs.edu/faculty/Pages/item.aspx?num=50852

*Nihon Keizai Shimbun*, 21 October 1998

————, 12 October 2001

Nishimura, Kiyohiko G. and Yuko Kawamoto, 'Why Does the Problem Persist? "Rational Rigidity" and the Plight of Japanese Banks', RIETI Discussion Paper Series 02-E-003, March 2002

Nordhaus, William D., 'The Mildest Recession: Output, Profits, and Stock Prices as the U.S. Emerges from the 2001 Recession', Cowles Foundation Discussion Paper no. 1368, Yale University, 2002, pp. 1–31, https:// cowles.yale.edu/sites/default/files/files/pub/d13/d1368.pdf

Ofek, Eli and Matthew Richardson, 'Dotcom Mania: The Rise and Fall of Internet Stock Prices', *Journal of Finance*, 58(3) (2003), 1113–38

Organisation for Economic Co-operation and Development (OECD), *OECD Economic Outlook*, December 2020, www.oecd-ilibrary.org/eco nomics/oecd-economic-outlook/volume-2020/issue-2_39a88ab1-en

Papaconstantinou, George, *Game Over: The Inside Story of the Greek Crisis*, Athens: Papadopoulos Publishing, 2016

Parker, George and Sebastian Payne, 'Rishi Sunak Extends Furlough Scheme to End of March', *Financial Times*, 5 November 2020, www.ft. com/content/8f9371a7-e8e2-4a73-b1b6-d2330bb224a3

People's Bank of China, *Wenzhou Private Lending Market Report*, 21 July 2011

Pickard, Jim, 'Gordon Brown "Apologises" for Claiming to Have Ended Boom and Bust', *Financial Times*, 21 November 2008, accessed 15 March 2022, www.ft.com/content/ba54c2c8-7a74-355a-9ede-52ef78e9a558

Purdy, Elizabeth R., 'Charles H. Keating, American Businessman', *Encyclopedia Brittanica*, 30 November 2021, accessed 24 January 2022, www.britannica.com/biography/Charles-Keating

Quinn, William and John D. Turner, 'The Dot-Com Bubble', in *Boom and Bust: A Global History of Financial Bubbles*, Cambridge: Cambridge University Press, 2020, pp. 152–69

Randewich, Noel and Lewis Krauskopf, '20 Years After Dot-Com Peak, Tech Dominance Keeps Investors on Edge', *Reuters*, 18 February 2020, accessed 25 May 2022, www.reuters.com/article/us-usa-stocks-dotcom bust-graphic-idUSKBN20C1J7

Rein, Lisa, 'In Unprecedented Move, Treasury Orders Trump's Name Printed on Stimulus Checks', *Washington Post*, 14 April 2020, accessed 20 September 2022, www.washingtonpost.com/politics/coming-to-your-1200-relief-check-donald-j-trumps-name/2020/04/14/071016c2-7e82-11ea-8013-1b6da0e4a2b7_story.html

Reinhart, Carmen M. and Kenneth S. Rogoff, 'Recovery from Financial Crises: Evidence from 100 Episodes', NBER Working Paper w19823, 2014

Reis, Ricardo, 'The Portuguese Slump and Crash and the Euro Crisis', *Brookings Papers on Economic Activity*, 46(1) (2013), 143–210

Revoltella, Debora and Pedro J. F. de Lima, 'Thriving in a Post-Pandemic Economy', VoxEU.org, 21 December 2020, https://voxeu.org/article/thriving-post-pandemic-economy

Richardson, Gary, 'The Great Depression: 1929–1941', Federal Reserve History, 2013, www.federalreservehistory.org/essays/great-depression

Richardson, Gary, Alejandro Komai, Michael Gou and Daniel Park, 'Stock Market Crash of 1929', Federal Reserve History, 2013, www.federalreservehistory.org/essays/stock-market-crash-of-1929

Rodrik, Dani, 'Globalization's Wrong Turn, And How It Hurt America', *Foreign Affairs* 98(4) (2019), 26–33

Rogoff, Kenneth, 'Can China's Outsized Real Estate Sector Amplify a Delta-Induced Slowdown?' VoxEU.org, 21 September 2021, https://voxeu.org/article/can-china-s-outsized-real-estate-sector-amplify-delta-induced-slowdown

Russell, Karl and Stephen Grocer, 'Do Recessions Always Follow Major Stock Market Downturns? Usually', *New York Times*, 18 March 2020, accessed 12 April 2022, www.nytimes.com/interactive/2020/03/18/business/coronavirus-stock-market-recessions.html?smtyp=cur&smid=tw-nytimes

Sablik, Tim, The Fed's 'Tequila Crisis', *Econ Focus*, Federal Reserve Bank of Richmond, 2017, accessed 28 February 2022, www.richmondfed.org/publications/research/econ_focus/2017/q1/federal_reserve

Schlesinger, Jacob, 'How Alan Greenspan Finally Came to Terms with the Market', *Wall Street Journal*, 8 May 2000, accessed 18 May 2022, www.wsj.com/articles/SB957740787830302I9

Schwartz, Herman M., *Subprime Nation: American Power, Global Capital, and the Housing Bubble*, Ithaca, NY: Cornell University Press, 2009

Sharma, Ruchir, 'There is Another Act to Come in this Market Drama', *Financial Times*, 6 June 2022, accessed 6 June 2022, www.ft.com/content/53c7a5a4-e183-493c-8d62-be0c79123f24

Shiller, Robert J., *Irrational Exuberance*, Princeton: Princeton University Press, 2000

Shin, Hyun Song, 'Reflections on Northern Rock: The Bank Run that Heralded the Global Financial Crisis', *Journal of Economic Perspectives*, 23(1) (2009), 101–19

Silber, William L., 'Why Did FDR's Bank Holiday Succeed?', *Economic Policy Review*, 15(1) (2009), 19–31, www.newyorkfed.org/research/epr/09v15n1/0907silb.html

Simon, Ruth, 'Margin Investors Learn the Hard Way that Brokers Can Get Tough on Loans', *Wall Street Journal*, 27 April 2000

Singh, Ajit, 'International Competitiveness and Industrial Policy', in Irfan ul Haque, ed., *International Competitiveness: Interaction of the Public and the Private Sectors*, Washington, DC: World Bank, 1990, pp. 41–4

Singh, Manmohan and James Aitken, 'The (Sizable) Role of Rehypothecation in the Shadow Banking System', IMF Working Paper WP/10/172, July 2010

Spiegel, Peter, 'Draghi's ECB Management: The Leaked Geithner Files', *Financial Times*, 11 November 2014

————, 'If the Euro Falls, Europe Falls', *Financial Times*, 15 May 2014

Stone, Brad, 'Amazon's Pet Projects', *Newsweek*, 21 June 1999

Stracqualursi, Veronica, 'Birx Warns US is "in a New Phase" of Coronavirus Pandemic with More Widespread Cases', CNN, 2 August 2020, accessed 20 September 2022, https://edition.cnn.com/2020/08/02/politics/birx-coronavirus-new-phase-cnntv/index.html

Sunak, Rishi, 'The Chancellor Rishi Sunak Provides an Updated Statement on Coronavirus', HM Treasury, 2020, www.gov.uk/government/speeches/the-chancellor-rishi-sunak-provides-an-updated-statement-on-coronavirus

Tam, Pui-Wing and Mylene Mangalindan, 'Pets.com's Demise: Too Much Litter, Too Few Funds', *Wall Street Journal*, 8 November 2000

Taylor, John B., 'Monetary Policy and the Long Boom', *Federal Reserve Bank of St. Louis Review*, 80(6) (1998), 3–11

Tham, Engen and Ziyi Tang, 'China Regulator Launches New Probe into Banks' Property Loan Exposure', Reuters, 18 August 2022, www.reuters.com/business/finance/exclusive-china-regulator-probes-banks-property-loan-portfolio-sources-2022-08-18/

Thornton, Jennifer and Sunny Marche, 'Sorting Through the Dot Bomb Rubble: How Did the High-Profile E-tailers Fail?', *International Journal of Information Management* 23 (2003), 121–38

Togoh, Isabel, '"I Can't Save Every Job" Warns British Chancellor with Plan to Help Millions of Furloughed Workers', *Forbes*, 24 September 2020, www.forbes.com/sites/isabeltogoh/2020/09/24/i-cant-save-every-job-warns-british-chancellor-with-plan-to-help-millions-of-furloughed-workers/

Tooze, Adam, *Crashed: How a Decade of Financial Crises Changed the World*, London: Allen Lane, 2018

Trade Association for the Emerging Markets (EMTA), 'The Brady Plan', accessed 14 October 2022, www.emta.org/em-background/the-brady-plan/

Treasury Committee, 'Oral Evidence: Spring Budget 2020', 16 March 2020, https://committees.parliament.uk/oralevidence/190/html/

Triffin, Robert, *Gold and the Dollar Crisis: The Future of Convertibility*, New Haven: Yale University Press, 1960

Trueman, Brett, M. H. Franco Wong and Xiao-Jun Zhang, 'The Eyeballs Have It: Searching for the Value in Internet Stocks', *Journal of Accounting Research* 38 (2000), 137–62

United Nations (UN) Economic and Social Council, *Progress Towards the Sustainable Development Goals: Report of the Secretary-General*, New York, 2022

University of Oxford, 'Facts About COVID-19 Vaccines', Vaccine Knowledge Project, 9 June 2022, accessed 20 September 2022, https://vk.ovg.ox.ac.uk/vk/COVID19-FAQs#Q6

Waiwood, Patricia, 'Recession of 1937–38', Federal Reserve History, 2013, accessed 17 August 2022, www.federalreservehistory.org/essays/recession-of-1937-38

Wamsley, Laureal, 'March 11, 2020: The Day Everything Changed', NPR, 11 March 2021, accessed 15 September 2022, www.npr.org/2021/03/11/975663437/march-11-2020-the-day-everything-changed

Wearden, Graeme, ' "I've Never Seen Anything Like It": 2020 Smashes Records in Global Markets', *Guardian*, 30 December 2020, www.theguard ian.com/business/2020/dec/30/ive-never-seen-anything-like-it-2020-smashes-records-in-global-markets

Wei, Shang-Jin and Xiaobo Zhang, 'Relationship Between the Chinese Housing and Marriage Markets', VoxDev, 5 July 2017, https://voxdev. org.topic.macroeconomics-growth/relationship-between-chinese-housing-and-marriage-markets

White, Lawrence J., *The S&L Debacle: Public Policy Lessons for Banks and Thrift Regulation*, New York and Oxford: Oxford University Press, 1991

Wildau, Gabriel, 'Retail Investors Bear Brunt of China's Stock Rout', *Financial Times*, 7 July 2015, www.ft.com/content/7a5341ce-2476-11e5-9c4e-a775d2b173ca

Willems, Michiel, '2021 in Review: Furlough is Government's Big Success Story, But Rishi Sunak's £69bn Lifesaver Comes at a Price', *City A.M.*, 27 December 2021, www.cityam.com/2021-in-review-furlough-is-governments-big-success-story-but-rishi-sunaks-69bn-lifesaver-comes-at-a-price/

Wood, Christopher, *The Bubble Economy: Japan's Extraordinary Speculative Boom of the '80s and the Dramatic Bust of the '90s*, London, Sidgwick & Jackson, 1992

World Bank, 'Debt Service Suspension Initiative', 10 March 2022, www.worldbank.org/en/topic/debt/brief/covid-19-debt-service-suspension-initiative

———, *World Development Report: The Challenge of Development*, Washington, DC: World Bank, 1991, https://openknowledge.worldbank.org/handle/10986/5974

Wright, Chris, 'Asia '97: The Financial Crisis that Left Its Mark for Good', *Euromoney*, 9 May 2019, accessed 19 August 2022, www.euromoney.com/article/b1f7pksth48x10/asia-97-the-financial-crisis-that-left-its-mark-for-good

Yeung, Jessie, Steve George, Tara John, Melissa Macaya, Meg Wagner and Mike Hayes, 'July 6 Coronavirus News', CNN, 7 July 2020, accessed 20 September 2022, https://edition.cnn.com/world/live-news/corona virus-pandemic-07-06-20-intl/h_f3005c39fdd5e19c7fd68148baef68e8

Yeung, Karen, 'China's 2015 Yuan Reform Sent Shock Waves Through Financial Markets, Now It's "Learning Its Lesson"', *South China Morning Post*, 12 August 2021, www.scmp.com/economy/china-economy/article/3144769/chinas-2015-yuan-reform-sent-shock-waves-through-financial

Yi, Wen and Iris Arbogast, 'Not All Bursting Market Bubbles Have the Same Recessionary Effect', Federal Reserve Bank of St. Louis on the Economy blog, 15 February 2021, www.stlouisfed.org/on-the-economy/2021/feb ruary/not-all-bursting-market-bubbles-same-recessionary-effect

Yueh, Linda, *China's Growth: The Making of an Economic Superpower*, Oxford: Oxford University Press, 2013

———, 'Europe's Economic Paths', BBC News, 26 May 2014, accessed 11 April 2022, www.bbc.co.uk/news/business-27572537

———, *The Great Economists: How Their Ideas Can Help Us Today*, London: Viking, 2018

———, 'The Limits of Star Power', BBC News, 29 October 2013, accessed 13 September 2022, www.bbc.co.uk/news/business-24723411

———, 'The Shadowy Threat from China's Lenders', BBC News, 6 March 2014, accessed 4 May 2022, www.bbc.com/news/business-26335304

Zarroli, Jim, 'Stocks 2020: A Stunning Crash, Then a Record-Setting Boom Created Centibillionaires', NPR, 31 December 2020, accessed 8 October 2022, www.npr.org/2020/12/31/952267894/stocks-2020-a-stunning-crash-then-a-record-setting-boom-created-centibillionaire

Zhou, Xin and Kevin Yao, 'China Local Government Debt Audit Finds $84 Billion Problem', *Reuters*, 4 January 2012, accessed 27 July 2022, www.reuters.com/article/uk-china-debt-idUKTRE8030M020120104

# Index

AAA credit rating 83, 127
Abe, Shinzo/'Abenomics' 64
aftermath phase
   Asian financial crisis (1997–98) 85
   Covid-19 crash (2020) 149, 161–2
   credibility and 1, 7, 27, 64–5, 79, 105,
     149, 181, 182–3, 189
   dot com crash (2000–2001) 79
   European Exchange Rate Mechanism
     collapse (1992) 27, 186
   global financial crisis (2008) 104–5,
     116–17
   Great Crash (1929) 6, 7, 79, 105
   Japan's real-estate crash (early 1990s)
     59–60, 64–5
   key lessons on 185, 189–90, 191
   next great crash and 9, 181, 182–3, 189
   savings and loans crisis, US (1980s) 41
Airbnb 80
Allied Irish Bank 94
Alphabet 79, 154
*amakudari* system 47–8
Amazon (online technology company)
   67, 68–9, 71, 73, 75, 79, 80,
   154, 158, 190
American International Group (AIG) 91
Anglo Irish Bank 94
'animal spirits' 71
Apple 72, 79, 154, 179
Arab–Israeli war (Yom Kippur War)
   (1973) 13, 31
Argentina 8, 15, 16, 24, 153, 156
Armenia 99
Asian financial crisis (1997–98) 7–8,
   9, 11, 19–26, 28, 62, 85, 133, 170, 188

Asmussen, Jörg 125
asset prices 3, 20, 22, 52, 59, 64, 71, 185
austerity measures 25, 100, 114, 117, 118,
   123, 129
Austria 5, 99, 127, 151

bailouts
   Covid-19 crash (2020) and 146–7, 150
   currency crises and 25, 27
   euro crisis (2010) and 8, 112, 113, 115,
     116, 117–19, 123, 124, 130, 132–3,
     134, 186
   global financial crisis (2008) and
     94, 95
   Japan's real-estate crash (early 1990s)
     and 62
   savings and loans crisis, US (1980s)
     and 41
Baker, James 50
balance of payments crisis 14, 15
bandwagon effect 71
Bankia/BFA 130
Bank for International Settlements (BIS)
   52, 55, 180
Bank of America 89–90, 96
Bank of Canada 98, 102, 127
Bank of England 18–19, 52, 95,
   98, 102, 110, 114–15, 127, 131,
   144, 150
Bank of Ireland 94
Bank of Japan 47, 51, 54–5, 59, 60, 62,
   98, 102, 127
Bank of Thailand 23
Bank of Tokyo-Mitsubishi 45
Bank Recapitalization Act, Japan 62

bankruptcy 22, 23, 30, 34, 37, 39, 41, 49,
    61, 62, 90, 112, 154, 170, 176
banks
    bailouts *see* bailouts
    bank holiday 4, 5
    banking crises 7, 8, 9, 65, 82, 84, 94,
        95–6, 98, 121, 164, 172, 177–8, 180,
        181, 185–9
    banking licence 167
    central *see individual central bank name*
    Covid-19 crash (2020) and 143–6, 150,
        153, 154, 157, 160
    currency crises and 22–5, 26, 28
    dot com crash (2000–2001) and 72
    euro crisis (2010) and 107, 109–35,
        187, 189
    failure of 3, 5, 20, 23, 30, 34–5, 49,
        55, 62–3, 65, 81, 95, 119, 133
    global financial crisis (2008) and 9,
        81–3, 84–5, 86, 87–105
    Great Crash (1929) and 3, 4–5, 6–7, 8
    investment banks 35, 81, 82, 83, 86,
        88, 89–90, 91, 99, 101, 146, 169,
        173–4
    Japan's real-estate crash (early 1990s)
        and 45, 46, 47, 48–9, 50, 51–2,
        53–6, 58–60, 61–5
    main bank system 49
    next great crash and 164–82
    offshore banking 7, 12–13, 175–6
    regulations 7, 13, 21, 23–4, 32–3, 34,
        39, 45, 48–50, 133, 135, 186–7
    runs on 4, 5, 35, 81, 88–9, 90, 122–3
    savings and loans crisis, US (1980s)
        and 29, 30–31, 32–3, 34–5, 41
    shadow banking 81–2, 85, 90, 164,
        167, 170, 171–3, 181
    'white knight' 94
Barclays 90, 95
Bar None 68
Barroso, José Manuel 130
Basel standards 28
BBC 81, 101, 172

bear market 3, 9, 72, 77, 103, 139, 140,
    174, 186, 190–91
Bear Stearns 88, 89
Belarus 99
Berlusconi, Silvio 124
Bernanke, Ben 93, 101, 127
Bezos, Jeff 68, 71
Biden, Joe 158, 159, 193
'Big Bang' deregulation of City of
    London, UK 13
'big short' positions 86–7
Bill and Melinda Gates Foundation 155
Birx, Deborah L. 152
Bitcoin 159
Black, Fischer 24
Black Monday (19 October 1987) 9, 51
Black Monday (28 October 1929) 3
Black–Scholes–Merton model 24
Black Tuesday (29 October 1929) 3
Black Wednesday (16 September 1992)
    18–19
Bloomberg TV 117, 118, 131
BMW 179
BNP Paribas 87, 88
bond market 24
    bond vigilantes 119
    Brady bonds 16
    Covid-19 crash (2020) and 143, 145,
        148–9, 157
    eurobond 125–6
    euro crisis (2010) and 110–35, 189
    global financial crisis (2008) and 87,
        91, 92, 97
    government bonds 16, 32, 53, 91, 92, 97,
        98–9, 110, 113–14, 120, 125, 135, 143
    Japan's real-estate crash (early 1990s)
        and 53, 56
    junk bonds 29, 35–7, 127
    next crash and 171, 175–6
    savings and loans crisis, US (1980s)
        and 29, 32, 35–7
    US Treasury and 16, 32, 91, 97, 98–9,
        125, 143

Boo.com 70, 74–6
borrowing
    Covid-19 crash (2020) and 147–9,
      150, 155, 157, 160, 161, 162
    currency crises and 15, 17, 21, 22
    dot com crash (2000–2001) and 76
    euphoria phase and 189–90
    euro crisis (2010) and 110–11, 113–14,
      116, 119, 120, 122, 192
    global financial crisis (2008) and 82–6,
      87, 91, 94, 97
    Great Crash (1929) and 2, 3, 5, 7
    Japan's real-estate crash (early 1990s)
      and 45, 49, 51, 52, 57,
      58–9, 60
    next great crash and 171, 172, 173,
      179, 180
    savings and loans crisis, US (1980s)
      and 32, 34, 39, 40
Bradford & Bingley 94
Brady bonds 16
Brady, Nicholas F. 16
Brady Plan 16
Brazil 8, 15, 16, 24, 98, 101, 102, 143, 144,
    156, 189
    Brazilian real 143
Brent Crude 140
Bretton Woods Agreement (1944) 12, 13,
    16, 98, 107–8
broker-dealer 82, 90
Brown, Gordon 90, 95
budget deficits 20, 28, 111, 113, 114,
    116, 117–18, 119, 123, 126, 128,
    130, 131
Buffett, Warren 93
Bulgaria 16, 100
bull market 71–2, 139, 158, 159, 160
Bundesbank 17, 51, 109, 122, 132
Bundestag 122, 123, 125
Burry, Michael 87
Bush, George H. W. 40
Bush, George W. 94
business software 80

CAC 140
*cajas* (Spanish regional mortgage lenders)
    129–30
Cameron, David 126
capital goods 178
capital markets 45, 87, 135, 169, 170
'cash-for-trash' 37
CDs (time deposits) 32–3
Centers for Disease Control and
    Prevention (CDC), US 139
central banks *see individual*
    *bank name*
Chapter 11 bankruptcy 154
Chile 15
China
    Belt and Road Initiative 180
    'common prosperity' 166, 176–7
    Covid-19 crash (2020) and
      138, 141–2, 145–6, 155–6,
      158, 161
    global financial crisis (2008) and 87,
      98–9, 102–4, 171
    next great crash and 8–9, 163–83
China National Petroleum 167
Cisco 77
Citibank 96
City of London 13
climate change 151, 193–4, 195
CoCos 133
collateralized mortgage obligations
    (CMOs) 83
Colombia 99
command economy 163
Commercial Paper Funding Facility,
    Federal Reserve, US 97
Commerzbank 92
commodity prices 4, 5, 13, 15–16, 102–4,
    140, 178–9, 190
    commodity super-cycle 102
    *See also individual commodity name*
Congress, US 4, 32, 39, 90, 93, 127,
    139, 146
Connally, John 12

contagion 5–6, 24, 26, 28, 115, 121, 122, 128, 134
Continental Illinois 34–5
COP26 climate summit 193
Coronavirus, Aid, Relief, and Economic Security (CARES) Act, US 145
Coronavirus Job Retention Scheme, UK 147–8
Coronavirus Response Investment Initiative, EU 146
corporate failure 22–3, 49, 62, 154
corporate governance 168, 169, 194
Country Garden 175
Covid-19 pandemic
 China and 138, 141–2, 145–6, 155–6, 158, 161, 163, 176, 179–80
 economic crash (2020) 8, 137–62, 163, 176, 179–80, 191–2, 195
Cranston, Alan 30
crawling peg 15
'creative destruction' 80
credibility
 aftermath phase and 1, 7, 27, 64–5, 79, 105, 149, 181, 182–3, 189
 Covid-19 crash (2020) and 149, 161
 currency crises and 18, 27, 28, 188–9
 dot com crash (2000–2001) and 79
 euro crisis (2010) and 115, 135–6, 189
 global financial crisis (2008) and 105
 Great Crash (1929) and 5, 6–7
 importance of 1, 5, 6–7, 9, 185, 187–9, 190, 191
 Japan's real-estate crash (early 1990s) and 64–5
 next great crash and 9, 173, 180–81, 182
 savings and loans crisis, US (1980s) and 41
credit cards 33, 142
credit crunch 7, 61, 91, 92, 185
credit default swaps (CDSs) 86–7
credit rating 35, 83, 88, 91, 113, 116, 127
 agencies 35, 113, 116, 127

crisis management, global 28
crony capitalism 22
CRRC 173–4
CSI 159
currency crises 11–28, 182–3, 187–8
 Asian financial crisis (1997–98) 7–8, 9, 11, 19–26, 28, 62, 85, 133, 170, 188
 European Exchange Rate Mechanism collapse (1992) 7, 11, 16–19, 27, 28, 107, 108, 186, 188
 Great Crash (1929) and 5, 7
 international financial market development and origins of 11–15
 Latin American currency crisis (1981–82) 7, 11, 15–16, 19, 20, 26, 27, 28
 speculators and 5–6, 13–15, 17, 18, 19, 25, 27, 28, 59, 182, 186
 three generations of 7–8, 11–28
current-account inflows 25–6
CyberRebate 67
Cyprus 8, 132–3, 134

Darling, Alistair 90
DAX 140, 159
debt
 brake 126, 147
 Covid-19 crash (2020) and 137, 143, 147–53, 155, 157, 159–60, 161
 currency crises and 13, 15, 16, 22, 23
 debt-deflation theory 5, 6
 debt-to-GDP ratio 111, 117, 129, 131, 173
 default 34, 35, 37, 83, 86–7, 91, 92, 112–13, 119, 122, 124, 129, 153, 159, 175–6
 dollar-denominated 85, 101, 189
 euro crisis (2010) and 109–34, 186, 189
 global financial crisis (2008) and 82, 85, 86, 91, 95, 96, 100, 101, 104
 Japan's real-estate crash (early 1990s) and 49, 53, 55–6, 58, 60, 65
 mutualization of 112

next great crash and 9, 164, 166, 167,
171, 172, 173, 175–6, 177–8, 180,
181, 182
recognizing risk posed by rising levels
of fuelled by euphoria 185–7, 189,
190, 191
restructuring 100, 112–13, 118, 120,
121, 123, 128, 134
savings and loans crisis, US (1980s)
and 32, 36
sovereign debt crises 7, 112, 127, 186,
189, 191
DeConcini, Dennis 30
default 34, 35, 37, 83, 86–7, 91, 92,
112–13, 119, 122, 124, 129, 153, 159,
175–6
deflation 2, 4, 5–6, 64, 73, 80, 84,
104, 183
deleveraging 5, 185
Dell 77
DeLong, Brad 73
Democratic Party, US 30, 93, 158
Deng Xiaoping 163
Denmark 98, 100, 107, 144, 147, 151, 156
deposit
ceilings 48
insurance 4, 5, 7, 29, 30, 34, 39, 46,
63, 88, 95, 133
Depository Institutions Deregulation
and Monetary Control Act (1980),
US 33
depression 64, 79, 81, 84, 105, 137,
141, 186
deregulation 13, 21, 33, 50, 51, 52
derivatives 91
d'Estaing, Valéry Giscard 108
Deutsche Bank 86–7
Dexia 94, 122–3
Dillon, C. Douglas 108
dollar, US
Bretton Woods Agreement (1944) and
12–13
Covid-19 crash (2020) and 143, 144

crawling peg 15
currency crises and 15, 20, 21, 22
-denominated debt 85, 101, 189
dot com crash (2000–2001) and 67, 79
euro crisis (2010) and 107–8, 113,
127–8
Eurodollar market 12–13
global financial crisis (2008) and 85,
91–2, 96, 98–9, 100, 101–2, 105
Great Crash (1929) 6
next great crash and 174, 175
savings and loans crisis, US (1980s)
and 29–30, 50–51, 53–4
world's reserve currency 12, 98, 102,
105, 108
doom loop 116–17, 119–20, 121, 125,
128, 130, 186
dot com crash (2000–2001) 8, 9, 67–80,
85, 161, 173–4, 186, 187
double dip downturn 6, 104
Dow Jones Industrial Average 2, 72, 77,
93, 103, 137, 139, 158, 160
drag-away loans 37
Draghi, Mario 130–32
Dresdner 92
Drexel Burnham Lambert 35, 36, 37

Eat Out to Help Out scheme, UK 150
e-commerce 67–9, 71, 75, 156, 160–62,
187, 192
*Economist* magazine 62
*eigyo tokkin* accounts 56
Emergency Banking Act (1933), US 4
emerging markets (EMs) 186, 188–9
Covid-19 crash (2020) and 142–3,
153, 159
currency crises and 11, 15, 16, 20, 21,
24–8
global financial crisis (2008) and 85,
100–102, 103, 104
next great crash and 169, 170, 180, 182
*See also individual nation name*
Empire Saving and Loan of Texas 37–8

energy crisis 190–91
environment, social and governance
    (ESG) 194
equities 22, 25, 52, 72, 73, 81, 94, 133,
    168, 174, 179, 185
Estonia 100
eToys.com 67, 68, 70–71, 75
E★Trade 76
euphoria phase 1, 185
    Covid-19 crash (2020) 137, 160
    dot com crash (2000–2001) 67, 71,
        72, 79
    euro crisis (2010) 134, 136
    global financial crisis (2008) 84, 85,
        104, 187
    Great Crash (1929) 2, 6, 187
    key lessons on 186–7, 189–90, 191
    next great crash and 9, 165, 181
euro 8, 17, 100, 107–36, 189
    crisis (2010) 8, 107–36, 142, 145, 148,
        152, 157, 186, 192
    eurobond 125–6
    peg 100
Eurodollar market 12–13
Eurogroup of eurozone finance ministers
    111, 113, 130, 134
*Euromoney* 60
European Bank for Reconstruction and
    Development (EBRD) 99, 100
European Banking Authority (EBA) 116,
    122–3
European Central Bank (ECB)
    Covid-19 crash (2020) and 144–5,
        156–7
    euro crisis (2010) and 107, 109, 116,
        117, 120, 121, 122, 124, 125, 127, 128,
        130, 131–2, 134, 135
    global financial crisis (2008) and 88,
        97–8
    Pandemic Emergency Purchase
        Programme (PEPP) 144–5, 156–7
European Coal and Steel Community
    (ESCS) 108

European Commission 100, 108, 115,
    125, 130, 146
European Council 109, 121, 125, 130
European Court of Justice 126
European Economic Community
    (EEC) 108
European Exchange Rate Mechanism
    (ERM) collapse (1992) 7, 11, 16–19,
    107, 186
European Financial Stability Facility
    (EFSF) 115, 120, 122, 123, 125,
    126, 128
European Investment Bank (EIB)
    99, 146
European Monetary System (EMS) 108
European Monetary Union (EMU) 107
European Stability Mechanism (ESM)
    115–16, 125, 126, 128, 130, 132, 133,
    135, 146
European Union (EU) 25, 99, 187, 192
    China and 177, 179
    Covid-19 crash (2020) and 146, 149,
        150, 151–2, 158, 159, 160
    constitution 109
    currency *see* euro
    financial transactions tax 126
    global financial crisis (2008) and
        99, 100
    single market 107, 135, 187
Eurostat 113
Euro STOXX 600 140, 159
Evergrande 175–6, 177
exchange controls 11–12, 13
exchange rates 7, 11–21, 23, 26, 27, 28,
    54, 98, 107, 108–9, 111, 170, 182,
    186, 188
Exchange Stabilization Fund 92
exports 13, 14–15, 25–6, 31, 45, 100,
    102–3, 164, 171, 174, 178–9, 186, 190

FAANGs (Facebook, Amazon, Apple,
    Netflix and Google) 79
Facebook 74, 79, 154

fairness, policies that increase 192–3
'fallen angels' 35–6
Fannie Mae (Federal Housing Authority) 82–3, 87, 92, 97
Fauci, Dr Anthony 139
Federal Deposit Insurance Corporation 30, 46, 95
Federal Home Loan Bank Act of (1932), US 30
Federal Reserve, US 2, 4, 6–7, 12, 15, 24–5, 46, 187, 191
   Commercial Paper Funding Facility 97
   Covid-19 crash (2020) and 141, 143–4, 154
   dot com crash (2000–2001) and 72–3, 78, 79
   euro crisis (2010) and 110, 114, 115, 117, 127, 131
   global financial crisis (2008) and 85, 89, 91–2, 93, 96–8, 101–2, 103, 104, 105
   Primary Dealer Credit Facility 96–7
   Term Asset-Backed Securities Loan Facility 97
   Term Auction Facility 96
   Term Securities Lending Facility 96
Federal Savings and Loan Insurance Corporation 30, 34, 39
Federal Trade Commission (FTC), US 71
Finance One 23
financial liberalization (1980s) 17
Financial Reconstruction Law, Japan (1998) 61–2
Financial Revitalization Act, Japan 62–3
Financial Services Agency (FSA), UK 63
Financial Stability Board (FSB) 28, 187
Financial Stability Forum (FSF) 28
Financial Supervisory Agency (FSA), Japan 47
Fintech 80
fire sale 5, 24, 39, 55, 89

First World War (1914–18) 2, 138
fiscal compact 126, 130, 135
fiscal policy 112, 125–6
fiscal stimulus 104, 145, 157, 171
Fisher, Irving 2, 5
Fitch 113
flexible working 192
flipping properties 37–8
foreign direct investment 21, 45
Fortis 94
four freedoms, EU single market 107, 135
Four Horsemen tech stocks 77
Fragile Five economies 101, 103, 189
France 6, 17, 50, 63
   Covid-19 crash (2020) and 140, 142, 145, 149, 150–51, 152, 156, 161
   euro crisis (2010) and 107, 108, 109, 111, 112, 113, 123, 124, 127, 132, 135
   global financial crisis (2008) and 87, 94
Freddie Mac (Federal Home Loan Mortgage Corporation) 82–3, 87, 92, 97
Friedman, Milton: *A Monetary History of the United States, 1867–1960* 4
Frugal Four economies 151
FTSE 140, 159
Fuji Bank 58–9
fund management industry 56, 169–70
furlough schemes 147–50, 157, 161, 192

G5 50
G7 50, 56, 62, 94, 95, 144, 159
G20 94, 101, 124, 143
Galbraith, J. K. 1
Garden.com 68, 70, 74
Garn-St. Germain Depository Institutions Act (1982), US 33
Gates, Bill 74
GDP (Gross Domestic Product) 6, 21
   China 163, 165, 173, 175–6, 179
   Covid-19 crash (2020) and 137–8, 141, 142, 144, 146, 147, 148, 149, 150, 151, 152–3, 155–6, 160, 162

GDP (Gross Domestic Product) – *cont.*
  dot com crash (2000–2001) and 77–8
  euro crisis (2010) and 111, 113, 114,
    117, 118, 119, 122, 123, 126, 129,
    130–31, 132
  global financial crisis (2008) and 85,
    87, 94, 99, 100
  Japan's real-estate crash (early 1990s)
    and 51, 53, 56, 62, 63
Geithner, Tim 122, 131
General Accounting Office, US 39
Germany
  Covid-19 crash (2020) and 140, 146–7,
    149, 151, 152, 156, 159, 161
  debt brake (*Schuldenbremse*) 126, 147
  ERM and 17–18
  euro crisis (2010) and 107, 108, 109–11,
    112, 113, 114, 116, 118, 120, 122, 123,
    124, 125, 126, 127, 130, 134, 135
  German Mark 7, 17, 108
  global financial crisis (2008) and 87,
    92–3, 94
  Japan's real-estate crash (early 1990s)
    and 50–51, 63
  reunification 17
Ghebreyesus, Dr Tedros Adhanom 139
ghost cities 165
Glenn, John 30
global financial crisis (2008) 8, 9, 28, 34,
    81–105, 112, 116, 117, 122, 127, 134,
    137, 140, 142, 146, 147, 151, 154, 159,
    160, 161, 163, 167, 170–71, 178, 179,
    187, 197
Global Investment Conference, London
    (2012) 131
globalization 7, 21, 50
gold 5–6, 12, 14, 107, 153
  gold bloc 6
  gold standard 5–6, 146
'golden age' of economic growth (1950s
    and 1960s) 31
Goldman Sachs 86, 93
golf courses 53, 54, 58, 59

Google 79, 80
Grand Hyatt Wailea Resort and Spa,
    Maui 54
Great Crash (1929) 1–7, 29, 79, 81,
    105, 187
Great Depression (1929–39) 2, 3–5,
    6, 7, 8, 29, 64, 84, 105, 137, 141, 186
'Great Moderation' (1990s–2000s) 27, 78
great recession (2009) 80, 81, 103, 119,
    141, 145, 153, 171, 173
Greece 8, 17, 107, 110–16, 118, 120–21,
    122, 123–4, 127–9, 132, 133–5, 139,
    151, 186, 189
green economy 151, 193, 195
green infrastructure 162, 193
Greenspan, Alan 72, 73, 79, 187
Grexit 121, 129
Growth Enterprise Board, China 168
growth forecasts 103

Halifax and Bank of Scotland (HBOS)
    92, 95
Hambantota International Port 180
Hanbo Steel 23
Hanks, Tom 141
Hashida, Taizo 58
Hashimoto, Ryutaro 61
Hawaii 54, 58
hedge funds 18, 24, 62, 86–7
herd immunity 152
herding behaviour 27, 173
Hokkaido Takushoku Bank 61
Hollande, François 132
Hong Kong 23
  Hong Kong Stock Connect
    programmes 179
Hoover, Herbert 4–5
'hot money' 11, 15, 21, 27, 28, 170,
    182, 188
House of Representatives, US 93
housing market *see* real-estate
Ho Yong Chung 58
HSBC 95

Hungary 99
hyper-globalization 21
Hypo Real Estate 94
hysteresis 148, 161

IBEX 140
Iceland 99
Inagawa-kai 57
income tax 31
India 101, 153, 155, 156, 189
Indonesia 20, 21, 23–4, 25, 101, 189
Industrial Bank of Japan's (IBJ) 59, 60
inequality 177, 193, 194
inflation 14–15, 17–18, 20, 27, 32, 74, 78,
    109–10, 154, 190–91
infrastructure 20, 32, 44, 70, 146, 162,
    171, 173, 180, 193
initial public offering (IPO) 67–70,
    72–3, 74, 75
innovations, impact of 2, 6, 35, 151, 192
Institute of International Finance 122
Intel 77
interbank market 91, 97–8
interest-only mortgages 84
interest rates 2, 187, 188, 190–91
    China 170, 172, 175
    Covid-19 crash (2020) and 143, 144,
      154, 160, 162
    currency crises and 15, 16, 17–19
    dot com crash (2000–2001) and
      72, 78, 79
    euro crisis (2010) and 112, 113, 121, 127
    global financial crisis (2008) and 82,
      85, 87, 91, 101, 103
    Japan's real-estate crash (early 1990s)
      and 50–51, 54, 63
    savings and loans crisis, US (1980s)
      and 31, 32, 33, 35, 36, 40
international financial market,
    development of 11–14
International Monetary Fund (IMF) 193
    Covid-19 crash (2020) and 142, 143,
      145, 159, 162, 191

currency crises and 12, 25, 186
euro crisis (2010) and 112, 113, 114, 115,
    122, 124, 128, 129, 130, 132, 133, 135
'Foreign Banks and the Vienna
    Initiative: Turning Sinners into
    Saints?' 99–100
global financial crisis (2008) and 82, 94
next great crash and 178, 179, 182
*World Economic Outlook* 162
internet economy 67–80
Iran
    Iran–Iraq war (1980–88) 13, 31–2
    Revolution (1978–79) 31
Ireland 8, 17, 87, 92, 94, 109, 110, 112,
    113, 116, 117–19, 120, 125, 127, 130,
    134, 186
irrational exuberance 68, 71, 72, 73, 79
Ishii, Susumu 57
Israel 13, 31
Italy 6, 17, 50, 110, 122, 124–5, 127, 132,
    139, 140, 149, 156
Itoman 58
Ito, Suemitsu 58

Japan 8, 21, 54
    Covid-19 crash (2020) and 142, 144,
      155–6, 161
    global financial crisis (2008) and 93
    Japan premium 60–63
    Japan rate 55
    real-estate crash (early 1990s) 9,
      43–65, 111, 163, 178, 182, 183, 186
    yen 50, 51, 53–4, 62
Johnson & Johnson 155
Johnson, Boris 141
JP Morgan 86
Juncker, Jean-Claude 111, 130, 134
junk bonds 29, 35–7
*jusen* (housing loan companies) 52
Justice Department, US 40

Kay, John 71
KB Toys 70

Keating, Charles 29
Keating Five 29–30, 40
*keiretsu* (business networks) 45, 52
Kennedy, John F. 1, 108
Kenya 180
Keynes, John Maynard 12, 71
Kia Motors 23
King, Mervyn 127
Klarna 80
Kohlberg Kravis Roberts &
    Company 36
Kohl, Helmut 107
Kurosawa, Hiroshi 60
Kyowa Saitama Bank 58–9

labour-surplus economy 44
Lagarde, Christine 94, 145
laissez-faire economics 50
Lamont, Norman 18
Latin America 99, 178–9, 188
    currency crisis (1981–82) 7, 11, 15–16,
        19, 20, 26, 27, 28
Latvia 99, 100
'lean against the wind' 181, 187
Lebanon 139
Lehman Brothers 81, 89, 90, 104
'lender of last resort' 132
Lenk, Toby 70
letters of comfort 36
leveraged buyouts 36
Lewis, Michael: *The Big Short* 87
Liberal Democratic Party (LDP) 46,
    59, 64
limited liability laws 34
Lincoln Savings and Loan 29
liquidity 28
    Covid-19 crash (2020) and 144, 146,
        191–2
    euro crisis (2010) and 110, 114, 121,
        123, 127, 128, 130
    global financial crisis (2008) and 82,
        88, 91, 93, 95, 96, 97–8, 102, 105, 187
    next great crash and 169, 181

Lithuania 100
Lloyds Bank 92
Lloyds TSB-HBOS 95
loans 3, 187
    Covid-19 crash (2020) and 143, 144,
        145, 146, 157
    currency crises and 15–16, 20–21, 22,
        23, 24–5
    dot com crash (2000–2001) and
        68, 78, 79
    drag-away 37
    euro crisis (2010) and 111, 113, 118, 123,
        127, 129–30
    global financial crisis (2008)
        and 82, 83, 86, 88, 89,
        97, 100
    Great Crash (1929) and 5
    Japan's real-estate crash (early 1990s)
        and 50, 52, 53, 55, 56, 58, 59, 60,
        61, 63, 64
    loan-to-value ratios 187
    next great crash and 167, 170, 171,
        172–3, 176, 177–8, 180
    non-performing/bad loans 60, 61,
        64, 86
    savings and loans crisis, US (1980s)
        and 8, 29–41
London Stock Exchange 179
Long-Term Capital Management
    (LTCM) 24–5, 62
Long Term Credit Bank 63
loss compensation 56–7
Louvre Accord (1987) 50–51, 54

Maastricht Treaty (1992) 107, 112,
    113, 160
    Growth and Stability Pact 111
Mackay, Charles 71
Macron, Emmanuel 150–51
Magin, Konstantin 73
main bank system 49
Major, John 18
Malaysia 20, 21, 23, 25, 133, 188

Management Coordination Survey 53
Mao Zedong 163
market capitalization 72, 76, 154
market friendly approach 43–4
mark-to-market convention 86
Martin, William McChesney 187
Mastercard 142
McCain, John 29–30
McLemore, Greg 68
Medvedev, Dmitry 117
mergers 48, 49, 63, 154
Meriwether, John 24
Merkel, Angela 112, 113, 117, 118, 122,
    123, 124, 126, 132
Merrill Lynch 76, 89
Merton, Robert 24
Meta 79
Mexico 15, 98, 99, 122, 143, 144
    peso 143
MIB 140
Microsoft 74, 77, 79, 154
Mieno, Yasushi 54–5
Milken Institute 37
Milken, Michael 35, 36–7, 41
Ministry of Finance (MoF), Japan
    45–9, 51, 53, 54–5, 57, 59, 60,
    61, 65
Ministry of International Trade and
    Investment (MITI), Japan 44–5
Mitsubishi 45, 93
Mitterrand, François 107
Moderna 155, 158
*mofu-tan* 47, 48
Mohamad, Dr Mahathir 25
monetary policy 17, 19, 47, 51, 97, 105,
    107, 110, 125–6, 135, 145, 154,
    188, 191
monetary support 3–4, 6, 101
money supply 4, 97
Mongolia 99, 165
Monnet, Jean 108–9
Monti, Mario 124–5, 132
Morgan Stanley 93, 101

mortgages 8, 29, 30–31, 32, 33–4, 37, 40,
    52, 81–9, 129
    brokers 86
    collateralized mortgage obligations
        (CMOs) 83
    interest-only 84
    market 81–2, 87
    mortgage-backed securities (MBS)
        83, 87, 89, 92, 96–8, 143
    sub-prime 8, 9, 34, 83–9, 95, 97, 98,
        100, 102, 105, 115, 146, 168, 174,
        178, 182
MSCI Emerging Markets Index 170
MUFG Bank 45
Mullins, David 24
mutual funds 32–3, 36, 92, 113
mutualization of debt 112

NASDAQ stock index 67, 70, 73, 76–7,
    78–9, 80, 154
National Bureau of Economic Research
    (NBER), US 77
National Institute of Allergy and
    Infectious Diseases (NIAID),
    US 139
negative equity 61, 63, 86, 87–8, 92
Netherlands 6, 17, 94, 109, 127, 151
Netscape 67–8, 72–3
    Navigator browser 73
net-zero carbon-emissions targets 194
New Deal 92
New Institutional Economics 193
New York Fed 24–5, 89, 91
New York Stock Exchange 67–8, 139
next great crash 8–9, 163–83
Nigeria 16, 178
Nikkei stock index 51, 53, 54, 55, 57
Nikko Asset Management 57
9/11 78, 85, 98
NINJAs (no income, no jobs or
    assets) 84
Nippon Credit Bank 63
Nishikawa, Yoshifumi 63

Nishimura, Masao 62
Nixon, Richard 12, 31
Nobel Prize for Economics 24, 127
Nomura Holdings 57
non-performing/bad loans 60, 61, 64, 86
non-tradable shares 168–9
Nordea 100
North, Douglass 193
Northern Rock 81, 88, 94
Nui Onoue 59

offshore banking 7, 12, 13, 175–6
oil 13, 15, 31–2, 35, 38, 39, 40, 44, 103, 140, 178
'old boys' network 48
Organization of Petroleum Exporting Countries (OPEC) 31
organized crime 43, 57–8
originate-to-distribute model 83
Outright Monetary Transactions 132
Oxford University/AstraZeneca vaccine 155, 158
Oxford Vaccine Group 155

Pakistan 99
Panhellenic Socialist Movement Party (PASOK) 111, 129
Papademos, Lucas 124, 125, 127
Papandreou, George 111, 123, 124
Paris Climate Change Accord (2015) 193
Paulson, Hank 90, 93
Pebble Beach resort, California 54
People's Bank of China 181
Pets at Home 75–6
Pets.com 67, 68–9, 74, 75
PetSmart 68, 69
Pfizer/BioNTech vaccine 158
pharmaceutical companies 155, 160–61
Philippines 16, 20, 23, 25
Plaza Accord (1985) 50, 53–4
Poland 16, 99
Portugal 8, 17, 110, 111, 112, 119–20, 127, 134, 157, 161

pound/sterling 5–6, 17–18, 19, 98, 188
poverty 134, 143, 164, 194
Powell doctrine 154
Powell, Jerome 141–2, 154
price controls 48
price makers/price takers 103
Primary Dealer Credit Facility, Federal Reserve, US 96–7
productivity 43, 44, 45, 78, 162, 167, 192
Project Birch 150
property taxes 31, 176–7
Prudential Securities 57

Qatar 95
quantitative easing (QE) 97, 101, 110, 114, 115, 143, 144–5, 150, 189
Quantum Fund 18

Rajan, Raghuram 101–2
Reagan, Ronald 50
real-estate 2, 7
    banking crises and 3, 185–6, 187
    currency crises and 21, 22, 23
    dot com crash (2000–2001) and 78–9
    euro crisis (2010) and 111, 116, 129, 134
    global financial crisis (2008) and 9, 82, 84–8, 92, 104, 105, 185–6, 187
    Great Crash (1929) and 3, 6, 7
    Japan's real-estate crash (early 1990s) and 8, 9, 43–65
    next great crash and 8, 164–8, 171, 173, 175–7, 180, 181, 182
    savings and loans crisis, US (1980s) and 31, 33, 34, 37, 38–9, 40
recapitalization 62, 65, 90, 93–4, 95, 96, 99, 105, 116, 117, 121, 123, 125, 126, 130, 166, 167, 181, 182
recession
    1917–21 137–8
    1927 2
    1937–38 'double dip' 6, 104
    Covid-19 crash (2020) and 141–2, 145, 153, 155–6, 159

credit crunch and 185
currency crises and 16, 17–18, 25–6, 188
dot com crash (2000–2001) and 8, 9, 68, 77–8, 79, 80
euro crisis (2010) and 107, 116, 117, 119, 133
global financial crisis (2008) and 81, 85, 88, 102–4, 153
Japan's real-estate crash (early 1990s) and 9, 55, 61
next great crash and 164, 171, 173, 174, 181, 183
savings and loans crisis, US (1980s) and 38, 39
stimulus cheques and 145, 157, 192–3
stock market decline and 9, 186
transformational 164
recovery 1, 185
  Covid-19 crash (2020) 150–52, 159, 160–62
  currency crises 26
  dot com crash (2000–2001) 77
  global financial crisis (2008) 174
  Great Crash (1929) 7
  Japan's real-estate crash (early 1990s) 63, 64
recycling 195
Reel.com 68
Regulation Q 13, 32, 33
remote working 154, 162, 192
renminbi 145–6, 170, 171, 172, 174, 175, 176, 179
repurchase/repo, market 82, 91, 110, 143
Republican Party, US 29–30, 90, 93
Reserve Bank of Australia 98
Reserve Bank of New Zealand 98
Reserve Primary Fund 91
Resolution Trust Corporation 40, 41
retail investors 76, 103, 168, 173, 174
Riegle, Donald 30
ringgit 25

risk 3, 20, 22, 26–7, 34, 35, 37, 39, 40, 49, 76, 83, 86, 87, 91, 93, 97, 114, 143, 170, 186
RJR Nabisco 36
Roaring Twenties 2
Roosevelt, Franklin D. 4–5, 7
rouble 24
Royal Bank of Scotland (RBS) 87, 94–5
Rubin, Robert 62
'rules of the game' 193–4
rupee 101–2
Russia 8, 16, 24, 117, 132, 155, 156, 164, 182, 188, 190–91
  Russia–Ukraine war (2022) 190–91

S&P 127
  500 77, 79, 139, 143, 153–4, 158, 159
SAIC Motor 167
Salomon Brothers 24, 56
Sammi Steel 23
Sanyo Securities 61
Sarkozy, Nicolas 94, 113, 117, 118, 124, 126
SARS epidemic 138
savings and loans crisis, US (1980s) 8, 29–41, 56, 83
Schäuble, Wolfgang 132, 134
Schilling 5
Schmidt, Helmut 108
Scholes, Myron 24
Schuman Declaration (1950) 108
Schumpeter, Joseph 80
Schwartz, Anna Jacobson: *A Monetary History of the United States, 1867–1960* 4
*schwarze Null* ('black zero' German balanced budget policy) 147
Second World War (1939–45) 6, 12, 43, 53, 61, 77, 137, 141
Section 13(3) emergency 91
securities 5
  Covid-19 crash (2020) and 143, 144
  currency crises and 13, 15, 24

securities – *cont.*
    euro crisis (2010) and 123
    global financial crisis (2008) and 83,
       84–5, 86–7, 88, 89, 91–2, 95, 96–7
    Japan's real-estate crash (early 1990s)
       and 47, 51–2, 57, 61
    next great crash and 167
    savings and loans crisis, US (1980s)
       and 29, 36–7
Securities and Exchange Commission
    (SEC), US 29, 37
securitization 31, 83–4, 86, 87, 88, 95
Senate Ethics Committee, US 30
shadow banking 81–2, 85, 90, 164, 167,
    170, 171–3, 181
shale oil 103
Shanghai Composite Index 103
Shenzhen, China 168, 177
Shiller, Bob 72
Singapore 23, 98, 144, 179
Slovakia 100
Sócrates, José 119
soft budget constraint problem 166–7
*sōkaiya* (professional extortionists) 57
Solow paradox 192
Solow, Robert 192
Somprasong Land 23
Soros, George 18–19, 186
South Africa 101, 143, 152, 156, 189
South Korea 20, 23–4, 25, 44, 63, 98, 144
sovereign debt crises 7, 112, 127, 186,
    189, 191
Soviet Union 163–4
Spain 8, 17, 87, 94, 110, 112, 119, 122, 127,
    129–31, 132, 134, 137, 140, 149,
    152, 188
Spanish flu (1918) 137, 140, 141
speculators 5–6, 13–15, 17, 18, 19, 25, 27,
    28, 59, 182, 186
Sputnik V 155
Sri Lanka 180
stagflation 190
Stark, Jürgen 122

state-owned enterprises 164, 165, 166–7,
    168–71, 173, 181
Steinbeck, John: *The Grapes of Wrath* 3–4
Stheeman, Robert 150
stock market 185, 186, 190–91
    Covid-19 crash (2020) and 137, 139,
       140, 153, 158, 159, 160–61
    currency crises and 21, 23
    dot com crash (2000–2001) and 71–2,
       77, 79
    global financial crisis (2008) and 103
    Great Crash (1929) and 2, 3, 4, 6, 7, 9
    Japan's real-estate crash (early 1990s)
       and 43, 51–2, 53, 55, 56–7, 59, 62,
       63, 64
    next great crash and 164, 167–9, 173,
       174–5, 179, 180
STOXX 600 140, 159
stress tests 116–17, 122–3, 135, 187
Stripe 80
structured finance 83
sub-prime mortgage lending 8, 9, 34,
    83–9, 95, 97, 98, 100, 102, 105, 115,
    146, 168, 174, 178, 182
Sumitomo 58
Sumitomo Mitsui Bank 63
Summers, Larry 62
Sunak, Rishi 147, 150, 157
Support to Mitigate Unemployment
    Risks in an Emergency, EU 146
supra-national regulatory
    supervision 187
Sustainable Development Goals, UN
    (2030) 194
swap lines 98, 102, 127, 144
Swedbank 100
Sweden 17, 18, 98, 99, 100, 151
Swiss National Bank 98, 102, 127
Syntagma Square, Athens 120

Tablita (fixed exchange rate) 15
Taiwan 44
taper tantrum 101, 189

tax
euro crisis (2010) and 112, 116, 117–18,
125–6, 130, 133, 135
global financial crisis (2008) and 93
income tax 31
Japan's real-estate crash (early 1990s)
and 46, 52, 53, 56, 57, 59, 60, 61, 65
property taxes 31, 176–7
savings and loans crisis, US (1980s)
and 31, 34, 38
Tax Reform Act (1986), US 38
technology 44, 67, 70, 73–4, 75, 77,
78–9, 80, 81, 154, 158, 159, 160,
161–2, 192
Term Asset-Backed Securities Loan
Facility, Federal Reserve, US 97
Term Auction Facility, Federal Reserve,
US 96
Term Securities Lending Facility, Federal
Reserve, US 96
Texas, US 38–40
Thailand 20, 21, 22–3, 25
Thai baht 23
TheGlobe.com 70
TheRealReal.com 68
'3-6-3' business 31
thrifts 30–41
Tokuyo City Bank 61
Tokyo University 47
Tokyu Corporation 57
Toys 'R' Us 70, 71
trade deficit 14, 50
transformational recessions 164
transition economies 163–4
Treasury Committee, House of
Commons, UK 147
Treasurys, US (bonds) 32, 97, 98–9,
125, 143
Treaty of Lisbon (2007) 109, 112
Trichet, Jean-Claude 115–16, 120
Triffin dilemma 107–109
Triffin, Robert: *Gold and the Dollar Crisis*
107–9

troika 113, 114, 116, 118, 120, 121, 123,
124, 130, 135
Troubled Asset Relief Program (TARP),
US 90, 93–6
Trump, Donald 37, 137, 145, 158
Turkey 8, 24, 101, 188, 189
Twain, Mark 80

UBS 88
UK
'Big Bang' deregulation of City of
London 13
Covid-19 crash (2020) and 139, 142,
144, 147–50, 152–3, 156, 157, 158,
159, 160, 161, 192
departure from gold standard (1931) 6
euro crisis (2010) and 107, 114, 115,
118, 126
European Exchange Rate Mechanism
collapse (1992) and 7, 11, 16–19, 27,
186, 188
global financial crisis (2008) and 8,
81–2, 87–8, 90, 92–6, 97
next great crash and 179
Ukraine 99, 190–91
unemployment 2, 3, 6, 191
banking crises and 185
Covid-19 crash (2020) and 8, 141, 142,
146, 147–8, 149, 151, 157
currency crises and 17–18, 19, 20, 188
dot com crash (2000–2001) and 78
euro crisis (2010) and 116, 119, 123,
129, 134
global financial crisis (2008) and 100
Japan's real-estate crash (early 1990s)
and 51, 62
United Nations 153
Global Compact 194
United States of America (USA)
190–91, 192–3
Covid-19 crash (2020) and 137–62
currency crises and 12–13, 15, 16, 20,
21, 22, 24, 25

United States of America (USA) – *cont.*
    dot com crash (2000–2001) and  69,
        70, 71, 72, 74, 75, 76, 77–8, 79
    euro crisis (2010) and  107–8, 111, 113,
        114, 115, 116, 117, 121, 122, 125, 126,
        127, 131
    global financial crisis (2008)  8, 9,
        81–105, 168, 186, 187
    Great Crash (1929) and  1–7, 29, 79,
        81, 105, 187
    Great Depression (1929–39) and  2, 3–5,
        6, 7, 8, 29, 64, 84, 105, 137, 141, 186
    'Great Moderation' (1990s–2000s) and
        27, 78
    Japan's real-estate crash (early 1990s)
        and  46, 50, 53, 54, 56, 62
    next great crash and  173, 174, 175,
        177, 178–9, 181, 182
    savings and loans crisis (1980s)  8,
        29–41, 56
universal basic income (UBI)  192
University of Oxford's Jenner
    Institute  155
US Treasury  12, 16, 32, 62, 90, 91, 92,
    93, 96, 97, 98–9, 105, 108, 117, 122,
    125, 131, 143, 148

Van Rompuy, Herman  125, 126, 130
venture capitalists (VCs)  69, 76
Vienna Initiative (2009)  99–100
Volcker, Paul  15, 191
voting  118, 195
V-shaped recovery  25, 77

Wainwright, Julie  68
Wall Street, US  3, 35, 37, 81

*Wall Street* (film)  35
Walsh, James  57
Webvan.com  68, 69–70
Weibo  173
Weidmann, Jens  122
welfare state  149–50, 193, 194
Wenzhou, Zhejiang province  172
West Texas Intermediate (WTI)  140
WhatsApp  80
White, Harry Dexter  12
'white knight' banks  94
Wilson, Rita  141
Wilson, Woodrow  137
Woodsmall, Eva  68
work–life balance  192
World Bank  12, 94, 99, 100, 153, 179
    *Development Report* (1991)  43–5
World Health Organization (WHO)
    137, 138, 139, 155, 156, 161
Wuhan, China  138

Xi Jinping  176

Yakuza  58
Yamaichi Securities  61
Yellen, Janet  103
yen  50, 51, 53–4, 62
Yoshihisa, Ojimi  44

Zambia  159
Zapatero, José Luis Rodríguez  119
Zhejiang Brothers Printing
    Company  172
Zhou Feng  172
Zoom  192
Zuckerberg, Mark  74